IN THE LINE OF FIRE

IN THE LINE OF FIRE

Personal Memories
of a Documentary Filmmaker

Antony Thomas

UNICORN

ACKNOWLEDGEMENTS

There's not enough space to thank all those who helped me through my career and during the writing of this book. My personal list must begin with my grandparents, Elsa and Eddy, as well as Bigvai Masekela, who treated me as his son, and opened my eyes to the realities of township life during the apartheid era.

I am hugely grateful to Tony Essex, Charles Denton, David Fanning, Roger James, Marie Natanson and Sheila Nevins for giving me so much support and encouragement throughout my career, and I would also like to thank those who provided valuable help and advice during the preparation of this book. The list includes my brother Rufus and my sister Kay, Nancy Abraham, Marcus Beale, Piers Brendon, McDonald Brown, Michael Carroll, Paul Cartledge, John Cleare, Nigel Crewe, Nick Cull, Richard Dawkins, Jennie Havord, Celia Hayley, Heather Holden-Brown, Jim Hougan, Rollin Kennedy, George Newton, Nick Newton, Benjamin Pogrund, Alan Rosenthal and Ian Strathcarron. Finally, I would like to give extra-special thanks to two dear friends for the time they devoted to this book – Elizabeth Klinck, for all her help with picture research and copyright negotiations, and Miranda Hearn, who went through every draft from start to finish.

Published in 2022 by
Unicorn, an imprint of Unicorn Publishing Group LLP
5 Newburgh Street
London
W1F 7RG
www.unicornpublishing.org

Every effort has been made to trace copyright holders and to obtain their permission for the use of copyrighted material. The publisher apologises for any errors or omissions and would be grateful to be notified of any corrections that should be incorporated in future reprints or editions of this book.

ISBN 978 1 914414 33 6
10 9 8 7 6 5 4 3 2 1

Design by newtonworks.uk
Printed by Fine Tone Ltd

CONTENTS

FOREWORD

On 26 January 1978, the front page of the *Daily Express*, a British tabloid, was dominated by a single photograph that captured the moment when an executioner's sword struck the neck of a kneeling figure. A huge crowd had gathered to witness this very public event, which was flagged with the headlines: DEATH BY THE SWORD. THE PRICE OF LOVING A PRINCESS.

The whole of the third page was devoted to the testimony of Barry Milner, a 25-year-old carpenter from Yorkshire, who had been working in Saudi Arabia at the time and had taken the enormous risk of photographing the execution with a small Instamatic camera, hidden in a cigarette box. The 'sickening scene' he witnessed that day was, in fact, a double execution.

The first to die was 'a tall, slim girl, dressed in black robes. They knelt her down by this pile of sand. Then two men – policemen or soldiers – drew their pistols, aimed, and each shot her three times. She staggered and fell backwards onto the sand. Her body twitched for a few seconds, then she was still.'

The next to die was a young man, who had been forced to watch the killing. 'Suddenly, the sword fell, and as it struck the victim's neck, my trembling hand pressed the button on the hidden camera. It took five more blows from the sword to kill the husband.'

Milner is then quoted as saying: 'the thousands in the square, some of them children, threw up their arms and cheered. I felt sick. The whole scene was incredible. It was as if it was happening in bygone days.'

This execution had taken place six months earlier but had not been reported anywhere until Milner returned to Britain with his photographic evidence. Before they published the story, *Express* journalists had done some research and provided the basic 'facts'.

'The brutal, public execution in the name of Allah was taking place in the medieval, walled city of Jeddah in Saudi Arabia. The victims were Princess Misha'al, granddaughter of King Khalid's older brother and a young student with whom she had eloped. Their crime: he was a commoner, and their marriage defied the Islamic family code.'

Under graphic headlines, different versions of this story appeared in magazines and newspapers across Europe and the US, but it was an account, given in private by a senior member of the Saudi government, which I found so compelling that I decided to leave for the Middle East and investigate.

As a result of this, I not only found the truth about the death of this princess, but also discovered that her story had stirred the emotions of many of my Arab friends, particularly women, who gave me insights into their lives and experiences they had never shared before. As they had trusted me to record these discussions on condition that they would never be identified, we decided on a docudrama, *Death of a Princess*, strictly based on the original transcripts, but with names, ages and professions changed to protect our sources.

The final result was described as 'the biggest single incident on an international scale, involving a television film, since television was created'. The Saudis reacted furiously, dismissing the British Ambassador and putting enormous pressure on the co-producing countries not to show the film. Only Britain, the US and the Netherlands stood firm, and the furious Saudi response only succeeded in attracting huge audiences to the broadcasts.

Ten years earlier, our whole team had been condemned to death in a military camp in Zambia. Now I was back 'in the line of fire', coping with vicious attacks from MPs and sectors of the press.

But, for most of my career, my programmes raised no hackles and received wonderful reviews, although, in some cases, the personal impact was just as great. One of them changed the course of my life.

From the full range of documentaries, made over a fifty-two-year career, I have singled out the subjects that affected me deeply and remain relevant to this day: the pernicious effects of racism; the 'seamless border' between intelligence and crime; the last colonial wars in Africa; the conflicts in the Middle East; the rise of Islamic extremism; the politicisation of evangelical Christians in the United States; and the origins of fake news – to mention a few.

Instead of skipping from subject to subject, I have tried to bring all these disparate experiences together by taking a personal approach and using every opportunity to bring the reader 'behind the camera', where I share the difficulties, the dangers and the moral problems we often faced. For instance, is deception ever permissible to gain access to an important story, and if exceptions can be made when dealing with repressive regimes or dubious organisations, can deception ever be right when dealing with ordinary people?

The most important lesson, learnt at the very start of my professional career, was that I should never embark on an important subject without rigorous research 'on the ground', and there have been times when my whole approach to a sensitive subject has been changed by everything learnt during those months of research.

While I am not afraid to share my feelings in commentary, I have never taken on the role of presenter, or relied on experts to provide the basic 'facts'. Wherever possible, I have tried to give a voice to people whose lives are directly affected by the issues involved and allowed them to tell the story through their own experiences. I am still convinced that this is the most powerful and responsible way to deal with an important subject.

During my lifetime, there have been enormous changes in attitudes towards race, sexuality, gender equality and class difference, and to reflect that fully, I decided that I would not confine the book to my career but begin the story in that very different world of the 1940s and '50s, when I was a child.

On a personal level, this was also a time of extraordinary turbulence, which probably gave me the best possible preparation for the career I would eventually follow. Not only was I experiencing life and mixing closely with people at the highest and lowest levels of society, I was also gaining important insights into human behaviour through the many family breakups and reconciliations I witnessed, and learning at a very young age that there are several sides to every story.

In the midst of all this turmoil, there was one short interlude of peace and security with my grandparents in South Africa. It was an experience that would have serious consequences. Sadly, by that time, they had both passed away.

Chapter One

THAT NIGHT ON TWIST STREET

Hillbrow. Street after street of high-rise apartments, dominating the heights north of Johannesburg and reaching down to the railroad track that separates the city's residential and commercial zones.

It was 1962 and, like many young whites starting out on their careers, I had chosen a Hillbrow bedsit as my first home. I had just graduated from Cambridge and was back in the country I loved.

When deciding to return, I believed – or wanted to believe – the message I was receiving from several sources, including my father, who had settled in the country twelve years previously. It was the notion that apartheid had evolved from crude discrimination into something entirely different. Black South Africans were now being granted self-government in independent homelands and encouraged to make their own contributions in industry, commerce and broadcasting. In schools across the country, their children were being taught their own history in their own languages.

It was a narrative that took me to a dangerous place.

Everything came to a head on New Year's Eve 1964. On that night, a huge crowd had gathered on Twist Street, Hillbrow's main thoroughfare, where the scene I witnessed at one of the main crossroads was breathtakingly. Blacks and whites were packed closely together; some of them even holding hands, as they waved their arms up and down in unison, chanting 'Happy! Happy! Happy!'

After a year of disillusion and self-doubt, I was suddenly experiencing what 'my country' could be and rushed to join the celebrations.

Minutes before midnight, police drew up in cars and vans, doors were flung open, and uniformed officers jumped out with German shepherds on the leash.

Instantly, blacks and whites separated. On the white side, there was a sudden sense of shame, as though they had been caught red-handed, committing an indecent act.

But there was one man, standing near me, who refused to move: a tall, elderly African with both hands resting on a beautifully carved stick. In African society, these are often heirlooms, passed down from generation to generation – gifts of enormous significance.

When the police saw that he was holding his ground, three of them (and a dog) headed straight for him. 'Move, kaffir! Move!' ('Kaffir' is the South African equivalent of the N-word, and just as demeaning.)

The old man didn't remonstrate or even glance in their direction, but stood there in silence, back straight, eyes staring ahead. One of the policemen immediately shoved him in the direction of the other Africans. He stumbled and his stick fell to the ground. A second policeman grabbed it and, with an enormous effort, broke it across his thigh.

At that moment, something happened to me that I have never experienced before or since: a feeling of uncontrollable rage. I believe they call this 'red mist'. Suddenly, I became a vicious, fighting animal, lashing out at the police without any thoughts about the consequences for the elderly African or for me.

And, of course, the police reciprocated. Thankfully, they did not take it out on the old man, but we were both arrested and shoved into a waiting police car.

Bruised and bleeding, I sat beside my new companion, while whites, who had been linking hands with their fellow countrymen moments earlier, were pressing against the car and shouting abuse at us through the closed windows. It was as if they had been woken out of a dream, a sweet dream, and now they were furious.

As we sat together, I pulled out a couple of cigarettes, lit one, and handed it to my companion, who took a deep drag.

It was an act of intimacy that incensed the whites even further. The car started to rock, and the police immediately moved in. I was pulled out, taken to another vehicle, and eventually driven to the nearest police station. When I asked where they had taken the elderly African, I was told that he was not guilty of any violence (true) and had already been released, something I was only able to confirm days later.

But the case against me was serious. I was guilty of assaulting two police officers, and the duty sergeant at the police station demanded an immediate statement.

What followed was as much of a surprise for him as it still is for me.

I explained that I was a film director, working for the Department of Information (i.e., South Africa's propaganda ministry). I also warned the sergeant that I would be drafting a detailed report about police behaviour that night and submitting it at the highest level. If the officer wanted authentication, he should call this person at any time after 8.00am, and I scribbled a name and number on a scrap of paper.

I was released at 8.15am.

It had been an extraordinary journey. In June, I had been invited to a private meeting with the Prime Minister, Dr Verwoerd. Six months later, I was in one of his jails.

How on earth did I get there in the first place?

****

I was born in India. When I was two years old, my parents divorced, and at the height of the war, Sheila, my mother, took me on the dangerous sea journey to England so that we could join her mother in an isolated slate cottage on the edge of Salisbury plain.

Mother and father in their India days.

Sheila was just twenty-three years old at the time, strikingly beautiful, yet filled with anger and capable of lashing out at me if I ever put a foot wrong.

After she broke with my father, she had formed a close friendship with another expatriate, Rufus T. Burton, a rising star in the American oil industry. They had stayed in touch by letter and the occasional telegram, but Rufus, as my mother told me later, 'blew hot and cold'. She now faced two possibilities; a new and exciting future with someone she loved, or life in a remote country cottage, where she had virtually no contact with anyone her own age. It was a time of enormous uncertainty and tension, but everything changed – at least for me – shortly after my third birthday.

I remember that moment very clearly. I had been banished to my room for reasons I cannot recall, and was lying in bed, idly peeling paper off the wall, when my father's parents walked into the room and introduced themselves.

'But you mustn't call us Grandpa and Granny. It makes us feel so old! I'm Elsa and this is Eddy'. At this point I was lifted off the bed and given a big hug, something my mother had never done.

I don't know what discussions followed this visit, but on a wet winter's night, my mother delivered me and a suitcase, packed with all my belongings, to Elsa's and Eddy's flat in Hove on the Sussex coast.

It was the beginning of a new life.

Elsa and Eddy created an atmosphere of openness and trust, wrapped in an all-embracing – literally all-embracing – love. In difficult times we had a ritual of throwing our arms around each other and shouting out: 'The three of us against the world!'

Theirs was a marriage of equals, where the conventional gender roles were often

With Eddy and Elsa.

reversed. Elsa, then in her late fifties, was the natural leader – impulsive, generous and strong-willed. She believed that anything was achievable if you set your heart on it, and it was a principle that would shape every decision I would make in life.

Eddy, a retired bank manager, was twelve years her senior and always a calming influence – quiet, sensitive and cautious.

I had been living with them for over a year when Sheila appeared at the flat in Hove. Apparently, Rufus had cabled a proposal of marriage and an invitation to bring me with her to the United States. ('Will you and yours join me and mine this side?' were his actual words!) I was in shock, but before the discussion went any further, Eddy guided me to my bedroom, where I stayed until my mother was ready to leave.

There are two versions of what happened next. According to my mother, she consulted my father in India and her own mother, and they both agreed that it would be kinder to leave me in the care of my grandparents.

Eddy had a different version. Apparently, Elsa booked an immediate meeting at the US embassy in London and was so persuasive that the consul finally gave Sheila a choice – a single visa for her or staying in Britain with me.

As I would learn later, no adoption papers or letters of agreement had been drawn up, and my mother had the legal right to reclaim me whenever she wanted. I am sure this was a major factor in Elsa's and Eddy's decision to leave England in 1946 and take me on the seven-thousand-mile sea journey to South Africa, a country they remembered fondly from their travels in the thirties.

Tickets were booked well ahead of time. The flat in Hove and most of the contents were sold and we moved into Green Gates, a quiet and secluded guest house on the edge of Worthing, a seaside town twelve miles from Hove. Most of the other guests were elderly, long-term residents, and the place had the feel of a retirement home.

The three of us had barely settled in when my father cabled with the news that he and his second wife, Molly, were on their way from India. This would be the first time in eight years that Eddy and Elsa had seen their only son.

From occasional remarks between Eddy and Elsa, I was aware of the tensions between them and Robert, known to his friends as Tommy. He had started his career at the main Cardiff branch of Lloyds Bank when Eddy was manager, but in 1930, at the age of twenty-one, he applied for a transfer to the bank's Calcutta (Kolkata) branch.

Eddy and Elsa had visited him there during his second year and were not impressed. Tommy had always been a keen sportsman, but now he seemed to be taking things to extremes. As well as managing his own football team and devoting entire days to cricket, he had taken up polo with a passion. Of even greater concern was his reputation as a womaniser and notorious practical joker. On one occasion he had driven half a dozen goats through the basement of Calcutta's Grand Hotel and into the lift, shutting the gate after them. It was clear to Eddy and Elsa that their son was not taking his career seriously, but their hopes rose when he returned to the family home in Whitchurch, a suburb of Cardiff, on his first leave.

The practice in colonial India was for British expatriates to take a six-month break every five years, which was time enough for Tommy to form a close relationship with Sheila, who lived with her parents a few doors down from Eddy's and Elsa's.

Sheila was a child of twelve when Tommy had last seen her. Now she was a beautiful seventeen-year-old, and Tommy was immediately attracted, but that was not the only factor. There was pressure from both families to bring this couple together. Eddy and Elsa were hoping that Tommy, once married, would finally settle down, while Sheila's parents were planning to separate, and wanted to get their only child off their hands.

In June 1938, Tommy and Sheila were married in St Paul's Anglican Cathedral in Calcutta. Four years later, they separated. Although Eddy and Elsa were progressive in so many respects, their attitude to divorce was absolutely in line with the values of the time, and it didn't help the situation when they heard that Molly Harrison, the woman Tommy had chosen as his second wife, was herself a divorcee.

Their visit to Green Gates, in the summer of 1946, was a disaster from the start. The two of them seemed determined to present themselves as a thoroughly modern couple, morally and physically different from Elsa, Eddy and the elderly residents of Green Gates.

Tommy was now in his mid-thirties, but still had the physique of an athlete. With his predilection for shorts, his Errol Flynn moustache and dark brown hair, brushed back and Brylcreemed to his scalp, he seemed cut out for the part he intended to play, but it was Molly who took the lead role. Six years Tommy's senior and still a glamorous figure, she chose dangerously low-cut necklines and Katherine Hepburn slacks, which she even wore at dinner. She was also a strong character – almost, but not quite, a match for Elsa – and from the very beginning, she did her utmost to provoke her in-laws, while Tommy was happy to follow her lead.

It was the practice at Green Gates for the newspapers of choice to be laid out every morning on the guests' breakfast tables. In this highly conservative milieu, the *Daily Telegraph* and the *Daily Mail* were the popular choices, but Molly and Tommy ordered the *Daily Worker*, the Communist Party daily, which sat on their table for all to see.

At one stage during their stay, they took me away for a few days, and it did not make things easy when I returned to tell Elsa that Molly had shared a bath with me and Tommy had given me my first shot of whisky.

The next surprise was the arrival of Nigel Harrison, Molly's son by her first marriage. A shy, withdrawn fifteen-year-old, Nigel spent most of his time alone in his bedroom, painstakingly constructing model aircraft. Elsa was horrified to hear that Molly had farmed him out to her in-laws, and that this was the first time she had seen him since he was two years old.

An even greater crisis was precipitated by a casual remark from an old India hand, who checked in shortly after Molly's and Tommy's arrival. 'Such a coincidence to find Molly Golton here', he told Elsa. 'We met a couple of times in Lahore, you know.'

Elsa corrected him. 'Molly Harrison, I think you mean.'

The truth soon emerged. Tommy was Molly's third husband. After her divorce from Nigel's father, she had married Sydney Golton and given birth to another son, who was my age. He was being brought up in Jersey by Sydney's parents, and Molly had made no plans to see him.

Elsa was appalled; not only by the double divorce and the subterfuge, but also by Molly's cold-hearted attitude towards her two sons. The only compensation she could take was the certainty that someone with Molly's feelings towards children was hardly likely to press Tommy to reclaim me.

How wrong she was!

I don't recall how and when Molly's and Tommy's visit ended. My next clear memory is the train journey with Eddy and Elsa to Southampton, passing bombed-out buildings on the greyest of grey winter days. For the next four years, it would remain an enduring image of England.

The three of us sailed on the *Carnarvon Castle*, a passenger liner that had been converted to a troop ship during the war but was not yet restored to its original state.

The ship was crammed to bursting point; thousands of people, desperate for a new life in a sun-lit paradise far, far away from the grim realities of post-war Britain. All male passengers had to sleep in a single, massive cabin with rows of bunks stacked on top of each other and served by ladders that ran from floor to ceiling. Eddy, who had just turned seventy, was given a bunk close to the floor, while Elsa and I shared a cabin with half a dozen women and their children. It was always noisy, and as we moved towards the equator the heat became insufferable.

Finally, on a still summer's night, two weeks after we had left Southampton, we docked in Cape Town, where friends of Eddy's and Elsa's met us and drove us to our new home – the Radnor Hotel, Green Point.

Today, Green Point is a densely packed Cape Town suburb, and the Radnor is no more, but in 1946 it stood in glorious isolation, an art deco creation with a huge garden and, beyond that, an open common running down to the sea.

We had only been there for a few days when Eddy and Elsa bought a black Ford Prefect, the first car they had owned since the outbreak of war. (Number Plate CA 48875, as I well remember.)

Cape Town is one of the most beautiful cities in the world. Its setting at the foot of Table Mountain is breath-taking, and now we were free, free to explore the city and its surroundings; free to take the cable car to the top of Table Mountain; free to drive through the glorious winelands to the east or follow the mountain road south to Cape Point, stopping on the way at beaches we sometimes had to ourselves. It was the most wonderful chapter of my childhood, and I fell deeply in love with South Africa.

At that stage, of course, I had absolutely no understanding of politics or any experiences that might have made me aware of the injustices and tensions in this country. The few thoughts I had were shaped by my grandparents.

Unlike many of their class and generation, Eddy and Elsa were not racists. They didn't believe that non-whites were of inferior stock. The worst that can be said is that they were complacent. They understood that the basic problem for the majority in this country was lack of education and opportunity, but they also believed that the British Empire was an altruistic institution, steadily raising standards across the vast territory it administered. One day, they were sure, there would be genuine equality. It was only a question of time.

But how much time? That was never said.

The National Party victory in the 1948 elections came as a shock to them both. Part of this, of course, was resentment that the leadership of the country had been taken away from the largely British United Party and was now in the hands of 'ignorant' Afrikaners.

There was also a strong response to the Nationalists' political slogan. 'Apart Hate', Elsa kept repeating, shaking her head in disbelief, but it wasn't long before we were distracted by more personal issues.

Six thousand miles away in Calcutta, Molly and Tommy had made a decision. The violence that preceded and followed partition finally convinced them that it was time to leave.

They had originally thought of Kenya, but a couple they befriended on board ship persuaded them that South Africa was the country of the future, and instead of disembarking at Mombasa, Molly and Tommy remained on board until they reached Durban, the next stop. A big factor in this decision was an invitation from their new friends to stay with them in their family home in Pietermaritzburg, the provincial capital of Natal, and to use this as a base while they assessed local conditions and opportunities.

Molly came from a wealthy family, and the money was there to buy Tommy a partnership in the Pietermaritzburg branch of a stockbroking business headquartered in Johannesburg.

Eddy and Elsa had been kept in touch with all these developments, and I could tell from their reactions that the atmosphere was improving. When we received news that Molly and Tommy had bought a home in Pietermaritzburg and would be settling there, a big decision had to be made. Should we join them?

Elsa and I were dubious, but Eddy felt strongly that this was the right thing to do. I was only nine years old, and they were an elderly couple. Anything could happen in the future, and it was important that I be given a chance to form a good relationship with my father and stepmother. Who knew when I might need them?

In August 1949, we uprooted and sailed to Durban with our faithful Ford Prefect in the ship's hold. It was the only time I can remember when Eddy had prevailed.

Molly and Tommy were at the port to meet us, and immediately suggested lunch together at a seaside hotel before we set off for Pietermaritzburg.

This was not the same couple that had burst into our lives three years earlier, and I was excited to see the change. Molly and Elsa got on so well that they decided to travel to Pietermaritzburg together in the M&T Studebaker, while Eddy, Tommy and I followed in the little Prefect.

Within a matter of days, I was registered as a weekly boarder in a prep school a few miles from Pietermaritzburg, while Elsa and Eddy moved into a country hotel nearby. It was agreed that I would spend alternate weekends with each couple and that holidays would be similarly divided.

All seemed to go well at the start, but on one of my weekends with Tommy and Molly, he suggested that we should stop at his office on our way back to school. Molly, who normally accompanied us, would be staying at home. I assumed that my father had to catch up with some work. It certainly didn't occur to me, as I kissed Molly goodbye, that this was the last time I would see her for eleven years.

Once inside his empty office, Tommy flicked on the lights and gestured me to a couch. I had a sudden premonition.

'Has something happened to Eddy – or Elsa?'

He shook his head. 'No. They are both well, but I want to talk about something that affects all of us.'

He sat beside me, and I felt a tightening in the stomach.

'Antony, you are very happy here. You are doing well at school and really settling in, but the situation is different for Eddy and Elsa. They love Cape Town and I know how much they miss it. For their sakes, I feel they should go back.'

'I don't understand what you're saying.'

A long speech followed. Tommy wanted me to know that I was *his* son and that the time had come to 'phase your grandparents out of your life' and live permanently with him and Molly. 'Of course, you can always visit Eddy and Elsa – maybe two or three times a year.'

I was completely unprepared for this. Everything seemed to be going so well between the two couples. Why this sudden demand to break us apart? I was speechless, but the expression on my face must have told Tommy everything he needed to know.

At this point, he changed tack and presented me with some hard facts. For the first time in my life, I learnt that no adoption papers had been drawn up and Eddy and Elsa had no legal right to keep me.

'Those rights belong to your mother and father.'

I managed to whisper: 'But Molly isn't my mother.'

Then came the final shock. Tommy had been in touch with Sheila, who was now living in the United States. She was willing to grant Molly and Tommy the full legal rights to adopt me.

I don't think I said another word on the drive back to school.

Immediately Tommy had dropped me off, I told the housemaster that I had to deal with an emergency, a family matter, something very private. Could I please use his phone? He had the good grace to leave the room. Once I was alone, I called Elsa and told her everything that had happened.

'So, what do you want to do?'

'I never want to see them again.'

'That's very serious. Are you sure you mean it?'

'Yes.'

'Then we'll make a plan.'

A couple of days later, I was playing with friends during a class break when one of the boys ran up and pointed to the steep bank of trees that rose up on one side of the yard.

'Someone up there wants to see you.'

I knew at once who this would be and climbed the bank. There was a dirt road at the top where Eddy and Elsa were waiting with the Ford Prefect parked beside them. The roof rack was loaded with luggage.

'Go back down,' Elsa said. 'Pick up as many of your things as you can without arousing suspicion and join us here.'

'Where are we going?'

'Cape Town.'

It was a journey of almost a thousand miles, and it took the better part of a week. As we passed through areas of ravishing beauty – the Transkei, the Garden Route – we often entertained ourselves with boisterous singing. Our favourite was courtesy of Rudyard Kipling.

'On the road to Mandalay,

Where the flyin' fishes play,

An' the dawn comes up like thunder,

Out of China 'cross the Bay!'

Once we reached Cape Town, life quickly returned to normal. We were back at the Radnor, and I was readmitted to my old school. I don't know what communication passed between Eddy, Elsa and Tommy, but my father made no further attempt to reclaim me.

Nine months after we returned to Cape Town, our whole world crashed. Just a week after my tenth birthday, Eddy died of a sudden heart attack.

I was stunned by the news. Elsa, of course, was the dominant power in this relationship and the one who usually made the decisions that affected our lives, but Eddy had played an equally important role in my life. He was sensitive and perceptive, and seemed to have an intuitive understanding of any problems and difficulties I might have, even before I was able to articulate them myself.

In many ways, Eddy performed the maternal role, reading me bedtime stories, and quietly consoling me when things were difficult. Elsa's approach was different. From a remarkably early age, she treated me as an adult, sharing family problems and asking me to make my own decisions, whenever possible. This was a great compliment, but there were times when it was also helpful to have someone with whom I could share moments of weakness and doubt.

Eddy's death was a shattering blow to both of us, and Elsa seemed to age in an alarming way. Grief, of course, was the major factor, but she also had serious financial worries. With characteristic frankness, she told me that they hadn't prepared for a crisis like this. Now that Eddy's bank pension was suspended, all she could expect was a widow's allowance of four pounds a week and an additional two-and-a-bit pounds from the capital they had patriotically invested in 'War Loan', which had plunged in value. We certainly couldn't afford to remain at the Radnor. Our only option was to return to England, where she had relatives and friends to turn to.

I was devastated.

Neither of us considered returning to Pietermaritzburg and trying to re-establish relationships there, but this did not stop Elsa appealing to Tommy for help. To his credit, he offered to contribute £15 a month towards my upkeep (equivalent to £360 today). Not a huge amount, but enough to save us from dire poverty.

Elsa's plan was to go back to her childhood roots. She had been in touch with her eighty-six-year-old aunt, Louie, who lived alone in a large Victorian house in Norfolk, and a deal was struck. If Elsa was prepared to do the housework, shopping and cooking, we would both be welcome to stay with her for as long as we wanted.

Chapter Two

AGAINST ALL ODDS

During our time in South Africa, I was not aware of any attempts by Eddy or Elsa to communicate with my mother or she with them, but after Eddy's death, Elsa wrote to Sheila's mother, Margaret, telling her about our plans, and when we docked at Southampton in late August 1950, Margaret (or 'Panny' as the family preferred to call her) was at the port to meet us.

We had half an hour together in the waiting boat train before the start of a journey that would take us via London to Hunstanton and Aunt Louie. The atmosphere between the two grandmothers was cordial, if not exactly warm, and most of the time was spent catching up on family news. Panny had sold her country cottage and was now living in Salisbury.

For the first time ever, I learnt that I had two half-sisters, a half-brother and a stepfather, Rufus T. Burton, a senior executive in the American oil industry. After a short stint at company headquarters, he had returned to India with the family to take on the dual role of Head of Esso Standard Eastern and Regional Co-ordinator for the Standard Vacuum Oil Company.

All this seemed worlds away from the life Elsa and I were now facing, and we were both hungry and exhausted when we arrived at Aunt Louie's late that evening, only to find that the larder was almost empty. The following day, Elsa did a mammoth shop, but on her return, Aunt Louie singled out items she considered 'extravagant'. Elsa was given two choices: either take them back or pay for them herself. She chose the second option.

Elsa's first priority was to secure a place for me at the local council school, where the new term was due to start in a few days. We went there together to meet the headmaster, and after a short verbal test I was given a place. I liked the school and was happy to go there, but I could see that Elsa was troubled.

My greatest concern, though, was my great-aunt. Yes, she was mean, but she was also hostile, particularly towards me. She didn't like the frank and open way Elsa and I communicated with each other. In her opinion, it showed disrespect on my part and misjudgement on Elsa's. Children were to be seen, not heard, and they certainly were not supposed to contradict adults or to have opinions of their own.

My escape to school on the first day of term came as a relief, but when I returned that afternoon, I sensed Elsa's distress. She asked how the day had gone, but before I'd had a chance to reply, out came a stream of apologies and regrets. She felt she had let me down in the most shameful way. No member of our family had ever been to a state school. Haileybury, Oundle, Sherborne – any one of those would be right for me, but not the local council school in Hunstanton.

I almost screamed at her: 'But we can't afford them, any of them!' Aunt Louie rose to her feet and left the room in disgust.

The very next day, Elsa was off. Public school terms usually start a few weeks later than state schools, and she was determined to get me into a prep school of her choice before the beginning of the school year. I don't know how she managed this, but within a week, she had secured a place for me at Sherborne Preparatory School in Dorset. We packed our things and made the move, but the financial implications were serious.

School fees were nearly double the allowance Tommy was sending. To survive, Elsa would have to look for work as a cook and cleaner, focusing on farms, where I could contribute to my upkeep during the holidays by feeding animals, sweeping stalls and doing whatever odd jobs were required.

As she scrubbed floors and washed dishes, Elsa's dignity and self-confidence were never shaken. A typical example was her response to the Baxters, who had agreed to take us on during my first school holiday. I wasn't present during Elsa's first meeting with the family when terms were presumably agreed: three pounds a week for her and free board and lodging for both of us, provided I was always available for work on the farm.

It was only when we moved in that we discovered another condition. No food would be provided for the three resident servants – Elsa, me and Jill, a young Australian who took care of the horses. We would take our meals in the kitchen and could eat whatever was left over from the family table. I expected Elsa to walk out the moment she heard this, but she chose to express her anger in a different way.

When the time came for our first lunch, Elsa followed house rules and scraped the family leftovers onto our plates. Anything we rejected was put into two large dog bowls in a corner of the kitchen.

Later that afternoon, I became suspicious when Elsa started preparing two of my favourite dishes, roast lamb and treacle tart. As dinner time approached, the next surprise was to see her slicing the joint herself – a ritual that was always performed in the dining room by the head of the family. She then served the three of us.

By now we could hear the grumbles through the hatch that separated us from the dining room. Dinner was late, but Elsa was unfazed. Once she had served the three of us, she picked up the two dog bowls, walked round to the dining room, and plonked them on the high table.

There was a furious reaction, and we were told to leave at once, but it was already dark, and Elsa refused to move. We would pack our things and leave first thing the following morning, and not a minute before.

Hitch-hiking was Elsa's favourite means of travel, particularly on country roads where buses were few and far between. The procedure seldom varied. When a car approached, she didn't withdraw meekly to the side and gesture with her thumb. She strode into the middle of the road and waved the car down.

Reactions varied. Sometimes there was real anger, at other times, surprise, even concern. Whatever response she received, Elsa didn't ask where the driver was going, but explained, with great charm, where *we* were going. Nine times out of ten it worked, even when it meant a diversion for the driver.

These were the 1950s, and with all their faults – class and racial prejudice, misogyny, capital punishment; the list goes on and on – the one thing we did not have to cope with was the insane materialism that persists today. Certainly, the boys at Sherborne Prep didn't think any better of X when his parents swept up the drive in a Rolls-Royce Silver Ghost, nor did they think worse of Thomas when his grandmother stepped off the bus in a moleskin coat that had seen better days.

During the 1951 spring holiday, Panny forwarded two letters from Sheila; one was addressed to Elsa, the other was a warm and affectionate letter to me. It included a graphic description of the dangerous sea journey we had taken together from India at the height of the war, but I had no recollections of this. For me, memory started – albeit in brief flashes – during my time with Sheila and Panny in the cottage on Salisbury Plain, but that period was barely mentioned.

The letter ended with an invitation. Sheila and the children would be spending the coming summer months in the Grange, 'a lovely country hotel with a beautiful garden' on the edge of Salisbury, where they could all be close to Panny. It would be wonderful if I could join them during my summer holiday.

I put the letter down and stared blankly at Elsa.

'Well?' She asked.

'I don't want to see her.'

'Are you sure?'

It was a repeat of the conversation we'd had two years previously in response to Tommy's ultimatum, and once again, I was sure.

'Very well!'

The letters were ignored.

The following year, the invitation was repeated, but this time Elsa was not content to stay neutral.

'All you have to do is meet them. After that, it's your decision, but please give this a chance.' In a separate letter to Elsa, Sheila had offered to cover my school fees. To her credit, Elsa did not share that with me at the time, as she knew it would force my decision, but even without that incentive I agreed to meet the family.

Arrangements were made for Sheila to visit me as soon as she arrived in England in early June. It was during school term, and for some reason it was decided that we should meet at the school swimming pool.

This was the first time I had seen my mother in eight years, but I spotted her immediately. Now in her early thirties, Sheila was more striking than ever, and several school masters had gathered round her, but as soon as I approached, she abandoned them to welcome me with the first hug I could remember.

As we meandered back and forth along the edge of the pool, Sheila chatted about the family. My sisters, Linda and Kay, were now five and seven, and little Rufus (nicknamed 'B') had just turned three. 'They would all love to meet you.' It was an offer I couldn't resist, and we agreed that I should come to Salisbury for the first week of the summer holiday.

Years later, Kay told me that it was not until Sheila was driving them to the station that they learnt they were about to meet their elder brother. They were still confused when I ran up the platform towards them and stared at me in silence as my mother introduced them, one by one. It was only when we were walking along the river towards Panny's house that they managed to pluck up enough courage to ask all the questions that were confusing them. Why hadn't they met me before? Where had I been living and with whom? Was I finally coming to live with them? Questions, questions, questions, in spite of Sheila's repeated calls to shut up and stop bothering me.

I am not sure whether I would have continued seeing my mother if she had been childless, but I had fallen in love with my three siblings, who stuck firmly to me for the rest of the day. Before long, they had a nickname for me – 'Ants', and when I walked into the girls' bedroom at the Grange to say my good nights, Linda immediately burst into a fit of giggles. Pointing to her sister, she shouted out, 'Ants, she says she wants to marry you!' Poor Kay cringed with embarrassment.

To this day, Kay and B have remained close friends, but my mother would always be an enigma. She was certainly very gifted. On the wall of my bedroom, there is a street scene she painted when was she was just fifteen years old. The details are beautifully observed; it really looks like the work of a mature artist.

According to both Panny and Elsa, Sheila had done remarkably well in her school days, both academically and in sport, and as I got to know her better, I recognised many other qualities. She had an extraordinary ability to relate to people across boundaries of class and race, and it was no surprise to learn that she had been heavily involved in charitable work and politics, particularly in India. She felt passionately about the country's right to independence, but as a unified state, and had formed close connections with the two men who would shape the future of the subcontinent. I have never been able to corroborate this, but I heard from two sources that my mother was entrusted with chauffeuring Jinnah, the future leader of Pakistan, to a final secret meeting with Nehru in the hopes of reaching an agreement that would avoid partition.

It was always hard to understand how someone who related so well to people of all classes and backgrounds could become such a different person in the family context. As Kay once put it to me: 'She was a wonderful person to have as a friend, but a very difficult person to have as a relative.'

In her own home, Sheila could be a tyrant. Neither Eddy nor Elsa had ever hit me, and I was shocked by my mother's outbursts of violence against her own children, the smacking and shouting. Her relationship with Rufus was equally tempestuous. At one stage during his retirement, he walked out of the house and stayed out for nearly a year. Apparently, he spent most of his time fishing in Pakistan!

The problem, I am sure, was one of deep frustration. If my mother had been born a generation later, she might have had a successful professional career, but those opportunities were not readily available to a young woman growing up during the Great Depression. Despite her academic promise, she was taken out of school when she was fifteen and was also discouraged from pursuing her interest in sport. Apparently, there was a popular misconception at the time that women who took strenuous exercise risked sterility.

For Sheila and many young women like her, the only purpose and option in life was to marry and raise children.

All these thoughts and observations would become clear over time, but on that first day in Salisbury with Sheila and the children, I knew that my three siblings would always play an important part in my life.

Elsa and I had agreed that if all went well at that first meeting, I should stay with the family for the first week of my summer holidays. After that, we could divide the time on an equal basis – one week with Elsa, one week at the Grange. But once that was put into practice, I was genuinely torn. Whomever I was with, I always hated the departures, but it was the pattern we would follow for many summers.

After the breakup with the Baxters, Elsa had found a job as cook and cleaner on a farm near Sherborne. The Dales treated us fairly. As long as I did my bit whenever I was on the farm, there would always be food for me and a place to sleep, and no objections were raised when I took time off to visit the Grange.

In those journeys back and forth, I was oscillating between two entirely different worlds. The Grange was a first-class country hotel, set in a huge garden with a tennis court and a putting green. Our days there were gentle and leisurely, and we were (almost) treated as guests of honour, because of the length of the bookings.

Conditions were very different on the farm, but neither Elsa nor I felt any resentment. In her case, this was remarkable, especially in the light of Sheila's original promise to pay my school fees. If that had been honoured, Elsa would not have been forced to work as a servant in her old age, but it never was.

Elsa made no mention of this until my relationship with the family was firmly established. When she did, I insisted that she raise the matter with Sheila, but Elsa was adamant. She was not prepared to beg, and I had to promise to respect her wishes and never to mention this to my mother. In part, it was a matter of pride, but I also sensed Elsa's fear that she might not survive long enough to support me all the way through school and, hopefully, university. A time might come when I would be totally reliant on this family, and we shouldn't do anything to upset that relationship.

At fourteen, I entered Sherborne senior school on an exhibition. This barely took the edge off the higher fees, but once again, I was told not to mention this to Sheila.

Tommy, my father, was continuing with his monthly payments of £15, and when he wrote to tell us that he and Molly would be coming to England the following spring, Elsa was equally insistent that I should not make any pleas for additional support.

It would be Molly's and Tommy's first visit since the Green Gates fracas, nine years earlier. Apparently, the two of them planned to go their separate ways for one week of the holiday. Tommy would be hiring a car and taking Elsa and me on a tour of the Cotswolds, while Molly would be spending the time with her parents in Yorkshire. Clearly, she had no wish to see Elsa.

The drive through the Cotswolds brought back so many memories of those wonderful times with Elsa and Eddy, touring the Cape in our little Ford Prefect. The countryside we passed through may have lacked the grandeur of the South African landscape, but the medieval towns and villages in their distinctive yellow limestone and the rolling hills and grassland had a charm of their own. Although it was only a one-week break, it was the first holiday Elsa and I had enjoyed together since we had come to England. Tommy took care of everything, allowing us to explore and meander wherever we pleased.

This was very different person from the father who had summoned me to his Pietermaritzburg office to tell me to 'phase your grandparents out of your life', and when we were alone together on the first evening of the tour, I began to understand why he and Elsa had developed such a fractious relationship. He couldn't believe the way I had interacted with her during our travels that day; how I had interrupted, contradicted and even broken into one of her stories with, 'Oh Elsa! You do exaggerate.' Nor could he believe Elsa's response. There wasn't a touch of anger. If anything, she seemed to enjoy the banter.

I had such a strong feeling that the freedom, love and respect I had been given as a child was Elsa's act of atonement, her way of compensating for the strict, authoritarian upbringing she had probably imposed on her own son. I also felt I understood why, at the age of twenty-one, Tommy had decided to get as far away from his parents as possible and went out of his way to shock and defy them when they came to visit him in India. There seemed to have been so many tragic misjudgements and overreactions on both sides, culminating in Molly's and Tommy's provocative performance at Green Gates. Now, at last, mother and son seemed to have reached an accord.

The following month, Sheila wrote to tell us that Rufus had reached the heights of his profession. The family would be leaving India and returning to the United States, where Rufus was about to take up the post of Executive Vice President of the Standard Vacuum Oil Company, and I was invited to join them for the December holiday. It would be my first Christmas away from Elsa, but she insisted that I should seize this opportunity.

After a twelve-hour crossing in a Boeing Stratocruiser, we landed at New York's Idlewild Airport (later JFK). It was the height of the McCarthy era, and as the immigration officer stared down at this fifteen-year-old, he asked, in all seriousness:

'Are you a member of the Communist Party?'

'No, Sir.'

A brief pause, and then: 'Have you ever been a member of the Communist Party?'

I wish I had said: 'Yes, but when I was five, I read Yakovlev's account of the failures of the collective farm policies and handed in my party card.'

I did not, of course, and only managed another shy 'No, Sir.'

The family was living in a luxurious home, close to the sea in Southport, Connecticut, where I met my stepfather Rufus for the first time. He was an imposing figure, well over six feet tall and now in his early fifties. Although he was always friendly towards me, we spent very little time together. Rufus worked a six-day week, leaving home in the dark to begin the long commute to the company's headquarters in New York's Rockefeller Centre, and sometimes staying away until eleven o'clock at night. His heart and soul were in his job, not his home. That was Sheila's territory.

I have some marvellous memories of that first holiday in America, but Sheila's occasional flashes of anger and violence against the children continued to upset and anger me. It would take another year before I found the courage to intervene, threatening my mother with 'a punch in the face' if she hit little B again.

Looking back from this distance, I am amazed that Kay and B were not damaged by their childhood experiences. When they became parents, neither of them followed their mother's example, and ever since have maintained close relationships with their children and, subsequently, their grandchildren. Our sister Linda was the only casualty. Sadly, she has had many problems, and is now being looked after in a home in Connecticut.

Less than a month after my return from America, my housemaster called me out of class to tell me that Elsa had suffered a heart attack. I was free to visit her at the local hospital and left at once.

I was expecting the worst, but Elsa sat up in bed as soon as I entered the ward and did her best to assure me that this was only a mild attack. The bad news, though, was that she would have to retire from domestic service.

The Dales kindly allowed her to convalesce on the farm, and when she had recovered sufficiently, she decided to leave the Sherborne area and move into a rooming house in Hove, where I joined her for my next holiday. Our situation was desperate, and we both knew it. Then something remarkable happened.

During my first holiday, we were having lunch together with the radio on. In those days, local announcements preceded the one o'clock news on the BBC's Home Service. At one point, Elsa suddenly pricked up her ears and gestured for silence. The announcer was inviting parents on low incomes to apply to the East Sussex County Council for grants to cover their children's boarding fees at state grammar schools. To qualify, they would have to show compelling reasons why their children could not register as day students, whose education was free.

Elsa had always felt strongly that I had to be a boarder, but this never felt like rejection. As she would say again and again: 'You can't spend your life with this little old woman. You need to be with people your own age.'

As soon as she heard the announcement, Elsa started taking down the details. I tried to explain that we were not eligible – I was in a private school, not a state school – but she wasn't listening.

Early the following day, Elsa took the bus to the council offices in Lewes and returned triumphant. I have no idea how she achieved this, but from that moment onwards, payment of all my fees was guaranteed by the East Sussex County Council; and not only through my entire time at Sherborne, but also until the end of my final year at university, provided I passed the entry exams.

This generosity seems extraordinary today, when students can find themselves with debts of over £40,000 on graduation. The difference, of course, is that only a small minority had ambitions to go to university in the 1950s. In a society still strictly divided on class lines, money was not the only factor. It was that sense of entitlement and self-confidence that someone with Elsa's background had in abundance, and in her case, this never faded. Whether we were scrubbing floors, sweeping stables or living in a cheap rooming house, she believed that I had an absolute right to expect the best education the country could offer. Today, those expectations are spreading throughout society, but sadly the state is no longer willing or able to provide the necessary funding.

I was fifteen years old when Elsa secured this grant. In the same year, there was another decisive moment, at least for me.

One afternoon, I wandered into the school library, which had just acquired a new set of Encyclopaedia Britannica. I pulled out a volume and opened it at random to find page after page of stills from the great film classics – Bogart and Bergman in *Casablanca*, Brando in *A Streetcar Named Desire*, Welles in *The Third Man*, which is still one of my favourite films. I was spellbound. By absolute chance, I had opened the Encyclopaedia at 'Motion Pictures', and at that moment I made a decision that would shape the rest of my life.

It was an absurd, childish decision, but it had a certain logic. This was my O-level year. From that point onwards, I would be forced to specialise. I loved acting and had a passion for literature and the arts, but I was also drawn to maths and science. Here in front of me was a potential career that seemed to bring every-thing together. I had no idea what role would be right for me – actor, director or technician – but I believed that all would become clear over time. The important thing was to keep every option open and work doubly hard to take A-level exams in as many subjects as possible.

I shared these thoughts with Elsa. As always, she listened respectfully, but there were bigger issues on her mind. Ever since her heart attack, I sensed her fear that she might pass away while I was still a schoolboy or become a burden to me when I was trying to make a start in life.

These thoughts were never expressed in words, only through her actions. As well as maintaining close contact with Tommy and Sheila, she encouraged me to accept Christmas invitations from school friends and their families and was thrilled when I received a telegram from Rufus, inviting me to lunch at the Savoy during his impending visit to London.

The contrasts between the Grange hotel and the Dale's farm were insignifi-cant in comparison to those I experienced on the day I left the rooming house in Hove to take the train to London. On arrival at the Savoy, I was greeted by a commissionaire in a black morning suit and top hat who opened the doors to another world. The colonnaded hallways with their massive chandeliers, the gilded archways and the overall sense of space and luxury took my breath away.

Rufus had suggested the Savoy Grill, and I arrived well ahead of time. As soon as I mentioned my stepfather's name to the head waiter, there was a respectful nod, and I was led across the spacious art deco interior to the table Rufus had booked. He arrived on the dot of time. 'This OK for you?' he asked with a smile, indicating the room.

I remember noticing that the price of a single vegetable was slightly more than Elsa and I paid for a whole meal in the local café where we occasionally ate, but I felt no resentment. If anything, I found this comparison rather funny and shared the joke with Rufus, who took it in the same spirit.

The following year, there was another sudden change, which I sensed the moment Elsa stepped off the train on one of her Sherborne visits. Hair and make-up had been carefully attended to, and much of her old vitality had returned. When I told her how thrilled I was to see her looking so well, she smiled, then, looking me straight in the eye, asked: 'What would you say if I told you I had fallen in love?'

His name was Bill Crowther, and he was from Dudley in the West Midlands. If it was alright with me, they planned to move into a Bournemouth hotel together, where I could join them as soon as term ended.

I was delighted and told Elsa that I really looked forward to meeting her new partner.

Bill was a widower, five years younger than Elsa. He was a remarkable man who had recently retired from a senior position in local government. Born into a working-class family, he had educated himself in libraries and working men's clubs and taken a degree in his late thirties.

Bill was in a position to look after Elsa and give her treats she hadn't enjoyed since our Cape Town days. They went to the theatre, cinema and concerts together. On Saturdays they sometimes went dancing. Their love was deep and genuine. It was also physical. One evening when the three of us went out for dinner, Elsa, who was usually abstemious, had a little too much to drink. When Bill slipped out to the gents, she leaned over to me and whispered, 'I never knew sex could be so much fun!'

There was a definite subtext to this wonderful relationship, which Elsa and I both understood. She now had someone she could rely on to take care of her for the rest of her days.

But Elsa was not the sole beneficiary. Thanks to Bill's generosity, I always had a place to stay and no longer needed to take holiday jobs. He also shared my interest in film, and one of his first gifts was membership of the local film society, which he had joined as soon as he and Elsa moved to Bournemouth.

Bill and I had long conversations together. As far as he was concerned, emotions stirred by great films like *The Third Man* and *Casablanca* were understandable, but I should think seriously about the best way to start my filming career.

Like Elsa, he believed that the first priority was to secure a good degree. Once that had been achieved, I should be prepared to work at any level available on a documentary crew and learn from first-hand experience. I could move to features eventually, but Bill felt he knew enough about me and the experiences I'd had to believe that documentary might be the right medium for me. How perceptive he was.

Thanks to Bill and my film society membership, I would have a thorough grounding in documentaries over the next two years – from early classics like *Nanook of the North* and *Battleship Potemkin* to the work of directors like Karel Reisz and Lindsay Anderson, who (in Reisz's words) were trying to 'convey their feelings in terms of people.'

****

In 1959, I gained a place at Queens' College, Cambridge, and was also awarded an exhibition – as I recall, it was worth about £100 a year. All the rest, including tuition fees and all living costs, was covered by the East Sussex County Council.

There was a twelve-week gap between the end of the school term and the start of the university year, and when Sheila invited me to spend that entire summer holiday with her and the family, Elsa and Bill urged me to accept. It would be a wonderful opportunity to get to know another country.

I wrote to Sheila, thanking her for the invitation and asking if she could possibly find me a casual job somewhere local, so that I could raise enough money to pay for two or three weeks of travel.

Her reply was not encouraging. Travel plans had already been made. Rufus had rented a house on a beautiful island off the coast of Maine, where we would be spending the first weeks of my holiday. By the time we were back in Connecticut, it would probably be too late in the season to look for a summer job.

I was disappointed, but still hoped that I would find some way to fund a few weeks of travel, with or without Sheila's help.

We drove to Maine a few days after I landed. The island was stunning, and I shall never forget our first evening there together. As we were sitting on the terrace, savouring the sunset, we spotted an elderly lobsterman, slowly punting his way across the shallows between us and a neighbouring island. Every now and then he would stop to lift a trap out of the water, extract the contents, and then drop it back with a soft splash. Sitting in the bow, watching his every move, was an equally elderly Indian lady, dressed in a sari.

Although I was pleased to be spending time with the family in this lovely setting, the isolation was making me increasingly restless, but everything changed when Rufus's sister, Eleanor, and her husband, Mac, breezed in. They had driven a thousand miles from Rockville, Indiana, a small midwestern town where Rufus's parents and most of his relatives still lived.

They were a warm, outgoing couple, who immediately sensed my problem and offered a solution. Why didn't I come back to Rockville with them when they returned at the end of the week? On the way, we could head for Buffalo, New York, nip up from there to Niagara Falls, and then follow the southern shore of Lake Erie as far as Toledo, Ohio, before heading down to Rockville, where I would be very welcome to stay with them.

I was thrilled at the suggestion.

'But how's he supposed to get back?' Sheila asked sharply.

Now it was my turn. 'Greyhound Bus. It's easy.'

'Do you have enough money for that? Food and accommodation included?'

'Yes.'

'How much did you bring with you?'

After a pause, 'Forty dollars.'

Sheila shook her head in disbelief. 'Not nearly enough. It's a stupid idea, and you shouldn't think of going.'

At this point Rufus intervened. 'I think Ants has reached an age when he should be allowed to make his own decisions.'

And off we went, but the trip nearly came to a disastrous end on our second day. Eleanor and Mac always travelled with their identity cards, and as I had my passport with me, they suggested that we should cross the Rainbow Bridge into Canada to get the best view of the Niagara Falls.

On our way back, we had to pass through US Immigration. When I submitted my passport, I was told that I had already used my single-entry visa and would not be allowed back in the country. It was a critical moment, but when Uncle Mac raised his right hand, everything changed. After a short exchange between him and the immigration officer in a language I did not understand, we were waved through.

It was left to Eleanor to explain what had happened.

'Mac had spotted the officer's signet ring and showed him his. They are both Masons, you see.'

Eleanor and Mac were wonderful company throughout the trip. They were also very generous and insisted on paying for all my meals and overnight stops. When we arrived in Rockville, my precious forty dollars were still intact.

The few days spent in that small Midwestern community were special. I was able to meet Rufus's parents and other members of the clan, but when the time came to buy the bus tickets, I told Mac and Eleanor I had decided on another plan. I wanted to see as much of the country as possible. Sheila and the family were now back in Connecticut, but instead of going straight there, I wanted to head south to New Orleans. From there, I would follow the Gulf Coast to Florida, before making my way back along the Atlantic Coast to Connecticut. By my reckoning, it would be journey of just over three thousand miles and probably take between three and four weeks.

Eleanor and Mac couldn't believe what they were hearing. There was no way I could make a journey like that with the money I had, but I told them I would hitchhike all the way and was confident that my forty dollars (worth about $300 today) would see me through. When they offered to contribute, I turned it down. It wasn't just the problem of imposing on them yet again. I felt that it would damage their relationship with Sheila and Rufus if they colluded with me in any way, but I assured them I would write to Sheila immediately, outlining the plan and promising to send her regular postcards on my travels.

On a forty-dollar budget, there was no way I could afford overnight accommodation, even in the cheapest motels. Instead, I slept on beaches, in bus stations, graveyards, parks and small-town jails, where permission to spend the night was seldom refused, but there was one occasion when I was turned out of my cell in the early hours to make room for some drunks who had just been arrested.

Keeping body and clothes clean was a challenge, particularly during the first stages of the journey when I was far from any beaches, but I did my best in 'rest rooms' at filling stations, and on one occasion was guilty of an illegal entry. While wandering through the lovely French Quarter in New Orleans, I noticed that the gate to a walled garden had been left unlocked. Inside, there was an exterior stairway leading to a first-floor balcony. From there, I was able find my way into a bathroom where I enjoyed the first shower I'd had in ten days. Clean and refreshed, I walked away unnoticed.

It's a sad admission, but I feel it would be madness for any teenager today to set off alone on a similar journey. Even on my travels, there were some bad moments. One night when I was sleeping in a Greyhound bus station, I was woken up by two aggressive police officers. My suntanned skin and jet-black hair had obviously attracted their attention, and they suspected that I was a 'wetback' – an illegal immigrant from Mexico. On my travels, I was also propositioned by two (male) drivers, but those challenges were quickly overcome – a British passport in the first instance and some angry 'No's on the other occasions.

Apart from the chance to savour glorious scenery and visit places of historical interest, I had an opportunity to mix with people of all classes and backgrounds in a way that was not possible in 1950s Britain. Although Elsa and I formed close friendships with other servants working with us, in our dealings across shop counters and with porters and bus conductors (to mention a few), our accents defined us, and I frequently sensed hostility towards this 'little posh boy'. But in the United States, my clipped public-school accent (as it was then) raised no hackles. In fact, it was frequently appreciated, and I was often asked to 'say that again!' I also found that people trusted me and opened up to me in ways that no stranger had done before.

In those few weeks on the road, I feel I made the transition from childhood to manhood. I also believe it was an experience that helped shape my future career. My interest in the lives and opinions of the people I met was usually regarded as a compliment rather than an intrusion and, thanks to them, I was able to see the world from many different perspectives.

Of all those encounters, one really stood out. Denzel was an African American, who had graduated as a lawyer from the University of Chicago and was returning for a short holiday in the family home, a few miles outside Mobile, Alabama. He took me on a tour of the whole area, and I was shocked by the contrasts between the white and black districts we passed through and the looks we were receiving as we drove past in the same car.

At one point, Denzel showed me a 'crèche' for black children that consisted of a row of chicken huts surrounded by a high wire fence. As it was the weekend, the place was empty, but it was hard to imagine what conditions must have been like when the place was crowded with small children on a typical weekday.

I met both his parents, who were interested to know my background. In those days there was very little awareness of South Africa in the United States, and when I told my hosts about the country I loved, nobody raised questions about apartheid.

Twenty-three days after setting off from Rockville, I returned to the Burton family home, expecting a furious response from Sheila, but she was proud of me and had actually arranged for an interview at a local radio station. By defying her instructions and breaking the family rules, I seemed to have touched a rebellious streak deep within her and won her respect. It was a turning point in my relationship with my mother.

Chapter Three

CAMBRIDGE AND THE CONSEQUENCES

That first year at Cambridge was a time of momentous change on many levels. Issues of racial injustice, which I had started to think about seriously during my hitchhiking tour the previous summer, came to dominate the news, but the focus was not on the United States. It was on 'my country'.

During the Lent term, three major events followed in quick succession. On 3 February 1960, Harold Macmillan delivered his famous 'Wind of Change' speech to the South African parliament in Cape Town. Three weeks later, the first anti-apartheid demonstrations were held in Trafalgar Square, with protestors demanding a trade boycott. The following month, passions were further inflamed by the Sharpeville massacre, when the South African police fired on a crowd of several thousand protesting the laws that put any black or 'coloured' South African at risk of arrest and imprisonment if found in a designated white area without a valid passbook. Sixty-nine demonstrators were killed that day and more than twice that number were severely injured.

In the early years of apartheid, few people in Britain spoke out firmly against the South African regime and its policies. We were still an imperial power and racial segregation, in one form or another, was the norm throughout the Empire.

Well into the 1950s, British landlords were free to post notices on their front doors, making it clear that 'No Coloureds or Indians' need apply. It was also a time when close friendships across racial lines were rare and mixed marriage was almost unthinkable.

Nothing conveys the change in British attitudes – both within the country and towards South Africa – quite as powerfully as the story of Seretse Khama and Ruth Williams.

Seretse was the chief-in-waiting of the dominant Bamangwato tribe in the British protectorate of Bechuanaland. While studying law at the Temple in London, he met 24-year-old Ruth Williams, who was working as a confidential clerk for a firm of Lloyd's underwriters.

In September 1948, the couple announced their engagement. Ruth was sacked from her job and her father turned her out of the house, but it was the response of the South African government that made the greatest impact. The National Party had been in power for just four months when news of this intended marriage reached the Prime Minister, D.F. Malan. He cabled the British government, describing the relationship between Seretse and Ruth as 'nauseating', and insisted they be forbidden to marry.

Under apartheid law, sexual relationships across racial lines were a criminal offence, and the idea that a mixed-race couple might, one day, be ruling a neighbouring country was more than the South African government could tolerate.

Faced with all these pressures, the Attlee government caved in. Seretse was warned that if he married Ruth, he would be banned from his own country, but the couple had already made their wedding plans and would have gone ahead regardless, if the clergyman who had originally agreed to hold the service hadn't lost his nerve. He referred the matter to the Bishop of London, who refused to allow the marriage to take place in any church in his diocese.

On 2 October 1948, Seretse and Ruth were married in a London registry office, and the British government carried out its threat. Seretse was forbidden to return to Bechuanaland.

In South Africa, National Party organ *Die Transvaler* crowed: 'While trying to prop up with words the whitewashed façade of liberalism, the British government has had, in practice, to concede to the demands of apartheid.'

But the era when the apartheid government could impose its will was fast coming to an end. The transformation began in the mid-Fifties as one former British colony after another was being prepared for independence and a new Commonwealth of Nations began to rise out of the ashes of empire. In 1956, Seretse was allowed to return to Bechuanaland on condition that he renounce his claim to the tribal throne, but that did not prevent him from engaging in politics, and when the Bechuanaland protectorate finally gained independence and the new country of Botswana was born, Seretse Khama was the first elected president.

Any member of the South African government who failed to understand the significance of these changes was left in no doubt when the British Prime Minister, Harold Macmillan, delivered his famous speech to the South African Parliament, making it clear that his government would continue to grant independence to all Britain's possessions in Africa. He was equally clear that 'there were aspects of your policies which make it impossible for us to give South Africa our support and encouragement without being false to our own deep convictions.'

Threatened with expulsion from the Commonwealth, South Africa finally withdrew in October 1960.

Tommy and I had corresponded regularly since our Cotswolds tour, and when these political pressures began to build, he insisted in letter after letter that the situation in South Africa was being grossly misrepresented. Bill Crowther took a different position. He was radical, with firm views on everything from nuclear disarmament to the misused powers of advertising. He was also strongly critical of apartheid, but Elsa and I shared the same feelings for South Africa and weren't sure whom to believe.

These debates came to a sudden end in the spring of 1960. Elsa and Bill had decided to take a flat in Cambridge to be near me, but within days of moving in, Elsa started losing her voice and having difficulty swallowing. A local doctor assured her that this was nothing serious – a minor obstruction in the throat – and she was booked for a routine operation at Addenbrooke's Hospital.

Bill and I accompanied her there on the day and agreed to return in the early evening when Elsa would have recovered from the anaesthetic.

That afternoon, I was in the main court of Queens' rehearsing the part of Friar Lawrence in the college production of Romeo and Juliet, when I caught sight of Bill waving for my attention across the court. I asked the cast to excuse me and ran over. He had just received a phone call from the hospital and the news was bad. As soon as the surgeon started to operate, he realised that Elsa had severe throat cancer.

Bill had a taxi waiting and we went straight to Addenbrooke's.

By this time, Elsa had been moved into a private ward, and I was shocked to see the transformation. She couldn't speak, and when I took her hand, she simply shook her head. It was a gesture that told me everything I needed to know, even before we saw the consultant. 'I'm afraid there is nothing further we can do', he told us. 'You can visit her whenever you like, and if there's a sudden change, we'll call you.'

Bill and I received the final summons three days later, at 2.00am, and stayed with Elsa until the end.

Her funeral was heart-breaking. The hearse developed mechanical problems on its way to the crematorium and arrived, bumping and shuddering, some ten minutes later than the appointed time. The duty clergyman was waiting for us at the door of the chapel, clipboard in hand. After a few sharp words about our timing and his heavy schedule, he hustled us inside and gabbled through the service in double time.

This was certainly one of the worst moments of my life. Grief was compounded with a sense of shame. Was this the best we could do to commemorate a life like Elsa's – just two of us in the congregation and a clergyman who had never met her and whose main concern was his schedule?

I wanted to shout 'Stop!' and tell the pallbearers to take the coffin out of the chapel; something I'm sure Elsa would have done in similar circumstances, but I lacked her courage. The best I could do was to take her ashes with me and spend the next few days tracing her surviving friends in Whitchurch, the Cardiff suburb where she and Eddy had spent most of their married life. A date was set for a second funeral service at St Mary's, the local parish church.

Several old friends were present when Elsa's ashes were buried in the grave of her second son, Peter, who had died in 1919 when he was just six months old.

I had kept Tommy up to date. He could not get away in time for either funeral and suggested instead that I might like to join him and Molly for a September holiday together in Spain's Costa Brava. He was sure I needed a proper break.

There had been no communication between Molly and me since our flight from Pietermaritzburg eleven years earlier, and I was not looking forward to seeing her again. I had always believed that she was the author of the ultimatum Tommy had delivered in his office on that terrible Sunday afternoon, but soon after I received his invitation, Molly broke her silence with a long, tender letter. There were no recriminations, no references to the past and – most important of all – not a word against Elsa. On the contrary, Molly acknowledged everything my grandmother had done to secure me the best education England could offer.

This was a very different Molly from the stepmother who had refused to meet either of us five years earlier. In the letters that followed I learnt that she was now in touch with both her sons. Nigel, the shy fifteen-year-old, who had spent most of his time at Green Gates shut away in his bedroom making model aeroplanes, had pursued his passion and signed up with the Royal Air Force on his sixteenth birthday. It was a ten-year commission, and as soon as his time was up, Molly had invited him to South Africa, where he was now working in Tommy's office.

Molly was also in touch with her second son, Rodney, who had not seen his mother since he was two years old and had now been invited to join me on the Costa Brava holiday. He was my age and worked in a London bank. We actually met for the first time at Heathrow Airport. There was so much to catch up with, so many gaps to fill, that we hardly stopped talking during the entire flight.

Molly, it seemed, was starting to develop strong maternal feelings at a relatively late stage of life, though perhaps there was a simpler explanation. This was someone who could not relate to children.

She and Tommy were waiting for us when we touched down at Alicante Airport. Apart from her hair, which was now a soft blue, she had changed very little, but was obviously struck by the transformation that had taken place in the little buck-toothed nine-year-old who had kissed her goodbye eleven years earlier.

As the four of us were settling down to dinner, Molly touched my arm affectionately and told me that she and Tommy would like me to spend my coming Christmas holiday with them in South Africa. I was delighted to accept.

Molly and Tommy had a beautiful but simple thatched home in the hills above Pietermaritzburg. Christmas in South Africa comes in mid-summer, at the peak of the holiday season. Tommy had closed his office for three weeks, and Molly had filled the diary with social engagements.

Clearly, they were doing their best to entice me back to South Africa, but I was troubled by the political situation. I hadn't raised any of these issues during our short break in Costa Brava, but Tommy was a passionate walker, and we had many opportunities to discuss politics during our long hikes together.

Summer is the rainy season in most of Southern Africa, and there were times when we had to find shelter from a sudden storm. Just as suddenly, the rumbling thunder would roll away, the sky would clear, and the smell of wet veldt and blue gum would fill the air. What affected me so much was the sense of boundless space; a landscape rolling grandly towards distant mountains that seemed to melt into the sky. In moments like this, my feelings for South Africa were overwhelming, but I needed to hear the truth.

Tommy supported the ruling National Party, which, he believed, had the only practical solution for the country's future. Apparently, an Act of Parliament had already been passed which would turn whole areas of South Africa into self-governing tribal homelands.

In his opinion, the tribe was the only coherent entity in African society. By failing to respect this and granting independence to countries defined by colonial borders, the imperial powers were storing up serious problems for the future. People with different histories, languages and cultures were either being lumped together or split apart by these arbitrary boundaries.

I agreed. That was a real problem, but could we talk about the present: pass laws, strict segregation, 'whites only' and 'black only' signs everywhere you look?

Tommy repeated the mantra I would hear again and again. Yes, we all acknowledge that apartheid started out as a crude form of discrimination, but it was now evolving into something completely different. In schools, black children were being taught their own history in their own languages, and opportunities were open to them, right up to university level.

And Sharpeville? Sixty-nine protestors shot dead?

It was a terrible tragedy, but I had to understand that a hostile crowd of over five thousand protestors had converged on that police station, and the sad truth is that our police force contains a high proportion of those who are most resistant to the changes this government is making.

I still wasn't sure, but as the final days approached, one thing was certain. The thought of leaving the country I loved and returning to Cambridge was painful.

****

The sudden loss of Elsa and the conflicting emotions about South Africa were serious enough, but there was another problem during my first year at Cambridge: my tutor.

Ever since I made the decision to work in film, I had hoped to maintain a balance between science and the arts, but after taking O-Levels, was forced to make a choice. The best I could do was to work on chemistry, physics and higher maths to scholarship level, while taking an English A-Level on the side. Now that I was at Cambridge, I wanted to restore the balance.

My English tutor was appalled. I had been awarded an exhibition, based on my maths and science results. If I switched to English – or so he implied – I would be taking college money under false pretences.

For someone like me, who had enjoyed such strong support and encouragement throughout childhood and adolescence, it was hard to deal with this level of hostility, especially when it came from the one person who would be at very centre of my studies for the next three years, but I stood firm.

My tutor was not the only problem. Those who read English at Cambridge in the early sixties may disagree with me, but I found the course stultifying. Every week we had to submit an essay. The subject might be a single Shakespeare play or the works of three minor poets, but in all cases the trick was to provide a clever synthesis of the fashionable critiques of the day. Creativity and originality did not seem to be high on the agenda, and the composition of the University's English department reflected this. Of the seventy-plus professors and lecturers, few were involved in what most of us would regard as creative writing. Amongst this small elite, one person stood out: the great C.S. Lewis.

His first lecture was unforgettable. The subject was Chaucer's *The Canterbury Tales*, and Lewis focused on one minor character – the Clerk of Oxenford. Here was a young man who spent whatever money he had on books and was so engrossed in his studies that he was friendless and penniless.

Lewis used this story as a warning. He predicted an explosion in the number of university undergraduates over the coming decades and a time when even the best degrees would no longer guarantee life-long security in a prestigious career.

We should learn from the Clerk's mistakes and start thinking beyond university. What were our real aims in life? What were our greatest dreams? Those were the questions we should be asking ourselves, and when we felt we had the answer, we should focus on that, even if it meant never attending another lecture.

It is hard to exaggerate the impact this lecture had on me, but in my first year at Cambridge, I was not prepared to follow Lewis's advice. For Elsa's sake, I was determined to work hard and secure a good degree, but my tutor's hostility never let up until I finally crumbled, securing a miserable 'third' in the preliminary exams at the end of my first year.

Elsa never lived to hear this result, and now that she was no longer with me, I felt ready to follow the great man's lead. I began commuting back and forth to London, where I managed to persuade a film editor and two production managers to let me observe work in progress.

I frequently took the last train back to Cambridge, arriving at the college long after the gates were shut. The high fences were an easy climb, but one night the spike at the top of a railing pierced the sole of one of my shoes. I shouted out: 'Oh God!' and out of the darkness came the reply: 'No, this is not God; merely his representative on earth!' It was the college Dean, but he never took the matter further.

During my time in London, I also paid several visits to the South African embassy, where there was a whole collection of pamphlets with English translations of articles written by a group of Afrikaner intellectuals, who had come together in what would be known as the 'Verligte' ('Enlightened') movement.

Their message was a repeat of everything I had heard from Tommy but set out in much greater detail. I learnt that the Transkei, a whole segment of the north-eastern Cape covering an area larger than Switzerland, would soon be granted independence as the 'homeland' of the Xhosa people. There were long articles about the cultural sensitivity of Bantu education, as well as Bantu achievements in commerce, drama, music and broadcasting.

'Bantu', by the way, translates as 'people' in several African languages. When I was a child, white South Africans usually described themselves as 'Europeans' and, in polite society, blacks were called 'Africans', but this was unacceptable in National Party circles. Weren't we all Africans?

Throughout this literature, little mention was made about the daily indignities of pass laws and segregation, just a warm and rather vague sense that independent homelands and rising standards of education and achievement among all racial groups would eventually transform South Africa into a federation of self-governing states, but one author was less complacent, and his message really affected me. As he saw it, a fundamental struggle was taking place between those who were determined to make these positive changes and those who were clinging to the old ways. Occasionally, those backward elements would strike back, as they had done in Sharpeville, but they would not be able to stop the forward momentum.

I fell for it. All of it.

During those embassy visits, I was also told that South Africa had a thriving film industry, but it was far too early for me to contact any of the companies involved. At this stage, I had nothing to show. I couldn't even be sure that I had the ability to become a filmmaker.

Bill and I had remained in constant touch since Elsa's death. He was aware of my strong feelings for South Africa but couldn't believe that this was a country experiencing fundamental change.

He was equally consistent with his advice on my career. I should learn my craft here, even if it meant starting at the lowest level. Of course, I could always pay the occasional visit to South Africa, but if I was serious about filmmaking, I shouldn't think of moving there until I had something to show for myself, and a job to return to in Britain if things didn't work out well.

It was the best advice I could have been given, but instead of going through all the stages that Bill suggested, I decided to make that journey in a single leap. I had already spent many hours observing filmmakers in action and believed that I had grasped the rudiments. The rest would be up to me. I would have to be guided by my instincts and learn as much I could from my mistakes.

As I look back, this decision seems unbelievable, but it was the route I followed. If I could find an important subject, I was prepared to invest every penny I had inherited from Elsa (£1,800 in all) to produce and direct my own film.

I did not have to go far to find a deserving cause.

Children's Relief International, a Cambridge-based charity, provided annual seaside holidays for children in a DP (Displaced Persons) camp on the outskirts of Hanover. At the time, I knew nothing about the DP situation and was shocked to hear that these were people who had been displaced during the final years of the Second World War. Virtually all of them came from countries that had been absorbed into the Soviet bloc and, for many reasons, were unwilling to return.

While the millions of Germans who had fled from the East had been quickly integrated into West German society, refugees from Hungary, Poland and the Balkan states were still living in camps, sixteen years after the end of the war.

It was a story that had to be told.

A team was assembled which included two Cambridge friends: Harris, who was fluent in German, and Malcom, who lived just below me in the Fisher Building at Queens'. Both of them were thinking seriously about a future in filmmaking. We would be joined by Ian and Yousef, who had just completed the camera course at the London School of Film Technique in Brixton.

It still seems incredible that the four of them were prepared to put their trust in a 'director' with no filmmaking experience and agree to work without pay in the hope that the finished film would be good enough to give all of us screen credits that mattered. Accommodation in Germany was free, courtesy of the British Army, which had a camp on the outskirts of Hanover. All other expenses would have to be covered by my inheritance.

In the summer of 1961, we set off for Germany in an old Volkswagen camper van. The first two days were spent meeting camp residents and familiarising ourselves with the surroundings – rows of single-storey brick buildings, each containing sleeping and living quarters for up to eight families. Within each block there was a communal kitchen and separate male and female shower rooms and lavatories.

On day three, equipment was unpacked; our old Newman Sinclair camera was locked onto the tripod, and we were ready to go. The dream that began in a school library five years earlier had finally come true, but I had much to learn.

My first mistake was to be too controlling. We started with 'establishing shots' of the camp, which I handled as a theatre director might have done. With the wave of an arm, I signalled the moment when the curtain was rising. On cue, DPs 1 and 2 would come out of that door and walk towards the gap between those two huts. DP3, who had been waiting with a basket of wet laundry, would start hanging clothes on a line, while DPs 6, 7 and 8 would do this and DPs 9 and 10 would do that.

At the start, no one in the team questioned this approach. In this pre-digital age, we were all aware of the cost of film, and since every second was precious, it seemed right that key images should be carefully constructed, but we soon realised that this was the wrong approach. It was not the feeling that we were faking something that did not exist – I don't think any of the shots gave a false impression of the camp – it was the implicit arrogance that was so troubling. No matter how gentle and polite we were, the fact remained that we were giving orders to people whose lives had been torn apart. Instead of learning from them, we were simply telling them what to do.

We soon agreed on a new set of rules. When filming exteriors, we had to choose camera positions that gave a good sense of the layout of the camp and the daily activities. Once in place, we had to wait for the right moments. Direction should go no further than 'Would you mind coming out of that door again?' or 'Please carry on as you were doing before.' It would be a much slower process, but we knew it was right.

Interiors, at least in those days, were a different matter. Because of the slow film speeds, virtually everything had to be pre-lit, which left little room for spontaneity, but there again, the same principles had to apply. Our responsibility was to reproduce moments we had actually experienced and which we knew were a genuine part of camp life.

Even at this early stage, I was beginning to understand that documentary filmmaking – or at least the kind of filmmaking I wanted to do – had to be a gentle, almost intimate process; no tantrums, no shouts of 'Action!' and 'Cut!'. The director's role was to listen and learn, to be quiet and attentive.

We heard many personal stories from the people in the camp, but I had neither the experience nor the equipment to do something that would become so important in my later work – to give a voice to ordinary people. We had primitive sound gear, and our old Newman Sinclair camera was far too noisy to permit filmed interviews. The best we could do was to try to make the key points in commentary and add music and sound effects at the editing stage.

In spite of these limitations, I felt that I had been given a taste of what might be possible in the future. People in the camp trusted me and confided in me. Some spoke reasonable English; others would ask a friend to interpret, but however we chose to communicate, I had a real sense that an interview, conducted sensitively, could be a therapeutic experience for those involved. Two people almost welcomed the chance to talk frankly about their collaboration with the Nazis. Clearly, this was something they were still trying to resolve in their own minds and, of course, everything they said remained confidential.

****

In that final year, I scarcely bothered with my studies. At this stage, I was running the university film society and commuting regularly to London, where a professional editor, who had become a close friend, was devoting her weekends and evenings to the DP film.

While all this was happening, Tommy was making plans for my return to South Africa. He had been introduced to Billy Boxer, the CEO of a cinema chain with its own studio on the outskirts of Johannesburg, producing documentaries and commercials. Once I arrived in South Africa, he would be prepared to meet me and look at my work.

Meanwhile, we had decided on a very ambitious programme for the premiere of the DP film. In the spring of 1962, we would hold a festival of films in Cambridge's Arts Cinema under the banner 'A New Generation in World Cinema'. With help and guidance from David Robinson, film critic of the *Times*, contributions were invited from film schools across Europe. Some of the Hungarian and Polish films were outstanding, and although not in the same class, the DP film did attract the attention of Mme Théodora Olembert, a producer who made the occasional short documentary for cinema release. I was very excited when she approached me after the screening and suggested a meeting in London, where we could discuss a way to take the film forward.

Two days later, Mme Olembert received me in her spacious apartment, overlooking Regent's Park. She was a large lady in her mid-fifties with a preference for spacious, flowing gowns, and emphasising every point she made with extravagant gestures. Yes, she felt that the DP film had great potential and would like to take it over completely. For a start, the film needed a re-edit, which she would entrust to her good friend, Oswald Hafenrichter, editor of *The Third Man*. I was thrilled at the suggestion.

My departure for South Africa was just three weeks away, and it had always been my plan to take the DP film with me, but Mme Olembert persuaded me to let her continue working on her stronger version, which she promised to send me on completion. In the meantime, there were laboratory and other outstanding bills that I had to settle before my departure, but instead of dealing with these myself, she suggested that I deposit the necessary funds into her account and leave it to her to deal with all payments. It was important that everyone should know that the project was now in the hands of someone with her experience and reputation. She would, of course, be covering all future expenses herself.

This final pay-out relieved me of virtually all the money I had, but at least I didn't have to worry about travel costs, and in June 1962, I left for South Africa on a £10 immigrant ticket.

Not long after my arrival, red demands were forwarded to me from my former Queens' College address. Every bill I had covered was still outstanding, and when Mme Olembert failed to respond to my messages, I contacted my friends in the DP team, asking them to get in touch with her. She insisted that she had never come to an arrangement with me and denied that I had entrusted her with any money.

Tommy could hardly believe my naivety. I had turned everything over to this woman without any written agreement. From six thousand miles away, legal action against her would have been difficult and costly. The only option was to cut my losses and pay the bills again. Very sensibly, Tommy refused to lend me the money (approximately £750), but he did offer to guarantee an overdraft with a set time limit.

The one consolation for Tommy was that I had learnt a valuable lesson. He had always regarded filmmaking as 'a dodgy business'. Now, perhaps, I would be a little less gullible when the next con artist appeared.

Fortunately, I was never put to that test again, but over the years I came across other Olembert victims, including an aspiring young screenwriter who was told that the commentary he had written for one of her documentaries was 'rubbish' and she would be commissioning someone else to rewrite it. He received no payment, but several years later, when he was in a cinema in San Francisco, the Olembert film popped up unexpectedly as part of the programme. He swore that the commentary was his, word for word, but no writer was credited.

The other example was even more outrageous. When I was finally back in England, I shared my Olembert memories with Marjorie Cummins, a dear lady, then in her late sixties, who used to type the final drafts of all my documentary proposals in those pre-computer days. We were amazed to discover that we had both fallen into the same trap. Olembert had engaged Marjorie to do all her secretarial work for a full month, but when the day came for payment, she strode across her luxurious apartment in her flowing gowns, threw open her fridge, which was virtually empty, and told Marjorie: 'I am destitute. Take whatever you want.'

The loss of the DP film was not only a loss for me, but also for Children's Relief International, who wanted to use it in their charitable appeals, and for every member of the team, who had worked without pay in the hope of having something to show potential employers.

With nothing to bring to my meeting with Billy Boxer, I had to begin my career at the lowest level, making two-shot commercials, where a typical script might read: Best possible exterior of Mrs van de Merwe's hairdressing salon. Best possible interior of Mrs van de Merwe, styling a client's hair.

There were, of course, financial problems as well. To reduce the debt as quickly as possible, I took a second job. By day, I worked at Alpha Studios, by night as a waiter in the Pianola Restaurant, close to the railroad track at the bottom end of Hillbrow and a favourite haunt of Johannesburg's (white) demi-monde – pop musicians, artists and even the occasional prostitute, accompanied by her pimp.

Backstage, the white waiters and black kitchen staff worked as a team, and at times it was easy to forget that we were living in a segregated society where the customers we served were prevented by law from inviting any non-whites to join them.

At Alpha Studios, the atmosphere was even more relaxed. Many of the company's commercials were made for the African market, and when a black cast was in the studio, they would sit chatting to us between takes, as all actors and models like to do when they are on set.

Without any real experience at this stage of the hard edge of apartheid, it was too easy to become complacent and believe the *verligte* narrative that we were living in a fast-changing society, where crude discrimination was being replaced by something entirely different.

Four months into my new job, I was invited to a gathering of film people in Pretoria, the capital. Among the guests were two members of the Department of Information – Hennie Momberg, a gentle Afrikaner giant in his late fifties and his chain-smoking, hyperactive English-speaking colleague, Errol Hines.

(Hennie, by the way, was the person whose name and number I would give to the Hillbrow police sergeant on New Year's Day 1964.)

At some stage in the evening, I was introduced to them both. After we had exchanged pleasantries, they asked if I had seen any of their films. Yes, I had. What did I think? I felt they were missing the point. Surely it was time to make a film that showed how apartheid was evolving, and to take that message not only to the world, but just as importantly, to whites in this country, many of whom were still stuck in their old ways.

Hennie nodded and suggested a meeting at the Department of Information in Pretoria to discuss this further and asked me to bring an example of my work. I was not expecting this and had to admit that I had nothing to show them, except a short trailer of my DP documentary, but they were undeterred.

In the meeting that followed I offered my version of the *verligte* narrative and described the kind of sequences one might use to make the main points. Hennie immediately picked up the phone and, after a quick exchange in Afrikaans, suggested that we should all go to the top floor together. He would like me to share my thoughts with Dr Wentzel du Plessis, the Secretary of the Department of Information, and a man regarded in Nationalist circles as one of the country's leading intellectuals.

Du Plessis, an intense little man his late fifties, nodded slowly as he took in what I had to say. Then, after a long pause:

'So, why don't you make a film that explains our policies fully and properly?'

From this distance, it is still hard to believe that I agreed to this. At the time, I had never visited a black township or sat down in some private place with any of the black actors in the studio or the black kitchen staff at the Pianola and talked to them in confidence about their daily experiences, but agree I did, and from that point things moved quickly.

The government was in session in Pretoria, and I was invited to meet the Prime Minister, Hendrik Verwoerd, a charmless and rather intimidating figure. Frankly, I cannot remember much that passed between us. I don't think he had been properly briefed or had any real idea what all this was about, but he did brighten up at the final handshake, and wished me well with the project.

I formed a partnership with Hans Wagner, an experienced cameraman, and recruited David Kalahote as our interpreter and production manager.

David was impressive. He had a degree in English literature, spoke several African languages and had originally come to my attention when he was modelling for a commercial. It was clear to me at the time that he had talent for greater things.

And off the three of us went, with a tiny budget, to make a documentary with the unflinching title: *Anatomy of Apartheid*. I was 22 years old.

The lessons learnt from that experience would shape everything I did for the rest of my professional life.

Chapter Four

THE PROPAGANDIST

Watching *Anatomy* all these years later is a difficult experience.

The whole tone at the start is radical and fiercely critical of the treatment of black South Africans prior to 1948, as the commentary makes clear.

'1935, 1940, 1945. A nation develops into the premier industrial power on the African continent. First, thousands and then, enticed into mining, commerce and industry, hundreds of thousands of Bantus leave to sell their labour in the white cities.'

'The homelands become labour pools, nations no longer.'

'The industrial revolution of South Africa followed Europe's pattern in every detail but one – here the new proletariat was a black proletariat; the new slum, exclusively a black man's shanty town'.

Apparently, everything changed when the National Party won its first election victory. In the words of a white interviewee:

'When the new government came to power in 1948, it set into motion a three-phase plan to give back to the Bantu his independent livelihood, his own art and education, his full self-identity through self-government.'

Anatomy flouts every principle of documentary filmmaking I now hold dear. It was a case of starting with a preconception, and then looking for the best ways to illustrate it.

This may be acceptable in advertising and drama, but is absolutely wrong in documentary, particularly when dealing with a serious political subject. However great the challenge, the first priority is to gain the trust of ordinary people; to hear their personal stories, in strict confidence wherever necessary; and to get a real sense of their daily lives and the problems they face. And that work must not stop until the evidence uncovered and the experiences people have shared are confirmed again and again. If done properly, it is a process that can require months of research.

Let's return to that 'three-phase plan' and examine the second phase – education. The film tells us:

'In 1954, a far-reaching education act was passed: its ambition, to facilitate instruction and self-expression by giving back to the Bantu their most precious raw material: language. Children, who once had to learn the names of Europe's emperors by heart, now heard the stories of their own historical leaders in the languages they spoke at home.'

This commentary is supported by images of a spacious playground and a classroom, where black children are participating enthusiastically in a question-and-answer session in Xhosa.

I can't remember the process we went through, but I imagine we phoned some important person in the Department of Bantu Affairs, who recommended a particular school in Soweto (South West Townships).

You cannot do that. You must speak to teachers, children and their parents. You also have to visit a number of different schools and attend classes, all of which I did later, when I got to know Soweto well. There were schools with no libraries, classrooms without electricity or desks for the children to work on, and class sizes were massive – sixty, sometimes eighty, to a room.

Teachers, parents and even some of the children were well aware of the reasons for this. The state was spending ten times more on the education of a white child than on a black child of equivalent age, and these statistics were not difficult to verify. Some of those I spoke to could even quote Dr Verwoerd's words when he introduced his Bantu Education Act in his role as Minister of Native Affairs.

'There is no place for [the Bantu] in the European community above the level of certain forms of labour. What is the use of teaching a Bantu child mathematics?'

Purely and simply, Bantu Education was a system designed to prepare black children for a subservient role in society. There were classes I attended later, where young girls were being trained in the 'arts' of cleaning and scrubbing.

'A far-reaching education act to facilitate instruction and self-expression'?

But there was another appalling omission in *Anatomy*. Nowhere are we given any sense of the daily humiliations: the 'whites only' benches, transport, shops, lifts, restaurants and entrances to flats and offices.

I had gone into this project firmly believing the *verligte* narrative that apartheid was evolving into something completely different. In the relatively relaxed atmosphere of the Pianola and Alpha Studios, it was (almost) possible to believe that an era of 'crude discrimination' was coming to an end, but once we were 'on the road', reality hit me hard and at a very personal level.

David Kalahote and I formed a close friendship. A handsome young man in his late twenties, David was superb in his job of translator and fixer. He also took his work seriously, never complaining about his own situation or criticising the line we were taking, but through him, I had many powerful experiences of the daily humiliations of 'petty apartheid'.

The first shock was the way David was treated in the hotels where we stayed. When he phoned ahead to make the advance bookings, race had to be specified: two whites, one Bantu.

Somehow, David was able to take all this in his stride. On our arrival at the first hotel, he stayed in the van, while Hans and I checked in at reception and collected the keys. 'The Bantu room', we were told, was at the back.

'And the key?'

'There's no key.'

I went with David as he drove round to the back, where there was a squalid dormitory that already had six occupants.

Unbelievable! We had to find somewhere else. David just shrugged and smiled. 'There's no hotel within twenty miles, and it's unlikely to be any better. Don't waste your time.'

We were finally able to get a vacant staff room, but it was a poor compromise.

Fortunately, most of our filming was in the Johannesburg/Pretoria area, and David could return to his Soweto home in the evenings, but the daily humiliations never ceased. Since we could not eat together in restaurants, we tended to use roadside diners. Most of these had eating areas for whites, while blacks were served through a hatch at the side of the building.

The procedure seldom varied. Hans or I would go in through the front entrance, place orders for the three of us and then eat with David in the parked van, but the looks we were given by some of the passing whites were unforgettable.

There was one incident I found particularly shocking. I had asked David if he could get permission for us to film the Orlando West police band, Soweto's finest, in action. The officer in charge was white and a man with a fearsome reputation, but David was confident he could deal with him. He set off on his own, dressed formally in suit, tie and a grey trilby, while Hans and I were filming an interview in Johannesburg. Mid-morning, David called us. The band had been booked for the afternoon and we could film for as long as we liked.

He had chosen an open space for filming, and when we arrived, the band was ready and waiting. How had David managed to persuade the (white) commanding officer to lay all this on for us?

David suddenly clasped his hands together in self-parody and began playing the role a bowing, cringing sycophant. 'Goie dag, Baas! Hou gaan dit met u?' ('Good day, boss. How is everything with you?'). At that point, he threw his trilby on the ground and stamped on it.

'You did that? You humiliated yourself in front of that arsehole! Why?'

Without a touch of resentment, David explained that this was the message the white police officer most wanted to hear. 'The greatest gift you can give a man like that is to tell him you know you're his inferior. And we got the band in return!'

I was in shock, but worse was to come.

The key event of 1963 was the creation of the first 'independent Bantu homeland' within South Africa's borders, and the timing was a big factor in the Department's decision to commission *Anatomy of Apartheid*, where the central message was flagged up in commentary.

'The scene, the Transkei, a slice of South Africa, larger than Switzerland, twice the size of Israel; just one of eight emerging black states, so-called "Bantustans", to be shaped into a single South African Commonwealth.'

According to the film, the Nationalist government was merely following in the steps of the British, who had established protectorates for three tribal groups in Southern Africa – the Tswana, the Sotho and the Swazi. Between 1966 and 1968 these territories would be granted full independence and three new countries would be born – Botswana, Lesotho and Swaziland (or Eswatini, as it has been known since 2018).

But the situation in South Africa was very different. The Transkei, 'Homeland' of the Xhosa people, was the only coherent territory within South Africa's borders. The other seven putative 'homelands' were mostly scattered fragments, barely able to support the people who lived there. None of them would have been able to function as a viable state without a massive handover of white land to link these scraps together, but nothing like that was on the agenda.

As well as being a single entity, the Transkei also had a potential capital, Umtata. With its two cathedrals (one Anglican and one Roman Catholic), this sleepy little town had the right to call itself a city. It also had a potential parliament building – the 'Bhunga' – a splendid Victorian creation, set up by the British as a chamber where they could engage with the local tribal chiefs.

Wednesday 20 November 1963 was set down as polling day for the Xhosa people in the Transkei and townships across South Africa. Voters had two choices, the 'National Independence Party', which supported the Government's Bantustan policy, or the 'Democratic Party', led by Victor Poto, who took the same position as the ANC, that the policy was 'designed to consolidate the inhuman policies of apartheid'. If Poto won the elections, his first step would be to dissolve the Transkei parliament.

And win he did, with a significant majority, but the government in Pretoria was well prepared. Sixty-four seats in the new 'parliament' had been set aside for tribal chiefs, who were on Pretoria's payroll. Almost to a man, they swung in behind Kaiser Matanzima, the leader of the 'National Independence Party'.

The first parliamentary session was due to take place on 11 December. On the previous afternoon, Matanzima gave us a carefully prepared statement in defence of government policy, with a government minder present throughout the interview.

Matanzima was Nelson Mandela's nephew. They had studied together at Fort Hare University, where they had formed a close friendship, but this was the time of the Rivonia trial, when Mandela and nine other defendants were facing the death sentence, which was eventually commuted to life imprisonment. During the twenty-seven years Mandela spent in prisons, he consistently refused visits from the nephew he described as 'a sell-out in the proper sense of the word'.

When the 'minder' had left and the crew were packing the equipment, I mentioned the trial to Matanzima as gently as I could. What were his feelings towards his uncle? He looked me straight in the eye, then after a long pause he said, 'Let me show you something,' and dropped down on his knees.

Along the wall on either side of his desk was a set of low shelves, packed with cardboard boxes and elaborately wrapped parcels. Matanzima pulled one of them out.

'Twelve bottles of gin, by courtesy of Messrs Gilbey's of London. Thank you, Mr. Matanzima!', he said sarcastically.

Still on his hands and knees, he crawled along the length of the shelves, pulling out parcels and boxes in rapid succession and naming the companies that had heaped these gifts upon him. 'Thank you … Thank you … Thank you, Mr Matanzima!'

This was a man in pain, and the unstated message was clear.

'Thank you for being a collaborator.'

We were in the same boat.

The opening of parliament the following day was another telling experience.

Swearing-in had barely started when a chair collapsed under the weight of one of the tribal chiefs. Crack! More would follow throughout the ceremony. Crack! Crack!

The reasons for this fiasco became clear later. The Transkei was a 'country' with no industrial base. In its desire to present 'the Xhosa Homeland' as a viable nation, the government had offered generous grants to anyone prepared to set up a factory. The first takers were a Swiss couple, who submitted a plan to manufacture furniture. The application was accepted, and they were rewarded with an exclusive contract to supply the seating for the 'Bhunga'. Clearly, their work was not up to scratch!

After filming the start of the session, we set up our camera outside the 'Bhunga', where a large crowd had gathered. A German couple, Werner and Ziggy

Grünbauer, also commissioned by the Department of Information, had created a makeshift platform from where they hoped to get wide shots of cheering crowds. But this wasn't happening. I can see Ziggy now, in her outfit of white leather (trousers and zip-up jacket), lifting both arms in frustration and screaming out: 'Be happy, damn you! Smile!'

This was documentary filmmaking at its worst, and I was ashamed to be involved. Ironically, there was a moment of genuine enthusiasm at the end of the session, but Ziggy wasn't prepared to wait.

Three weeks later came the arrest on Twist Street.

As soon as I was released from jail, I phoned Hennie Momberg, my main contact at the Department of Information. I was sure that he would have been given a very partial account of the previous night's events and was braced for a row, but Hennie was his usual quiet, gentle self. Without a word of reproach, he suggested that we meet the following day.

When I walked into his office, I must have looked like someone who had stepped out of a boxing ring, but Hennie made no comment. All he wanted to hear was my version of the story. And out it all came.

But I didn't stop there. I needed to share other experiences that had made such a strong impression on me over the previous weeks, particularly the way David had been treated. I did not include my meeting with Matanzima, as that would have been a breach of trust.

Hennie's response was predictable and also very flattering. Couldn't I understand how important *Anatomy* could be in helping to end those injustices? Probably for the first time, we have a film that will make white people in this country aware of Bantu history and culture as well as the true meaning of apartheid.

In retrospect, statements like these seem ludicrous, but they did give me some comfort at the time, and those feelings were strengthened after the January press screening of the four Department of Information films that had been produced during the previous year.

Anatomy of Apartheid received rave reviews across the political spectrum. 'Brilliant' ... 'Sophisticated' ... 'Full marks' ... 'Positive and direct' ... 'South Africans will be enlightened by this picture'. With no hint of irony, one reviewer even wrote: 'This film shows very little influence of politics. It shows a situation that faces us all, whatever the party or colour.'

Although this was reassuring at the time, it seems obvious that something else was at work here. Any thinking white South African must have experienced moments of guilt about their privileged position in this segregated society. How comforting and reassuring to watch a film that took a completely different view of apartheid, presenting it as 'parallel development', respectful of black culture, language and history.

The following month, I had a very different experience. Hennie had asked the management of one of Johannesburg's main cinemas to slip *Anatomy* into the Saturday night programme ahead of the main feature.

This time, the film would not be playing to an audience of 'thinkers', but to a true cross-section of white society, who did not take kindly to all the talk about black achievement and self-government in independent homelands.

Within minutes, the booing started. A couple of people jumped to their feet and shouted at the screen, and the hubbub continued to the final credits and beyond.

Hennie and I slipped out immediately.

There could have been no clearer confirmation that my first completed film was a piece of worthless propaganda that had nothing to do with the realities of life and politics in South Africa. This feeling would be intensified when I experienced more and more of township life over the following months and years, but for the moment, the reaction of that cinema audience was sufficient. I had made an appalling misjudgement at the start of my professional career.

Hennie was also shaken, and in an unguarded moment as we were driving away, he told me that the film would not be shown again to South African audiences. His whole argument about 'educating the white electorate' had gone up in smoke, but that did not stop the Department's extensive use of *Anatomy* as a propaganda tool in Europe and the United States for nearly a decade.

Here was proof, if any were needed, that I had betrayed the basic principle that had set me on this career, the belief the documentary could be a powerful medium of education and a force for good, and my immediate impulse was to give up all filmmaking ambitions. I certainly could not continue working for the Department of Information, and in a meeting the following week with Hennie and Errol, his English-speaking colleague, I laid it all out.

'So, what do you intend to do as a living?'

It was a pertinent question. There was no television in South Africa at the time, and the Department had a virtual monopoly on documentary output. I knew I could probably get my job back making crass commercials for Alpha Studios, but at this stage, filmmaking was no longer a priority.

I loved this country and certainly had no thoughts of returning to England. Even in those brief visits to Soweto, I had developed strong friendships across the racial divide. David and I were very close, and I had been to his Soweto home and met his lovely wife, Ailsa, on several occasions. Another person I had come to know well was Bigvai Masekela, uncle of the famous jazz trumpeter, Hugh Masekela. In time, he would become almost a father figure to me.

Friendships like these were not going to be set aside now that there were no professional reasons for me to visit Soweto.

Without mentioning any names, I laid all this out in the meeting with Hennie and Errol. My work, I told them, was no longer the issue. Yes, I wanted to stay in the country, but only on condition that I could live my life here as any normal person should.

Errol was quick to warn me to stay within the law: no visits to Soweto without the relevant permits from the Department of Bantu Affairs. Hennie remained silent.

As I had hoped, I managed to get my job back at Alpha, and was confident that I would work out ways to deal with permits, but the first priority was to find a way to get back and forth to Soweto. I had never owned a car or taken a test. David or Hans had done all the driving when we were filming.

Finding a car was not a problem. One of the editors at Alpha was planning to return to England and wanted to make a quick sale of his Fiat 600. The next step was to get a provisional licence and book a test, but when I went to the relevant office, they told me that nothing would be available for the next four months.

'But we have a cancellation next Monday morning, if you think you can make it by then!' I ignored the sarcastic smile and booked the test. It was now midday Friday.

I phoned David and asked if he could suggest a driving instructor in Soweto who might be prepared to take me on for two days' solid tuition. Yes, Nick Muthana, a good friend of his, would be perfect for the job. Confirmation came back within minutes. A car would be waiting outside my apartment at seven o'clock the following morning.

Nick was bang on time, standing beside an aged estate car, with 'Muthana's Driving School' proudly emblazoned on a sign above the roof. He drove me out of the city and onto a mine dump, where he taught me the basics, and then we headed for the N3, the main road to Durban. Over that weekend, I must have spent twelve hours behind the wheel.

First thing Monday morning, we arrived at the test ground and were signalled to a parking space, where we waited until an elderly examiner in a khaki dust coat made his slow progress towards us. Nick immediately got out of the car and stepped back, leaving the passenger door wide open. Clearly, he understood the protocol.

The old man looked at me, at Nick, at the sign on top of the car, and then back at me. For a moment, he didn't seem sure what to do. Yes, this was a test ground for whites, but a white in a black man's car? After a long pause, he lowered himself into the passenger seat, shutting the door after him, and nodded at me to start.

I went through all the usual tests, and answered a list of questions, delivered in a thick Afrikaans accent. Then, after a long silence, the old man gave his verdict.

'Well, I can't fail you, 'cos you didn't do nothing wrong.' At that point, he looked me straight in the eye. 'But fuck me! You drive like a kaffir!'

On our way out, I repeated the story to Nick, who roared with laughter, and when I stopped at the junction with the main road and looked dutifully left and right, he shouted, 'Hey man! No more stopping at red lights and stop signs, no more hand signals and speed limits. Just drive like a kaffir!'

We had a drink in my flat before he set off. There was a lot to celebrate. Permits permitting, I now had the freedom to go to Soweto whenever I wanted.

Chapter Five

COMPROMISE

In the Sixties, the two main roads from Johannesburg to the south, the N1 to Cape Town and the N3 to Durban, gave Soweto a wide berth. The whole area was effectively hidden from view; it wasn't even marked on some of the maps.

Yet, at that time, Soweto covered an area of over forty square miles and had a population of nearly a million people. It was actually the second largest city in South Africa and over twice the size of Pretoria, the capital. By its very existence, it made a mockery of government policy.

How could anyone talk seriously about 'separate development' when almost every home, mine, factory, shop and restaurant in the Johannesburg area was totally dependent on the black labour force that travelled from Soweto every day?

House construction began in Soweto on a major scale in the mid-Fifties. *Anatomy* describes it as 'part of a massive programme of clearance and reconstruction, its starting point, the city slum. The achievement in the towns: new homes for over a million people in twelve years.'

The inference was clear. This was all about raising black living standards.

Conditions in some of the older Johannesburg townships were certainly rough, but the real problem was that these were places where blacks had legal title to land which bordered and, in some cases, intruded into white suburbs. Johannesburg's whites weren't having any more of this.

The 1954 Native Resettlement Act gave Parliament the right to annul all freehold rights of black landowners in townships like Sophiatown, Martindale and Newclare, which were subsequently razed to the ground, forcing hundreds of thousands of their former residents to move to new townships grouped together in Soweto, a comfortable distance outside the city limits.

In truth, living conditions hardly improved at all. Standard forty-square-metre houses were built without ceilings, inside doors, running water or sanitation. Few had electricity.

Transforming these places into homes was the job of the incoming families, but whatever they did to their properties, they had no rights of ownership. In Soweto's new townships, blacks were merely tenants.

The one exception was 'Dube village', which had been set aside for 'the thoroughly urbanised and economically advanced Native'. Here, larger plots were available on thirty-year leases and tenants were free to erect their own dwellings 'in conformity with approved plans'. It will come as no surprise that a row of Dube houses was featured in *Anatomy* to illustrate the outcome of that 'massive programme of clearance and reconstruction'.

The refusal to grant freehold rights was absolutely in line with government thinking and mythology. Blacks were there as temporary residents. One day, they or their descendants would be returning to their tribal 'nations' within a South African commonwealth, and there would be no further need for Soweto to exist. In that mythological new age, Johannesburg's whites would presumably be self-sufficient.

My early trips to Soweto were purely social: evenings spent with David, Ailsa and the Masekela family, but the circle quickly widened as I was introduced to relatives and family friends.

For the initial visits, I went through the full bureaucratic process and obtained the necessary permits from the Department of Bantu Affairs. When asked to give my reasons for the visits, I told the truth. I was a film director who wanted to revisit people who had helped me make a documentary for the government, but repeated visits made no sense to these bureaucrats, and my third application was refused.

I had anticipated this from the start and had already told David, Bigvai and the others that I would be happy to come in and out of Soweto without permission as long as they were sure they wouldn't be compromised.

It was well known that the townships were awash with informers, but there was surprisingly little anger about this. Everyone knew that blackmail was the favoured method of recruitment.

The strategy was to engage people living at key points in Soweto and offer them two alternatives: either they cooperate with the security police, or they and their entire families would lose their rights to stay in Soweto, in which case, their only option would be to return to their tribal 'homeland' where they could try and scratch a living from the land. Livelihoods, homes and any ambitions they might have had for their children would be destroyed.

With a system like this in operation, we all knew how easy it would be to trace my identity through the Fiat's registration number and report on everyone I visited, but David, Bigvai and the others were sure that they were safe to meet me as long as I didn't get involved in any political activities. I would be the only one breaking the law.

During those early visits to Soweto, I was struck by the complete lack of resentment towards me, and this easy acceptance extended far beyond the milieu of educated, middle-class Africans I came to know personally.

Wherever I went; walking the streets, popping into homes or visiting schools, I don't remember a single hostile response. People were curious about me, of course, but I was never threatened or subjected to tirades about the injustices they were suffering at the hands of my people. Sowetans met their daily challenges with extraordinary dignity and the same self-protective sense of humour that David and Nick, my driving instructor, had shown again and again.

Even when walking the streets after dark, I felt safe in Soweto, but today, it is sad to say, I would hesitate to walk through central Johannesburg in the middle of the day.

Looking back, I still feel as I did when I witnessed that brief moment of racial harmony when blacks and whites were celebrating the New Year together on Twist Street. In the early Sixties, I believe there was still an opportunity for all South Africans to come together, but the terrible events of the next two decades changed everything. Fortunately for all South Africans, they would eventually have Nelson Mandela as their first democratically elected leader. Without someone with his integrity, his profound insights and his commitment to peace, I believe that a bloody conflict would have been inevitable.

Of all my early Soweto memories, one really stands out: the dawn migration to the stations and waiting buses. The rush began at about half past four in the morning and peaked between the hours of five and six. I can still see those moments with absolute clarity – smoke rising from thousands of wood fires and mixing with the dust thrown up by crowds tramping the unpaved streets on their way to the trains and buses. By eight o'clock, the exodus was virtually over.

With parents away for up to fifteen hours a day, it was often left to the children to take on all household responsibilities. Usually, the eldest daughter assumed the maternal role – cleaning, shopping, preparing the meals and ensuring that her younger siblings went off to school on time, even if this meant playing truant herself.

As one parent put it to me: 'This has made my daughter a very big woman at an early age.'

****

It may seem extraordinary that an ambition that had gripped me so firmly in my teens had now been set aside. Although there were moments when I longed to continue as a filmmaker, I had lost faith in my own judgement, and now had a different priority – to try and live my life in this country as any normal person should – but it didn't take long to discover that the freedom to do this was conditional.

A couple of months after I had started my regular Soweto visits, I was summoned to a meeting at the Department of Information in Pretoria. Hennie and Errol were both present, and in the long session that followed, the two of them seemed to be performing different roles. Hennie, the gentle Afrikaner giant in his late fifties, seemed genuinely concerned about my future. Errol, his chain-smoking contemporary, was there to help me face the facts.

At the start of the meeting, Hennie asked me if I was aware of the work of the National Film Board of Canada. I certainly was. They had produced some out-standing documentaries over the years.

He went on to explain that the government intended to set up a South African Film Board, which would operate on the same principles and sponsor non-political films. Would I like to suggest a subject?

For a moment, I didn't know what to say, and it was left to Errol to break the silence. Did I really think I could carry on in the way I was doing if I simply threw this offer back in their faces? The inference was clear. If I refused to cooperate, those trips back and forth to Soweto would stop. All I could say was that I needed time to think.

It was a huge decision. Whatever Hennie chose to call the sponsor, funding would be coming from a government whose policies I rejected. Where would I find a non-political subject in a country where those very policies were having such a profound effect on people's daily lives, and if I did, would it have any value?

I consulted many friends. As expected, Bigvai and David were thoroughly in favour. If I was committed to staying in South Africa, why should I reject this offer? Did I regard crass commercials as an honourable alternative?

From this distance, I'm still not sure whether it was right to compromise, but compromise I did and, after weeks of research and travel, committed to a subject that didn't seem to touch any political issues but which I believed was worthy of a film: *River of Diamonds*.

****

The Orange River brings together three chapters in the history of diamonds in Southern Africa. It rises in Lesotho, at a high point in the Drakensberg, the mountain range that marks that country's border with South Africa. In 1957, diamonds were discovered close to the river's source at a place called Letšeng-La-Terai, approximately 10,000 feet above sea level.

By the time we were filming, hundreds of small-scale prospectors were washing and sifting gravel with the same tools and techniques that had been used since the 1870s.

From Lesotho, the river runs west into South Africa, cutting a deep gorge before it flows into the reservoir that feeds the Gariep Dam, the largest in the country. From there, it crosses the Great Karoo and meets its main tributary, the

Vaal. It was on a farm close to the junction between the two rivers that a superb white diamond was discovered by a Griqua shepherd boy in 1869. He sold it to an Afrikaans farmer for a stupendous price in the eyes of the poor shepherd – 500 sheep, 10 oxen and a horse. Ultimately, it would be bought by the Earl of Dudley for £25,000 and become famous as 'the Star of South Africa'.

As word spread, people of all races and nationalities stormed into the valley, where they worked side by side. According to one observer: 'Natives of every dusky shade streaked the show of white faces.'

From its junction with the Vaal, the Orange flows westward through the arid wildernesses of the Kalahari and the northern Cape, where it marks the border between South Africa and Namibia before reaching the Atlantic at Oranjemund ('Orange mouth'). Here, diamonds are mined from the land and the sea, and the whole area is sealed off by high barbed-wire fences, which are constantly patrolled.

Before committing to the film, I spent a whole month following the course of the river in my little Fiat 600, with occasional forays on foot to get a real sense of the immediate surroundings. Even though this was a subject that would avoid any serious political issues, it would at least give me an opportunity to express my love for the breathtaking landscapes that unfolded at every stage of the river's journey.

Once again, David would be working with me as fixer/translator, and it was my great good fortune to have Raymond Hancock, South Africa's finest cinematographer, as partner in this venture.

Raymond was a generous and ebullient forty-something-year-old, who would give me a visual sense I never had before. He made me aware of the subtleties of lighting and the effect of every lens in his armoury. Whether he was working handheld, tight and close to the prospectors at Letšeng-La-Terai, skimming down the Orange River in a helicopter or filming the cascades deep inside the Augrabies Gorge, Raymond always managed to capture something unique.

River of Diamonds was completed in July 1965, broadcast by the BBC and shown in cinemas across South Africa. The reviews were sensational. 'Equal to the world's best' … 'A near masterpiece' … 'A thing of beauty which effectively captures one dazzling moment of hope'. The film also won two prestigious awards.

Most of the credit should go to Raymond, but the film had real consequences for me. While in London for the BBC broadcast, I was told that the door was wide open if I wanted to pursue a career in the UK, but at that time I wasn't interested. Personal relationships in South Africa were far too strong, and our travels from Natal to the Atlantic Coast had rekindled a love of country that was as intense as anything I had felt as a child.

I believed that I had found an honourable compromise. The hard truth, though, was that *River of Diamonds* hadn't gone an inch beyond its dazzling surface to reveal the realities of contemporary life in South Africa. Another year would pass before I discovered what would happen if that boundary were crossed, but for the moment, I was happy and settled.

My friend Bigvai Masekela wrote in a letter to me: 'You are a part of the new South Africa that is becoming', and at the time, I really believed him. If people could build strong personal friendships across the racial divide, real change was possible.

But this showed no real understanding of the depth of prejudice on one side and the increasing resentment on the other. It also ignored the fact that very few South Africans had an opportunity to reach out across that divide without getting into serious trouble. After the success of *River of Diamonds*, I was in a unique position, and, knowing this, I pushed the bar as high as it would go.

By now, I had moved out of my bedsit and taken a larger flat in Clive Mansions, a charming and rather shabby 1930s building on Clarendon Circle at the top of Hillbrow. Here I had the space to receive my Soweto friends on home ground. I also felt confident enough to invite some of my white friends to join me at parties, jazz nights and, on one occasion, at a beauty competition which I had been asked to judge in Soweto.

It was a time of great happiness and tragedy. When Ailsa gave birth to a son, she and David asked me to be godfather to Antony William Kalahote, but shortly after the christening, Bigvai Masekela became seriously ill. It was cancer, and after several weeks of treatment in Baragwanath hospital, the family was told that nothing further could be done, and Bigvai was taken home. What I found so moving was their decision to leave me alone with him during his final moments.

I was also asked to speak at Bigvai's funeral, which was attended by hundreds of mourners. Sometime later, I was told that several reports of my speech had been sent to the Special Branch. Although I was never able to confirm this, I certainly knew the police were aware of my activities, and for that reason followed strict rules. For my friends' sakes, as well as my own, I was never politically active. The speech I gave at Bigvai's funeral was a heartfelt tribute to a dear friend I respected and admired, but there was no attempt to put his experiences into a wider context.

But on one occasion, I threw all caution to the winds.

Late one winter's night, six members of a notorious Soweto gang broke out of the Fort Prison in Johannesburg. Cars were waiting for them, and they quickly dispersed.

The following night I was sitting with David in his front room while Ailsa was working in the kitchen. Suddenly, we heard the back door open and Ailsa's nervous response. David shot to his feet, and I followed. The intruder was David's cousin, and a member of the gang that had broken out of the Fort the previous night. Naturally, he was surprised to see me, but he didn't threaten us in any way. All he wanted was a place to stay for a few days. Then he would move on.

I was terrified of the consequences for David and Ailsa if this man were discovered in their home. My little Fiat was parked outside, and I offered to drive him across the border into either Basutoland or Bechuanaland (as they were then). The choice was his, provided he agreed to come with me immediately.

It was sheer madness and would have made things far worse for David and Ailsa (not to mention me) if an informer were to see the two of us driving away together. It would have been even more serious if we had been caught at the border.

But David's cousin made it clear that he had no intention of fleeing the country. He had an important job to do here, and to make the point, he raised one hand with his forefinger extended.

'First, I'll take five of them. Then they can take me.'

He honoured his first promise and left David and Ailsa before dawn. Three weeks later, he was involved in a shootout with the police in Daveyton Township, forty miles from Soweto. He didn't reach his final score, but three white policemen were killed before he was finally shot dead.

For the first time, I had a real sense of the anger that was simmering below the surface.

Chapter Six

THE FABULOUS REEF

Hennie suggested the subject and the title of the next film: *The Fabulous Reef*. The idea was to make a companion piece to *River of Diamonds*; a film that would tell the parallel story of gold in South Africa, and this time Raymond Hancock was free to work with me.

Right from the start, it was clear to both of us that this subject could take us into dangerous territory. *River of Diamonds* only covered the first chapter of South Africa's diamond history, a time when people of all races were free to stake out their claims along the banks of the Vaal and often worked side by side. From there, the story leapt forward to the two most recent chapters – the diamond discoveries in the Drakensburg and along the Atlantic coast. Rather conveniently, the intervening chapters were omitted, as they would have taken us away from the river, but they covered a time when labour relations in South Africa were clearly defined.

Within two years of the first rush to the Vaal, diamonds were discovered on a farm some twenty miles south of the river. Three other discoveries followed in quick succession, but the most important find was on a farm owned by two Afrikaans brothers, Diederik and Johannes de Beer. Originally known as New Rush, it would soon receive the more dignified title of the Kimberley mine.

The four mines were clustered within a radius of two and a half miles, and by late 1871, forty thousand people had gathered in this remote and unlovely spot. Unable to cope with the rush, the de Beer brothers sold out, but their name will survive for as long as the diamond industry exists.

The working practices established along the Vaal continued during the early stages of the rush. At one mine, Bultfontein, white prospectors owned only a fifth of the licensed claims.

At this crucial moment, when South Africa was on the verge of an industrial revolution made possible by diamond wealth, all races were ready to cross that threshold together. But it was not to be. On the pretext that every black and mixed-race prospector was a potential diamond smuggler, whites took the law into their own hands and forced them to give up their claims.

From that point onwards, the only black workers welcomed on the mines were labourers, recruited from tribal areas and herded into compounds where they could be strictly controlled. It would be the model for all future employment in South Africa's mining industry.

But it was not only black and mixed-race prospectors who would have to forfeit their claims. From the mid-1870s onwards, whites were leaving the mines in droves.

By this time, the Kimberley workings had reached depths of up to 200 feet. The costs of clearing away debris, pumping out water and hauling material to the surface were spiralling. Small-time diggers could no longer cope with these challenges and sold out to powerful consortia with the resources to install steam engines to power the cranes and pumps that could lift material to the surface and drain the mines.

While all this was happening, gold was discovered in three separate locations. The most important find was in an area called Witwatersrand (White Waters Ridge), some 300 miles northeast of Kimberley. There, prospectors were able to trace a line of gold-bearing lode for thirty miles across the open veldt.

In time, people would understand that this outcrop was merely the lip of a huge elliptical bowl, 170 miles across and more than three miles deep, which had probably been laid down millions of years ago by a retreating sea. It would be the most important gold discovery in the world.

Everything that had happened in Kimberley recurred here, only faster and more dramatically. Thousands of fortune hunters poured into the Witwatersrand area, and the city of Johannesburg was born, but once again, only those with strong financial backing and extensive mining experience could take the plunge, literally as well as metaphorically, and sink shafts that would reach deeper and deeper levels. Those best placed to achieve this were members of a small clique of rich financiers, who had learned their trade and made their fortunes in the diamond fields.

But it was not just technical and financial expertise that put the so-called 'Randlords' in such a strong position. They also understood how to maintain the huge labour force needed for large-scale mining and, once again, agents were sent far and wide to recruit black workers, who would be confined in heavily guarded compounds for at least two years at a time.

As the historian Cornelis de Kiewiet wrote in 1929, modern South Africa was not built on diamonds or gold, but on the availability of cheap black labour.

I'm not sure what Hennie had in mind when he suggested the idea for *The Fabulous Reef*, but I made it clear from the start that this would have to be about the actual working and living conditions on the gold mines. If he didn't under-stand the implications, Raymond and I certainly did.

****

Looking back through documentary history, it seems clear that creativity and innovation can only follow where technology leads. In the 1920s and '30s, when great directors like Flaherty and Grierson were determined to make ordinary people the heroes of their films, we hear their stories only through narration, seldom from the people themselves. The same could be said about the factory workers and serving soldiers featured in the great wartime documentaries. It was a time when synchronised sound involved too much cumbersome equipment to be of any use, except in studio or near-studio conditions.

But the steady development of lighter and more flexible equipment in the post-war era would gradually transform the process. In the late 1950s, cumbersome 35mm cameras were replaced by light, self-blimped 16mm Arriflexes and Eclairs. Thanks to ever increasing film speeds, a time would come when a reflector or an open curtain could do the job that used to require intrusive lighting for all interior filming. With the advent of wireless technology, synchronised sound was achievable in almost any situation, and in the 1980s all these developments took a further leap forward with the advent of compact video cameras.

But back in the days of the DP film and *Anatomy*, we were barely at the start of the process, and spontaneous interviews were almost impossible. Whenever synchronised sound was needed, Hans, the cinematographer on *Anatomy*, would insert the camera into a cumbersome wooden 'blimp', which was difficult to operate. Under these conditions, an interview had to be a formal, static process. Lights, camera and recorder were switched on. David would step in with a clapperboard and, on cue, the interviewee would deliver a carefully prepared statement.

But were we getting anywhere near the truth through this process? It was a question that haunted me when we interviewed Kaiser Matanzima, the premier of the Transkei, who delivered a carefully prepared endorsement of government policy when the camera was rolling. It was only when he pulled out the gifts that companies and corporations had showered on him that I had a real sense of his feelings. But that moment was never captured on film.

Once I started working with Raymond Hancock, all kinds of opportunities opened up. He had the very latest lightweight equipment, and although there were no interviews in the diamond film, his use of available light and the unobtrusive way he operated convinced me that we should set ourselves a second ambition when telling the story of gold. Not only would we capture the actual working and living conditions on the mines, but by avoiding all the palaver of a formal interview, we might also get a true sense of the thoughts and feelings of ordinary miners.

****

At the time we were filming, the standard rate of pay for a black gold miner was twenty rand (£10) a month. During their entire time on the mines, they would have to live in guarded compounds, separated not only from their wives and children back home, but also from all contact with the outside world. Even the second-class citizenship of blacks with passbooks was out of reach. These were third-class citizens, filling jobs the locals refused to do at such a low rate of pay.

It was a system of recruitment based on the assumption that there would always be areas of Southern Africa where conditions were so desperate that people would have no choice but to accept such a low rate of pay. At that time, 370,000 Africans were working on the gold mines, and I was shocked to discover that a third of the labour force had been recruited from South Africa's 'Bantu homelands'.

In the deep mines where we filmed, they worked twelve-hour shifts; four days on, four days off. At these levels, the temperature of the rock face could be as high as 60 degrees Celsius, and even with all the ventilation systems running, seldom dipped below 50. The noise of drills, railroad cars and distant dynamiting was deafening.

At the front-line miners worked in pairs, bent double as they drilled into the narrow band of gold-bearing reef. Every now and then, they would pause to wet the surfaces and settle the silica dust that rose wherever the drill penetrated.

There is a famous statue in central Johannesburg of three miners working together; two blacks and one white. They are not crouched low, as miners must when drilling the reef, but are standing upright with all the space they need. The white miner is touching the drill with his right hand while his left arm is raised, as though he is pointing out the area where the black miners should aim the drill.

During our entire time underground, I never saw a scene remotely resembling this.

Whites were in supervisory roles, and at that time, they were being paid the equivalent of £300 a month, while their black companions received £10.

But the most telling moments weren't experienced underground, but in the hostels. Access was severely limited, but thanks to the discreet way Raymond operated, we were able to record frank conversations with individual miners without any official standing by.

There was no rancour or self-pity, just clear statements about the problems they faced at home and the reasons why the £180 they would earn on the mines was a life-saver.

One man told us that if the present drought persisted, he would have to return to the mines within two months, but if it rained, he would be able to spend six months with his family. Another spoke movingly about his concerns for his wife and children during these long periods of separation. Several miners were hoping to use the money they made to educate their children. 'At home you can get a job if you are educated, but for a man like me who is not educated, there are no jobs. The only place I can earn money is here in the mines.'

It was a sobering thought that one miner in three, coping with these living and working conditions, was a South African from a Bantustan.

As the film took shape in the editing, I felt I had found the path I wanted to follow in all my future work, but when Hennie and Errol came to the first viewing, they took a different view. Why weren't there any white miners in the scenes filmed at the gold face? All the hard work was being done by blacks.

Hennie even referred to the famous statue of the three miners, and asked why I hadn't captured a moment like that? I told him that this was something we had never witnessed, and I was not prepared to do any staging.

The tone became increasingly angry, and I left the meeting with a list of cuts that would have reduced the film to roughly half its original length. But, instead of following instructions, I invited two leading film critics to a private screening. They were asked not to make any reference to my row with Hennie and Errol, just to publish their honest opinions of the film.

When they appeared, their reviews were ecstatic:

'A work of genius … and I use the term guardedly' … 'Certainly the best South African film ever produced.'

As soon as he saw the reviews, Hennie demanded an immediate meeting. I had never seen this mild man in such a rage. I was ordered to hand over all the material and was told I would never be asked to make another film for the Department, which was virtually the only sponsor of documentaries in those pre-TV days.

'You can always be a hairdresser!' was his bitter comment.

And there was a further point he wished to make. If ever I planned to visit Soweto in the future, I would have to make proper applications to the Department of Bantu Affairs.

(I learnt later that the negative was handed over to another company who prepared a cut-down version of just thirteen minutes with the title *Vision of Gold*. Apparently, I am still credited as director.)

Looking back all these years later, I still have warm feelings towards Hennie. I'm sure that he stood between me and the Special Branch, and that I would have been in serious trouble without his protection.

Hennie was, of course, a paid government servant, whose job was to defend and justify apartheid, but I often wondered whether he was also in a state of conflict. Whatever the truth, he certainly understood everything I was going through during those difficult months before and after the screenings of *Anatomy*, and from that point onwards, I trusted him sufficiently to share all my thoughts and experiences. He never once reproached me or tried to defend the government's record. Instead, he did his best to find ways to allow me to continue as a documentary filmmaker, but as we would both discover, a 'non-political documentary' about life in South Africa during the apartheid era was a contradiction in terms.

I am sure that Hennie's rage had more to do with those reviews of *The Fabulous Reef* than with the actual content of the film. I had broken an unwritten compact between us by arranging this viewing behind his back. Those feelings were confirmed two years later, after I had left South Africa and was working for Yorkshire Television.

When making *War in the Zambezi Valley*, a film I will describe in the next chapter, I passed through South Africa and decided to see Hennie in Pretoria. It was a remarkably friendly meeting, and I felt encouraged to make an outrageous suggestion. Would the department allow me to return to South Africa to make a film for British Television about the gold mines? To put it bluntly, I was suggesting a re-make of *The Fabulous Reef*, and Hennie knew exactly where I stood on every issue. As far as his government was concerned, the only positive aspect would be the message that hundreds of thousands of people in countries across Southern Africa were reliant on the gold mines for their survival.

I expected outright rejection, but Hennie remained silent for a few moments. He needed time to think this through, and I was already back in England when he finally gave his consent. Yorkshire Television immediately agreed to allow me to return to South Africa to make *The Gold Run*.

The finished film was well received in Britain, but I heard later that there were serious repercussions within the Department of Information.

But back in 1966, the situation was very different: I had been banned from documentary filmmaking. Fortunately, I did not have to follow Hennie's advice and train to be a hairdresser. Acting was my second passion, and when Emil Nofal, the country's leading producer/director, heard that my filmmaking career was over, he asked me to audition for the part of Michael in *Wild Season*, a feature film he was planning.

Gert van den Berg, South Africa's most celebrated actor, was cast as Dirk Maritz, a trawlerman who owned two boats; one he captained himself, and the other was captained by his beloved son, Steve.

The story opens as Steve's trawler comes into port with three survivors rescued from a boat that had capsized in a storm. Steve's body is also on board. He had died in the rescue attempt.

Dirk decides to go to Johannesburg and meet his younger son, Michael, whom he hasn't seen since he divorced his wife eighteen years earlier, but any thoughts of asking Michael to take Steve's place are abandoned at that first meeting. 'He's too soft', he tells his friend Tom, once he is back at home. 'He's not like Steve. He doesn't belong here.'

Suddenly, Michael pitches up at the dock. He is determined to prove himself, and after all kinds of trials eventually wins his father's respect.

Unlike *Anatomy*, this was not a crude piece of propaganda. It was a warm, sentimental and rather old-fashioned film, but in some ways, it was more insidious. This didn't occur to me when they were filming my scenes, but when I saw the completed film for the first time at the premiere, it hit me hard.

Emil had created an all-white fantasy world. In the scenes filmed on the streets, in the bars and at the docks, there isn't a single black or 'coloured' in sight, not even in the role of a servant. One important scene between Dirk and Steve's widow, Marty, opens with shots of her frantically vacuuming and dusting, something I had yet to see a white woman do in her own home!

According to the critics, I now had two great careers ahead of me. The reality, of course, was that my future as a filmmaker was blocked, and it was questionable whether I could continue as an actor in South Africa without contributing to a dangerous fantasy. After five years of mistakes and compromises, surely the time had come to leave.

It should have been an easy decision, but it was not. In spite of all the political pressures, I still looked upon South Africa as my country. I had developed close friendships with like-minded people within all communities, and I was hopelessly in love at the time, but for complex reasons, we both knew that our relationship would not survive the move to England. And yes, there was a whole range of jobs in South Africa, from teaching to writing, that would not require the same kinds of compromises that came with film work.

Apart from these personal issues, there was a serious problem I would have to address if I wanted to pursue a filmmaking career in Britain. Without membership of the ACTT, the powerful union representing all those working in film and television at that time, there was no way I could work in either medium. The application process could take months, even years, and I was not in a good financial position. I had only just paid off the debts that Mme Olembert had loaded me with, and the cost of a purely speculative trip to Britain was a real concern.

While all these thoughts were churning in my mind, I received a telegram from Sheila, my mother, offering to buy me an open return ticket so that I could join her and the rest of the family in London to celebrate the wedding of my sister, Kay.

She concluded with: 'All longing your presence wedding. Your visit England may help clarify your future. Devotedly Ma.'

On this, Sheila was absolutely right.

The wedding took place in July 1967. By then, my stepfather Rufus was in semi-retirement, and he and my mother had taken a spacious flat in London's Park Lane, where they planned to stay until returning to the United States in September. My sisters Kay and Linda both had jobs in London while B, my younger brother, was finishing his final year in an English public school.

Kay's marriage to Hugh Wilson was a great occasion for all of us, but as soon as the couple left for their honeymoon, I got down to work.

Alan Sapper, the General Secretary of the ACTT, had a fearsome reputation, and when I visited his offices in Soho Square, I was pleasantly surprised to receive an invitation to lunch.

I told Alan everything, from *Anatomy of Apartheid* to the current banning order which had made it impossible for me to continue documentary filmmaking in South Africa.

'I want to be clear, are you banned from South Africa?'

'No. I could go back and work there tomorrow. I am only banned from filmmaking.'

Alan thanked me for being honest. Apparently, he had issued union tickets to people claiming that they had been banned from the country, only to discover later that this was untrue. At that point, I was promised a union ticket.

For the next week, there was a frantic scramble of phoning and letter writing to the three main television channels and a number of independent production companies, but the uncertainties didn't last long. One of the first people who agreed to see me was Tony Essex, the senior producer of the BBC's outstanding *Great War* series. It was a time of massive change within the ITV franchise, and Tony had just been offered the job of Head of Documentaries at Yorkshire Television, a new ITV company which would begin broadcasting in July the following year. When I showed him *River of Diamonds*, he had only one question. 'When would you like to start?'

The time had come to return to South Africa and prepare for a final departure.

Those goodbyes were difficult and emotional, and there was a moment when I nearly changed my mind, but in late September, I finally left for England.

Early the following year, I received shocking news from Soweto. David Kalahote had been murdered. I couldn't reach Ailsa by phone and there was no response to my letters. Only when I returned two years later was it possible to trace her and find out what had happened.

She and David had been at a party where the drink was flowing. When David started chatting to a young lady, her boyfriend suddenly came up behind him, pulled out a weapon he had made from a sharpened bicycle spoke, and stabbed David through the ribs and into his heart.

Without a word, all the guests, including the murderer, walked out of the house and into the night: only the owner's family remained. Two of them carried the body out and walked with Ailsa to the nearest crossroads, where they laid David down. One of them then went back to the house to phone an ambulance, while the other stayed with Ailsa until it arrived. David's death was reported as an attack by an unknown assailant at that very spot.

The whole incident was indescribably painful for Ailsa, but after my experiences with David's cousin, I understood why something as dreadful as this could happen. If you regard the police as your enemy, you do not involve them in any way. No one at the party that night was going to be subjected to a police interrogation, even if that meant letting the murderer walk free.

It was a dreadful epilogue to the most important and formative chapter of my life.

Chapter Seven

WAR IN THE ZAMBEZI VALLEY

Viewers in Britain today have a choice of over a hundred 'free-view' channels as well as streaming services such as Netflix and Amazon Prime, but in the late Sixties there were just three options, BBC 1, BBC 2 and ITV (Independent Television), and between them they had a monopoly.

Tony Essex was in his early forties when he was chosen to run Yorkshire Television's documentary department, and I can honestly say that I have never known anyone so dedicated to his work and determined that the company he had joined would make its mark across the ITV network. He not only succeeded in doing this with documentaries, but also with three long-running drama series.

A chain-smoker who seemed to be at his desk or in the cutting rooms all hours of the day and night, Tony still found all the time needed to listen, guide and support me, and I owe him a huge debt of gratitude.

As a documentary director, starting out in British television, I did not choose my first subjects. They were offered to me, and I could either accept or refuse. Tony had enjoyed the visual razzmatazz of *River of Diamonds* and suggested that I should use a similar approach to tell the story of the M62, the Trans-Pennine motorway, which was in the final stages of construction. Sadly, there was a short breakdown halfway through the broadcast of *Motorway*, but the critics had seen the film at a special preview and their response was positive.

The next subject Tony suggested was much closer to my heart. He had been approached by the celebrated journalist, Nicholas Tomalin, with a proposal for a documentary about the guerrilla war against the Smith regime in Rhodesia. Nick had already settled on the title, *War in the Zambezi Valley*, and would perform the role of writer/presenter. Because of my experience as a filmmaker in Africa, I seemed a good choice as director.

It was 1968, a time when the magnificent Zambezi River marked the frontier between black and white Africa. To the north was Zambia, formerly the British protectorate of Northern Rhodesia, which had been granted full independence and membership of the Commonwealth four years earlier. To the south was Rhodesia, formerly Southern Rhodesia, where Ian Smith's white minority government had responded with a Unilateral Declaration of Independence. Britain, the Common-wealth and the United Nations immediately declared UDI illegal and imposed economic sanctions.

****

I flew out ahead of the rest of the team. My job was to go to Salisbury (today's Harare) and secure filming permission in Rhodesia, while Nick headed straight from London to Lusaka, the Zambian capital, where he had important contacts in the president's office and the headquarters of the Zimbabwe African People's Union (ZAPU), one of the main players in the nascent military struggle against the Smith regime.

This was my first visit to Rhodesia, and I was struck by the similarities and the contrasts between the political systems in that country and South Africa. In Rhodesia, there were no 'Blacks Only' or 'Whites Only' signs, but the suburbs were almost exclusively white and were served by townships that were entirely black. There was, however, a small minority of blacks who were able study up to university level and there were also sixteen black MPs representing ninety-five per cent of the population!

In truth, Rhodesia was still frozen in a colonial era when people, like my dear grandmother, sincerely believed that the British Empire was an altruistic institu-tion, steadily raising standards across the vast territory it administered.

But this was not the story Nick intended to tell. We were there to cover a white versus black war, and my job was to set up interviews with senior members of the Rhodesian cabinet and the military. It was a relatively easy task, thanks to a curious personal connection.

Molly, my stepmother, had a younger brother, Arthur Phillip Smith. According to her, he had hoped to qualify as a solicitor in England, but after he failed his exams, his wealthy father bought him a large tobacco farm in what was then Southern Rhodesia. Apparently, this did not do well either, but by the time of my visit Phillip had other priorities. He was now the Minister of Education in Ian Smith's cabinet and spent most of the time in his Salisbury home, leaving the management of the farm to others.

Phillip and his wife, Betty, were in their late fifties, a quiet and gentle couple who not only helped with introductions, but kindly invited me to stay with them during my time in Salisbury. I was frank about the film we intended to make and even shared the title, but like most white Rhodesians, the Smiths felt that the present situation could hardly be described as a war. According to them, every attempt 'the terrorists' had made to cross the Zambezi had been foiled, a claim that George Harman, the Minister of Defence, repeated later in his interview with

Nick: 'We are completely on top of the situation, and I have no doubt that if the terrorists come, they will be met with a very hot reception.'

When filming started, we were allowed to accompany Rhodesian troops right up to the Zambezi valley, where there had been three incursions in the previous two years. In every case, we were told, the army had managed to kill or capture virtually every guerrilla who had crossed the river. One enthusiastic sergeant major even took us along the same route that 'an old African game-tracker' had guided him and his men during the latest incursion. The track led to a hilltop where they had spotted a group of 'terrorists' hunkering down in a gully below. For our benefit, the sergeant major re-enacted his own role in the ensuing battle, firing wildly as he rushed down the slope before pulling the pin on a live grenade and tossing it into the gully.

It was no surprise that Kenneth Kaunda, the President of Zambia, took a rather different view and accused white Rhodesians of serious complacency. In his interview, he compared the present struggle to the time when the Viet Cong were dismissed as 'a mere handful of agitators' and predicted that, within two or three years, this would be a conflict on the same scale. Now was the time for the British government 'to quell [white Rhodesia's] rebellion against the Queen and the British people and save all the bloodshed that is going to come.'

Nick also interviewed George Nyandoro, the general secretary of ZAPU, who claimed that the war had already reached the stage Kaunda was predicting. Apparently, ZAPU fighters were 'eighteen miles outside of Salisbury and nearly all over the world', which he quickly corrected to 'all over the country'.

I felt strongly that these contradictory messages from the opposing sides were insufficient, and Nick certainly agreed that we needed to balance the bombastic displays by Smith's forces with equivalent scenes on the other side, perhaps shots of guerrillas training in their camp. More importantly, we needed to talk to some of them individually about the experiences that had motivated them to leave their families and communities in Rhodesia and take up arms against the Smith regime.

But there was a major problem. In all his public statements, including his interview with Nick, President Kaunda strongly denied that there were any guerrilla camps in his country. Nyandoro of ZAPU also stuck firmly to the official line. There was no point in seeking his permission to film in camps that did not exist in Zambia.

Looking back, I can hardly believe our naivety, but we were determined to find a ZAPU camp and take it upon ourselves to win the trust of the fighters who were based there.

The Smith Government probably knew the precise locations of the main camps, but this information was not made public for the obvious reason that 'the terrorists' would move to another location as soon as they knew their camp had been spotted, and it was unlikely that we would have made much progress had it not been for a curious discovery I made during my time with Phillip and Betty.

Theirs was a typical colonial house of the 1930s, which had a lavatory at the side of the building with its own separate entrance, presumably for the use of servants. I popped in there one day and saw that there was no lavatory roll; just sheets of typed and hand-written paper, nailed to the wall. On glancing through these, I was astonished to discover a number of confidential government briefings.

Later that day, when Phillip and Betty were out of the house, I returned for a careful search and finally came across a reference to an intelligence report about a guerrilla encampment some six miles outside Lusaka. The exact location was not entirely clear, but when the time came, there was enough information in that document to encourage us to spend a whole day following dirt roads and talking to local villagers, until we met an elderly African who guided us to a rough track leading off into the bush. He assured us that if we followed this for three or four miles, it would take us to a camp where guerrillas were living and training. By this time, it was nearly dark, and we decided to return the following day.

There were four of us in the team: Nick, me, Peter Jackson and Brian Ranger. Peter was a superb cameraman and the two of us would work together on eleven films. Brian had not worked with me previously and, after our experiences on that fateful day, I certainly understand why he didn't volunteer to join us on our next African project! Like Peter, he was an excellent technician, but unlike the rest of us he had two careers. He was a fine sound-recordist and a successful conjurer.

We set off in the early morning, and I still find it hard to believe that we never considered the risks we were taking. Here we were, four young whites, unaccompanied by anyone the guerrillas knew or trusted. We didn't even have an interpreter, yet we believed we could charm our way into a guerrilla encampment and be allowed to conduct interviews and film military training. If that was not serious enough, we were attempting this in a country where the very existence of these camps had been denied by the President himself.

We turned off the main road and followed the track we had been shown the previous evening. After several miles there was a sharp turn, and we suddenly faced a fortified gate with a single guard. It was a moment I will never forget. The man was wearing military fatigues and had a Mohican-style strip of hair running down the centre of his shaved skull. As soon as we came into view, he raised his rifle and shouted at us to stop the van and get out. The noise quickly attracted others, and within minutes we were surrounded by a dozen fighters, all in military uniform. One of them had a pistol tucked into his belt, another was covering us with his rifle and – the most melodramatic touch of all – a third was holding a large assegai spear.

Who were we? Why had we come here without any warning?

We did our best to stay calm and tried to explain that we were here to tell the story of their struggle to the British people, but this had no effect. The van was thoroughly searched, and we were ordered to hand over our passports.

There was one precious moment of comedy amidst all the fear and confusion. When conjurers are performing a difficult trick, they instinctively crack jokes and chatter to distract their audience at the most critical moments. For some reason, Brian used to keep his passport in a small bag containing his overnight essentials, which always stayed with him when we travelled. Faced with a fighter shouting at him for his passport, Brian released all his fear and tension in a wonderful comic patter: 'Now what have we here? A pair of pyjamas! Would you believe it? Blue and white stripes! And below that? Yes, a little toiletry bag! Not in the best condition, I have to admit. And here? Aha! My passport!'

Once the passports had been collected, we were ordered to march in single file into the camp with our hands on our heads. A large crowd started to gather round us; fighters wearing uniforms in distinctively different styles. I assumed that these were an indication of the different countries that had provided their equipment and training – Russia, China or Cuba.

Finally, we were ordered to line up in front of a high wooden stockade and made to stand absolutely still. Our escorts withdrew to the sides but kept us covered as two teams moved in to set up machine guns some thirty feet in front of us.

It was a hot day, and we were fully exposed to the sun, but I managed to stay still with my eyes closed for what seemed like an age. It's hard to explain this, but I felt drugged, disengaged from everything that was happening around me and absolutely calm, until I was suddenly woken out of this trance by shouting, and opened my eyes to see a group of men pushing their way to the front of the crowd.

The two teams of gunners immediately jumped up and began to argue with the intruders. I don't understand a word of Shona or Ndebele, but I'm sure these new arrivals were members of a faction that believed that our deaths would have far more serious consequences than the decision to let us go.

It took a while, but eventually the message got through. The crowd quietened down, the machine guns were moved, and one of the men who had argued for our release summoned an escort to take us back to our van, with a warning never to return to this area again. When we asked about our passports, he gave us the name of a contact at State House, the President's residence, where they would be ready for collection the following morning.

For the first few minutes of the drive back to Lusaka, the four of us barely said a word, but finally I got my thoughts together and made a heartfelt apology. Nick immediately seconded me and congratulated Peter and Brian for their courage and self-control. We were sure that if any of us had broken down and pleaded for mercy, we would have been treated with contempt, and the guns might have started firing.

We were back at our hotel in Lusaka by mid-afternoon, and the time had come to discuss our next move. Obviously, we had no camera coverage of anything that had happened at the camp, but we could not leave the country without reference to this. Once our passports had been reclaimed the following day, I felt that Nick and I should go back to the point where the track to the camp left the main road, so that he could do a piece to camera describing what had happened. It was still a dangerous option, and I felt strongly that Peter and Brian should not be involved. They would have to trust me with the camera and the recorder.

Nick agreed, and although the others argued strongly that we should stay together, we both insisted that this was the only way forward.

The following day, the four of us went to State House with no idea what kind of reception we would receive or the conditions that might be imposed before our passports were returned. On arrival, we gave the name of our contact, and within minutes, a young man appeared and handed them over with hardly a word spoken.

An hour later, Nick and I were in the van and on our way. Peter and Brian had agreed to call the British High Commission in Lusaka if we had not returned to the hotel by 5.00pm.

As soon as we reached the spot, Nick took a final look at his script while I set up the equipment.

Once the camera was rolling, I could scarcely believe what Nick was saying. In this new version, everything had happened during the first evening. Instead of turning back when darkness was approaching, we had driven straight up to the fortified gates with headlights on. Apart from the switch from day to night, the early details Nick described were exactly as I remembered them – the guard with the Mohican hair-cut, the fighters who surrounded us and searched the van. Nick even told the story of Brian's pyjamas, but everything that followed was censored. There was no mention of the march through the camp, the line-up in front of the machine guns or the long wait while the guerrillas argued about our fate.

In Nick's version, we never entered the camp and the atmosphere remained relaxed and cheerful. 'These were kind men,' he tells us, 'and finally, after about twenty minutes, in some cases, of deeply philosophical argument, when they were threatening to detain us, but otherwise very, very courteous indeed, they let us turn around and drive back to Lusaka.'

After all my experiences in Soweto and on the mines, I am sure that if we had entered that camp with the necessary clearances and been free to talk to the people there, we would have found many who were 'kind' and 'very courteous.' We might even have engaged in some 'deeply philosophical argument', but because we had burst in without permission, we had not experienced anything like this.

Nick was a fine journalist, who felt as strongly as I did about the injustices in Rhodesia, but that did not give us the right to invent conversations that never took place. Why couldn't he describe what had happened on that day? When I raised this, he insisted that we were not there to make a film about ourselves but to tell the much bigger story of the early stages of a race war.

That's fine, I told him. Omit the firing squad, keep in the stories of the Mohican haircut and Brian's pyjamas, and just say that our passports were taken, and we were sent away.

It was an absurd situation. Here we were, arguing with each other at the junction between the main road and the track to the camp. At any moment, a single guerrilla or, indeed, a whole truckload of them could have appeared, but as long as Nick stood firm – which he did – there was nothing I could do. He was the one who had been commissioned to present the film. My role was to support and advise, nothing more, and I finally got on with the job.

****

The finished programme was well received, and reviewers certainly accepted Nick's message that this was the story of 'a black/white war which had barely begun', but what troubled me was the lack of any evidence in the film to support this. It was a statement delivered by Nick in one of his pieces to camera. All we could offer were contradictory claims from the leaders on opposing sides. We hadn't come close to military action or given the viewer any sense of the motives and beliefs that drove the fighters on either side.

Throughout the history of television there have been some outstanding documentary presenters, and they certainly play a crucial role in historical documentaries, nature programmes and travelogues, but when it comes to important contemporary subjects, presenters should be careful not to use pieces to camera to fill crucial gaps in the story they are trying to tell.

As my career progressed, it became increasing clear that my duty was to get as close as possible to those whose lives were directly affected by the issues involved, and to allow viewers to make their judgements on that basis. I certainly had a presence through commentary and the occasional interview question, but I never worked with a presenter again on any contemporary subject, nor did I try to perform that role myself.

In spite of these differences, Nick and I remained good friends, working together on the commentaries of my next three films. Very sadly, he was killed by a Syrian missile while covering the Yom Kippur War in October 1973.

For reasons neither of us could have predicted at the time, Nick's overall message also proved correct. Eight years after our film was broadcast, the Smith Government began negotiations for majority rule. The decisive factor was the 1974 coup in Portugal which brought down the Caetano regime and led to the collapse of the last colonial empire in Africa.

Once the former Portuguese colony of Mozambique was granted independence, the new administration gave its full support to ZANLA, the military wing of Robert Mugabe's ZANU movement. The border between Rhodesia and Mozambique had now become a second front, which Smith's forces could not secure.

The story of Europe's last colonial empire was the subject of two documentaries I would make for Tony Essex after completing *The Gold Run*, and by now, I was free to choose my own subjects.

Chapter Eight

PORTUGAL, DREAM OF EMPIRE

It was April 1970, and eighteen-year-old Antonio Mendes was leaving his village in northern Portugal to become a soldier. After hugging his tearful mother in a final goodbye, he picked up a battered suitcase and followed the rough track through a village that seemed frozen in time. There was no electricity, no running water, no telephone line and not a vehicle in sight. The favoured form of transport was the donkey.

After stopping at the church to receive a final blessing from the village priest, Antonio continued on his way, passing women collecting water at the village spring and others digging and hoeing the surrounding terraces.

Before seeing these people again, Antonio would be trained to guard and perhaps fight and kill other peasants – black peasants – thousands of miles away in Africa, and unless government policy changed, he would be liable for three years' military service again and again without warning or limit, until he was forty-eight years old.

It was the price Antonio and hundreds of thousands like him were having to pay to defend the last colonial empire in Africa. Taken together, the three Portuguese territories of Angola, Mozambique and Guinea covered an area larger than Britain, France, Germany, Italy and Portugal combined. The struggle to defend this empire against five rebel armies was now costing Portugal nearly half her national budget.

How could the poorest country in western Europe continue to pay the price in resources and human life to defend its African empire and bring about essential economic and social reforms after centuries of exploitation and neglect?

Those were the questions we raised in two films with the shared title *Portugal, Dream of Empire*.

****

To find the answers, we needed complete freedom to film in Portugal and close access to the front lines in Africa. It would take the better part of two months to secure filming permission, and I am sure we would have failed without the help of

Anthony Allfrey, an English economist working as a financial advisor to the Portuguese government. Anthony trusted me to give an honest account of Portugal's wars in Africa.

Filming began in Portuguese Guinea, the poorest and most neglected of the three colonies. It had no known resources, and conditions were so challenging that no white settler had ever chosen to farm there.

Goaded into action by the rebel forces of the PAIGC (The Party for the Independence of Guinea and Cape Verde), the Portuguese were now spending more on development than at any time in the country's history, but in spite of these efforts, Bissau, the capital, was still a shabby, run-down colonial town dominated by a single building: the residence of the military governor, His Excellency General António Sebastião Ribeiro de Spínola. We were required to pay our respects here before filming could begin.

As we were ushered into his spacious office, the general rose from his desk to greet us. With his trademark monocle and braided white uniform, sixty-year-old Antonio Spinola seemed a caricature of an imperial governor, but first impressions were misleading. In the discussion that followed, he spoke passionately and frankly about past negligence and the race to catch up on lost time.

As he saw it, Africa was now facing two bleak alternatives: continuing white domination, as in Rhodesia and South Africa; or rule by one of the many Marxist factions, whose primary loyalty was to their tribe. In his view, only Portugal was offering a third way, one of genuine equality among people of all races, united under a single flag.

As if to prove the point, he invited us to join him the following day on a visit to a northern village, which the rebels had claimed as liberated territory.

Several hundred people had gathered close to the landing strip where we touched down, and as soon as Spinola stepped off the plane, the crowds cheered, and the drums started beating. He was hugged, embraced and lifted high on black shoulders.

One couldn't help wondering whether this was a performance staged for our benefit, especially when Spinola, after briefly losing sight of me, called out: 'Where's Antony?' But once I had assured him that I was right there with Peter, the cameraman, he was back in action. Whatever reservations we had at the time, it was hard to imagine the leader of a conventional white regime – an Ian Smith or a Hendrik Verwoerd – enjoying this kind of intimacy with black villagers.

The sense that we were on a carefully prepared guided tour continued in the days that followed. Every morning at seven o'clock on the dot, the same army captain would arrive at our hotel with two jeeps and their drivers.

On one of our first days, we were taken to visit rural schools. Apparently, more of these had been built in the two and a half years of Spinola's governorship than in the previous five hundred. Children of illiterate parents were now being taught to read and write, but not in their own languages, only in Portuguese.

The walls of every school we visited were decorated with propaganda posters, and on two occasions, the teacher signalled to the children as soon as we entered. On cue, they rose to their feet, and sang the Portuguese national anthem for our benefit. 'To arms. To arms. On the land. On the sea. To arms. To arms. To fight for the motherland, marching, marching against the guns.'

The authorities were also keen for us to film the work they were doing to create 'secure zones' outside rebel control. As protection against landmines, a network of tarred roads was being built across the country, and people in their thousands were being transferred from ragged mud villages into new settlements, close to the roads. Here they would enjoy living conditions they had never known before, but they would also be under Portuguese protection and therefore under Portuguese control.

Fair coverage of a war like this depends on access to both sides, but conditions in Portuguese Guinea were very different from those we had experienced in Rhodesia. Criss-crossing between areas controlled by the Portuguese army and the PAIGC guerrillas would have been impossible.

To a large degree, the problem was solved when we were given access to a documentary on the PAIGC that had been completed a few months earlier, and it was fascinating to see the similarities between PAIGC propaganda and the message the Portuguese hoped we would convey on their behalf. Both sides wanted to feature the new villages and schools they were creating and to boast their military success. The one difference, of course, was that the children in the rebel schools were being taught in their local languages, and portraits of Amilcar Cabral, leader of the PAIGC, replaced the Portuguese propaganda posters on classroom walls.

In his interview, Cabral accused Portugal of centuries of neglect and was not afraid to speak about the support he was receiving from the Soviet Union and Cuba, but he wanted to assure all those who were prepared to listen that 'we are not fighting for an ideology, for capitalism or communism in our country. We are fighting for the freedom and dignity of our people.'

Although Cabral's quiet and logical approach was impressive, I was determined that we wouldn't follow the path we had been forced to take with *War in the Zambezi Valley* by confining this film to a series of contradictory statements from leaders on opposing sides. As the days passed and trust was built, we started to get a sense of the human costs. Most important of all was permission to film in the military hospital in Bissau, which had been specially built to cope with the casualties of war. Here we were given freedom to talk to severely wounded soldiers on both sides of the conflict; troops caught in ambush, young men with limbs blasted by mines and – tragically – villagers caught in the crossfire.

Just as we were starting to go deeper into this important personal area, all cooperation suddenly stopped. The captain, who normally appeared at 7.00am precisely, didn't arrive until mid-morning, and when he did, all he had to say was: 'There are problems. No more filming.'

I couldn't believe what I was hearing, but the captain refused to answer my questions. When I asked to see General Spinola, he simply shook his head.

It took nearly three hours to get a phone connection to Anthony Allfrey in Lisbon. Communication was difficult over a crackling long-distance line, but I gathered that Anthony already knew that something was seriously wrong and wanted me to fly to Lisbon as soon as possible. He also suggested that the rest of the team should take the flights already booked to our next port of call, Luanda, the Angolan capital, and wait there for further instructions.

I managed to get to Lisbon late the following day and went straight to Anthony's house, where he showed me a copy of a letter written by a freelance director working for Yorkshire television whom I knew by name but had never met. It had been sent to a friend of his in Angola, who had immediately forwarded it to the authorities in Lisbon. In the letter, I was described as someone on the far left who could not be trusted to make a fair and unbiased film about Portugal's wars in Africa.

The idea that another documentary director, someone who had never exchanged a word with me, should try to sabotage my work came as a shock. What made this so much worse was the context. The letter had been sent when we were filming in a war zone, and it was clearly implied that my sympathies would have been with the PAIGC.

Anthony did his best to calm me down. He told me that the authorities had been unsure of the authenticity of this letter from the start. If they had really believed what was written there, all our film would have been confiscated. As a precaution, they had stopped any further filming.

Since my call from Bissau, Anthony had already taken two meetings with the military authorities and, at one point, had linked them by phone to Tony Essex, who assured all concerned that the letter had been sent out of malice and the accusations were false. What was required now was a further meeting where I could answer questions about the work we were doing and the approach we were taking. For Anthony's sake as well as mine, I gave honest answers, and by the end of that session my interrogators gave us the all-clear. I arrived in Angola a day ahead of the rest of the team.

****

Unlike Portuguese Guinea, Angola is rich in diamonds, oil, iron, coal and cotton; it is a country eminently worth fighting for.

As expected, the authorities there were as keen as General Spinola to highlight Portugal's 'colour-blind' policies. We were even invited to film a cocktail party, hosted by Colonel Augusto Vaz, the governor of Angola, whose guests included leading businessmen, doctors and university professors. The point he wished to make soon became clear. Amongst this élite, there were blacks, far fewer blacks than whites, but they were there.

For similar reasons, we were encouraged to film in the city slums, where, as expected, we would find a small minority of whites. We were also taken to the back-lands, hundreds of miles from Luanda, where Portuguese peasants were tilling the soil with their bare hands, a sight unique in Africa. Since the late Fifties, thousands of the country's poorest had been given land and free passage to Angola, but it was obvious that this attempt at enforced integration was not working. The whites kept to themselves in tightly knit communities, and none of those we met seemed to have any black friends. We also learnt that these white peasants had been migrating to South Africa in large numbers.

I needed to find someone I could trust, someone who could give us an objective account of those centuries of exploitation and neglect and put the massive changes now taking place into context.

Surprisingly, the person who came closest to fulfilling that role was Dr Manuel Vinhas, Angola's leading industrialist, who owned twelve factories and provided free schooling for the children of all his workers.

In a passionate interview, he came straight to the point: 'It's funny, if it were not a tragedy, to say that the biggest help given to Angola and Mozambique was terrorism, because it obliged us to work hard and not to lose any more time.'

Vinhas spoke frankly about the past, yet he still had hopes for the future. All that was needed now, he told us, was time; time to educate a new generation, to create new industries and to lift a country rich in natural resources to its full potential.

But how much time did Portugal really have? It was a question we asked ourselves again and again, especially when we were back in Lisbon, filming the departure of troop ships for Africa.

Of the thousands of relatives and friends crowding the quayside, the most striking were groups of peasants, clustered around religious banners dedicated to their patron saints. They had come from villages across the country to catch a last glimpse of young men like Antonio Mendes, who were about to risk their lives for a cause they barely understood.

As the military trucks moved in to offload soldiers below the gangways, the waving and shouting from the crowd reached fever pitch.

Soon, the ship was listing heavily as soldiers packed the decks on the port side, searching for their loved ones on the quay. Whenever contact was made, there was a frenzy of waving and blown kisses.

Finally, the horn sounded, moorings were cast off, and the troop ship slowly moved away. Only then did we feel the full emotional impact on this crowd.

****

Eighteen months after the broadcast, Manuel Vinhas called me from Lisbon. He wanted to discuss a matter that was too sensitive to be shared over the phone. Would I please join him at the earliest opportunity?

A meeting was arranged in the boardroom of a company owned by one of his associates. About a dozen people had gathered there, but Vinhas was the only one I knew. He gave me a warm greeting and also passed on General Spinola's best wishes.

I knew that the situation had deteriorated since our filming, due largely to the massive support that Fidel Castro was now giving the MPLA (the People's Movement for the Liberation of Angola) and the PAIGC in Portuguese Guinea, but I was certainly not prepared for what followed.

Choosing his words carefully, Vinhas explained that there would soon be a major change in the government of his country. In preparation for this, he would like me to make a series of films that would encourage the Portuguese people to regard Angola, Mozambique and Guinea as partner nations like Brazil, and not as colonies. Although the word 'coup' was never mentioned, it was clear that plans were afoot to bring down the Caetano regime and end the wars in Africa.

I thanked Vinhas for this kind offer but explained that the lessons I had learnt as a young filmmaker had taught me never to touch a political subject if the conclusions had been set down in advance. I wished them good luck and promised to treat this as a confidential meeting.

On 25 April 1974, young officers in the Portuguese army staged a coup that overthrew the government of Marcelo Caetano, and General Spinola was invited to serve as the country's new president. Under his leadership, press censorship was abolished, the secret police disbanded, political prisoners released, and political exiles allowed to return.

Portuguese Guinea was granted independence the same year and took the name Guinea-Bissau. Angola and Mozambique received their independence in 1975, but by that time Spinola had been replaced as president by General Francisco da Gosta Gomes, a more radical figure favoured by the young officers. Spinola's dream of a federation of states linked by language and a common culture would never be realised.

Chapter Nine

SURRENDER TO EVEREST

We must remember that the highest of mountains is capable of severity, a severity so awful and so fatal that the wiser sort of men do well to think and tremble, even on the threshold of their high endeavour.

George Leigh Mallory

Everest's greatest challenges.

It was October 1970, and I was deeply involved in the final edit of the Portuguese films, when the cutting-room phone rang. It was Chris Brasher from the BBC, asking if I would be free in the New Year.

'Yes. What did you have in mind?'

'We'd like you to produce and direct a documentary we are making about the international expedition that will be leaving for Everest in February. Are you interested?'

'Of course, but could we please talk about this later?'

We agreed to meet the following day.

It was only when Philip Shaw, the editor, had solved the problem we had been wrestling with that I started to think seriously about this proposal.

While I had great respect for the climbing community, a film about an Everest expedition seemed worlds away from the kind of subjects that were important to me. On a practical note, I had no climbing experience and couldn't see how I could perform the role of a 'hands-on' producer/director in that environment.

Chris Brasher had an impressive record: Olympic gold medallist, sports journalist, co-founder of the London Marathon and TV executive. The least I could do was to apologise to him in person, rather than over the phone, but when I gave my reasons, he simply shook his head.

What mattered most on Everest was the fitness and stamina needed to help the body adjust to lower and lower levels of oxygen. He knew I was an enthusiastic long-distance runner and, provided no unseen problems were revealed in the medical tests, he was confident I could cope.

Chris went on to explain that our operational centre during the key moments of the climb would be Advanced Base Camp, at roughly 21,000 feet (6,400m). The route to this camp would be marked and roped by the lead climbers, and it needed only basic mountaineering experience on my part to reach that level.

For coverage higher up the mountain, I could rely on a team of three cameramen, two sound recordists and an associate producer, who were all experienced climbers. In Chris's opinion, three of them were capable of reaching the summit.

All this was reassuring, but I had to be frank about my other concerns. By this time, twenty-eight climbers had reached the summit since the successful British climb in 1953. How could another Everest expedition have any real significance?

Chris explained that the mountain still offered two great challenges. The first was the *Direttissima*, the direct climb straight up the Southwest Face of Everest. Equally daunting was West Ridge Direct, which followed a narrow spine of rock, rising all the way to the summit at 29,029 feet (8,850m). So far, all attempts to reach the summit by these routes had failed.

But there was a third factor that made this expedition so exceptional. The climbers had been selected from twelve nations, seeking to prove, as Sherpa Tenzing once said, that the summit belongs to all men. Success on both routes would offer an inspiring example of international cooperation.

I was persuaded.

It took at least six meetings to decide on the equipment we would need. All of this had to be 'winterised' by the manufacturers and then tested in a 'mini-expedition' which Chris had planned in the Tyrolean Alps.

In the second week of January we arrived at the Austrian ski resort of Hochgurgl and after a night in a local hotel, set off at dawn with all our gear, almost filling the lift that took us to the top of a ski run. From there we traversed across the slopes and set up camp away from the skiing area, but had hardly settled in when the weather turned, bringing heavy snow and ferocious winds. John Cleare, the lead cameraman, warned me that these were the conditions we should expect at Advanced Base Camp, but there would be one crucial difference. Here we were unlikely to suffer the debilitating effects of oxygen starvation. Hochgurgl was at a height of only 7,500 feet (2,300m), roughly a third of the altitude at Advanced Base where I would be spending most of my time on Everest.

With or without the fear of oxygen starvation, I was already experiencing working conditions I had never known. We were, of course, living in a pre-digital age when everything had to be recorded on film. Cameras had to be started at very slow speeds to avoid the danger of the film snapping in these extreme temperatures, then reloaded in specially designed changing bags to protect the film from fogging in the glacial glare. The whole process was, in John's words, 'a bastard with numb fingers and in driving snow'.

But our time at Hochgurgl was not all doom and gloom. This was a great team to be working with, and during those five days in the Alps, we got to know each other well.

Although most of their time was spent testing equipment, they had also set up a climbing route on a rock pinnacle behind the camp where I was taught the rudiments: how to attach the spiked crampons that give one a firm footing in the ice, and how to abseil and use the carabiners which keep one linked to the guide ropes.

On the final day the weather improved and Norman Dyhrenfurth, the leader of the expedition, skied across the slopes to meet us. He was in his early fifties, tall and imposing in his full skiing gear. Most of his early life had been spent in Switzerland, but he was now a naturalised American and was best known for leading the 1963 Everest expedition when three Americans and a Nepalese Sherpa reached the summit.

I had always imagined that an Everest expedition leader would have the qualities of a military officer, someone with enormous self-confidence and very firm views, but Norman had none of those traits. He was gentle and diplomatic – a listener who seemed to value other people's opinions as much as his own.

Three weeks later we joined him and the British climbers on the final leg of our journey to Kathmandu, the Nepalese capital. Others were waiting to meet us at the airport, and for the first time, the whole expedition was together.

There were forty of us altogether: twenty-four climbers (including two climbing doctors), our seven-man film team, an oxygen expert, a Nepalese liaison officer, and Australian journalist Murray Sayle, who was covering the climb for the *Sunday Times*.

It was a joyful moment: old friends embracing each other, and some of the younger climbers excited to be meeting the stars of the mountaineering world for the first time. The mood was only slightly dampened when Elizabeth Hawley, the local Reuters correspondent, stepped out of a group of waiting reporters and challenged Norman with her own thoughts about this expedition.

'It strikes me that you have come to the highest mountain in the world. You have decided on the two most difficult routes, and you have chosen the most difficult way to do this with a group of people, not all of whom can communicate with each other. In fact, half of them can't communicate with the other half.'

Norman ignored this pertinent statement and assured all those present that 'as far as human relations are concerned, I am very optimistic.'

It took nearly three weeks to get all the supplies and equipment packed and organised before we were ready to embark on the 'march in' to Base Camp. The logistics were staggering: thirty-two tons of food and equipment, 300 oxygen cylinders, boxes of medical supplies and ten miles of rope. Roughly half of this load was flown to a small airstrip at Lukla, a seven-day march from Everest Base Camp. The rest would be carried all the way from Kathmandu on the backs of the expedition's 450 porters.

For the climbers, the Everest 'march in' was a gentle seventeen-day ramble through some of the finest mountain scenery in the world, a time to relax and acclimatise. For us, it was the first opportunity to work together as a team.

We used the time to form a good working relationship with the six Sherpas who would be supporting us throughout the climb and to find the best ways of coordinating three-camera coverage. Both here and on the mountain, we wanted to film tight and close to the climbers while simultaneously covering them from a distance to give a real sense of the scale and raw beauty of the surroundings and the challenges they were facing.

Even more important was the opportunity to get to know the climbers and gain their trust. At this early stage, I needed informal interviews with every one of them as well as scenes that would show how the climbers related to each other – whether on the march, in the mess tent or taking a riverside break for lunch.

Clearly, there would be no space for all this footage in the finished film, but as the climb progressed some members of the team were bound to come to the fore, perhaps for their summit victory or for giving their selfless support to others. When that time came, it was crucial that we had enough material to establish every one of them as a real person, not just a name.

All of us agreed that the most likeable member of this expedition was Major Harsh Bahuguna, a serving officer in the Indian army. He was in his early thirties, a warm, gentle and thoughtful person with close links to the Sherpas. In fact, he made me promise that, when the commentary was finally written, we would make it clear that *thirteen* nations were involved in this climb, not twelve, as stated in the publicity.

Harsh Bahuguna.

Harsh had seen the list and was shocked to find that Nepal was not included. 'Antony, no expedition has ever been organised to put a Sherpa on top of the mountain, but without their contribution, I doubt that anyone would have made it.'

Harsh had been on the 1965 Indian expedition when nine climbers reached the summit, but for reasons he still couldn't fathom, he had lost confidence when he was just 800 feet short of the summit and turned back. This time he was determined to make it, but as I would learn when we were alone together one evening, something else was driving him. 'As an Indian, I'm determined to show the world that we're equal to any of these European climbers.' This was not a proclamation for all to hear. He was quietly reading out a line he had just written in one of the letters he regularly sent to his wife and two young children.

Two other climbers also became good friends: Michel and Yvette Vaucher from Switzerland. Yvette was the only woman on the team and had dazzling credentials. She started rock-climbing in her early twenties and then took up parachuting, making more than a hundred jumps. In 1962 she married Michel, who was regarded as one of Switzerland's greatest mountaineers, and together they had accomplished some of the most challenging Alpine climbs.

I have a passable grasp of French, which was probably one of the reasons why we became good friends. The Vauchers hardly spoke a word of English and the same was true of the French climber, Pierre Mazeaud, and the two Japanese, Naomi Uemura and Reizo Ito. Other climbers from Austria, Italy and Germany had only a rudimentary understanding of English, and it was the same story on the other side. Of the eight English-speaking climbers, only two had any understanding of another European language: Peter Steele, the expedition doctor and Dougal Haston, who was notoriously quiet and uncommunicative.

Elizabeth Hawley had certainly foreseen the problem when she challenged Norman at the airport, and as I got to know the climbers better, I shared her concerns. Not only was there a danger of serious misunderstandings at critical moments, but there was also the possibility that language barriers would divide the climbers into cliques.

With our vast supplies of tents, food and equipment, we were following an Everest tradition that had been firmly established by the successful British expedition in 1953. You climb for as long as you can, hammering in pitons, securing ropes and setting up high altitude camps for the benefit of others, who take over when you're exhausted. There is an old saying, 'those who reach the summit climb on the shoulders of others', and once that is achieved, it is seen as a victory for the entire team.

All that would change in 1978 when two celebrated climbers, Reinhold Messner and Peter Habeler, reached the summit of Everest in a matter of days, without oxygen or any climbers or Sherpas to support them. The following year, Messner repeated the feat from the Tibetan side, but this time entirely on his own.

But our expedition was firmly set in that earlier age when unknown young men worked selflessly together, driven by the conviction that a summit success was a victory for the team, not just the individual. We certainly had our quota of unknown young men, including two Norwegians and several Americans, who had scrimped and saved to pay the $500 fee to join the expedition, but this group was heavily outnumbered by hard-core professionals with established reputations to maintain.

At the top of the list were the two Englishmen, Dougal Haston and Don Whillans. The previous year, they had made the first ascent of the south face of Annapurna, which was regarded as the greatest climbing achievement in the Himalayas at that time. Dougal was the director of the International School of Mountaineering in Leysin, Switzerland, while his partner, Don Whillans, a former plumber, was now making a good living lecturing on mountaineering. As a pair, 'they went like steam engines at high altitudes', and both were groomed for stardom.

Even those who did not make a living from climbing craved the fame and recognition a summit victory would bring. Pierre Mazeaud, a deputy in the French National Assembly, was determined to be the first Frenchman to conquer Everest, not only for the glory of the Republic, but because a triumph like this would probably secure him the role of France's Minister of Sport. For Yvette Vaucher, there was the real possibility that she would be the first woman to conquer Everest. 'I came here for the summit,' she told us, 'really for the summit'.

But could climbers like these really believe in the principle that a victory for one would be a victory for all?

There was another important factor: age. Most of the 'climbing stars' were in their late thirties and early forties and knew that this was probably their last chance of an Everest victory. But all these issues were casually overlooked in the holiday atmosphere of the 'march in', where the climbers enjoyed five-star treatment, thanks to Colonel Jimmy Roberts and his staff.

Roberts was co-leader of the expedition, with overall responsibility for the Sherpas, porters and supplies. He had served with the Gurkhas throughout the Second World War and had an outstanding military record. Since then, he had led scores of climbing expeditions to the Himalaya and pioneered tourist treks throughout Nepal. Now in his mid-fifties, Roberts would only be accompanying us as far as Base Camp, but as long as he was in charge, we would receive the same treatment enjoyed by the wealthy tourists on his guided tours.

At 11,000 feet (3,350m), we reached the snow line and had our first glimpse of Everest. Although the mountain was partially hidden by Nuptse, the summit was clearly visible, with a huge plume of cloud rising from it like frozen smoke. It was the first hint of the violence of the jet-stream winds that would make the final stages of the climb so daunting.

Three days later we were at Tengboche. At 13,000 feet (almost 4,000m), this is one of the highest human settlements in the world, and it was here that Dyhrenfurth called his crucial 'planning meeting'.

The climbers were free to choose their own routes, and by a happy coincidence there were equal numbers in each team. As Dyhrenfurth rattled off the names, I was struck by the division along national lines. The Face was dominated by Anglo-Saxons, but included the two Japanese climbers, Naomi Uemura and Reizo Ito. The Ridge climbers were mainly continental Europeans – French, Swiss, Austrian, German and Norwegian – with one American and Harsh Bahuguna, the only Indian on the climb.

Now was the time for Dyhrenfurth to nominate the leaders of each team. There were at least four potential candidates on the Ridge team, but for the Face there was only one obvious front-runner, Don Whillans. But the problem here was that this blunt and outspoken working-class Brit was not the kind of person Dyhrenfurth wanted to put in command, so he resolved both dilemmas with a fudge.

On this expedition, he explained in three languages, there would be no leaders, only coordinators. 'Since we are a very strong team and each route has top climbers who have done some of the greatest climbs in the world, it is not a question of this coordinator being the climbing leader, because obviously the others in the group are as good as he is.'

So, who would be making the crucial decisions as the teams reached the final, dangerous approaches to the summit? Norman Dyhrenfurth's diplomatic skills may have worked well in gathering money, support and recruits, but they would be severely challenged in the weeks ahead.

****

From Tengboche, it was a four-day trek to Base Camp at 17,600 feet (5,350m). As we drew nearer, all sights and sounds of life were gradually disappearing. We were entering a monochromatic world of black rock and wind-blown ice, and the increasing thinness of the air was having its effect.

It's a slow process, acclimatisation – accustoming the blood to less oxygen. Movement becomes increasingly slow, difficult and painful. There are frequent headaches, sleeping is difficult, and the voice hoarsens; but very slowly, the body adapts.

On 23 March 1971, Base Camp was established in its traditional place at the foot of the Khumbu Icefall. We were now over three miles above sea level and facing the most dangerous and demanding section of the climb: cliffs and towering blocks of ice, moving forwards and downwards continuously under the pressure of the ice behind.

The conditions in the Icefall that year were the worst in living memory. We had barely settled into the camp when we heard a loud roar and rushed out of our tents to see huge blocks of ice tumbling down, smashing everything in their path. It was an awesome warning that the holiday stroll was finally over.

There's a basic technique for getting through the Icefall. First, the best climbers explore the treacherous terrain to find the safest route. Then they screw in ice pitons and fix permanent guide ropes. Crevasses are bridged with logs and aluminium ladders, which are also fixed to the steepest ice blocks on the climb.

Today, Everest is a tourist venue, and at the start of every season paid professionals are sent in to secure the route, but in 1971 we had the mountain to ourselves, and that responsibility was ours. It took two weeks, twice as long as expected, to get the job done, and our high-altitude film team (John Cleare and Jerzy Surdel on camera, Ian Howell on sound) were there from the start. I joined them as soon as the work was completed and the Sherpas and porters were ready to move through with their loads.

Nothing I asked seemed too much for this team. When I wanted a powerful shot of heavily loaded porters crossing a deep crevasse bridged by a couple of logs, John Claire immediately abseiled down to the depths and captured a wonderful image of the porters, high above him against the sky and framed by two walls of ice.

In recent years, great films have made about Himalayan climbs, but the tools available today have transformed the process. Not only have digital cameras solved the problems our team faced when loading film but drones now offer the possibility of sweeping aerials and wide shots of the climbers that give a real sense of the awesome surroundings and put those tiny figures into context. Back in the 1970s, we had to climb to a distant point every time a shot like this was needed. On one occasion, I over-stepped the mark.

There was a notorious section on the route where a huge ice block was leaning several degrees over the path. The Sherpas were so wary that they would scatter votive offerings of rice to the gods before moving ahead at double speed until they were clear of the overhang.

As soon as I saw this, I suggested a camera position well away from the route, which would give the viewer a sense of the size of this overhanging ice block in relation to the tiny figures scurrying below.

Everyone on the team had enough climbing experience to know the dangers of wandering into uncharted areas of the Icefall, yet when you are working well together and morale is high, it is hard to be the one who steps out of line to complain that 'a great shot' is too risky. Without a word, the team followed me on a wide detour until we had a perfect view of the section we wanted to film. We must have spent half an hour there before turning back and had barely reached the main path when we heard an enormous crash. The whole area where we had been standing and filming was collapsing into the crevasse below.

It was the second time I had put the lives of my colleagues at risk, but on neither occasion do I remember anyone complaining. In both cases, they were grateful to have survived, but this experience was a turning point for me. The 'gung-ho' attitude had to stop, and I vowed never, never to take risks like this again.

****

At the top of the Icefall, the climbers and Sherpas established Camp One. Ahead of us was the legendary Western Cwm, and Everest was now clearly in view, hunching undramatically on our left.

The Cwm is the highest valley in the world, a desperate, claustrophobic trough, whose vertical white walls dwarf all within. When the skies are clear, the sun reflecting off the ice and snow can push the temperature up to 30 degrees Celsius, but once the clouds move in, this can plunge below freezing in a matter of minutes.

The Cwm is two miles long and half a mile wide. In good weather it's a safe climb, but when the snow falls, the beaten trails are obscured, and the many small crevasses become hidden man traps. The Swiss had christened the Cwm the Valley of Silence, a rather inappropriate choice in my view, since we were constantly aware of the creaking of the ice and the moaning of the wind high on the peaks above.

On 6 April, Advanced Base Camp (also known as Camp 2) was established at the far end of the Cwm at a height of 21,600 feet (6,600m). From now on, this would be the heart of the expedition and the operational centre for the two attacks on the summit. It would also be my home for the better part of two months.

From this point onwards, or so I thought, I would be removed from all the action. The best I could do was to keep in radio contact with the two teams filming on the

Face and on the Ridge. It never occurred to me at the time that the most moving and dramatic moments in this expedition would occur right here at Advanced Base.

The first party set off to attempt the *Direttissima*, the direct climb up the Southwest Face, a sloping wall of ice that starts at 40 degrees and steepens almost to vertical.

In six days, the two Britons, Whillans and Haston, and the Japanese, Uemura and Ito, with supporting Sherpas and climbers, had set up their first staging post, Face Camp 3, at 23,000 feet (7,000m) It was neatly sheltered by an outcrop that protected it from falling rocks and avalanches.

At the same time, the second party was attacking the West Ridge. Because he was familiar with Everest, it was decided that Harsh Bahuguna should lead the climb in partnership with Wolfgang Axt, an ultra-fit Austrian giant. After a tough start, the two of them finally managed to establish Ridge Camp 3 at 22,600 feet (6,900m). They also found a suitable site for Camp 4, while the other members of the team and the Sherpas continued to back them up with supplies.

On 16 April, Whillans and Haston returned to Advanced Base for a rest. John Cleare and Ian Howell came down with them and the two Japanese climbers took over the lead of the Face team. By now, Jerzy Surdel, our Polish cameraman, had already returned from West Ridge in a state of exhaustion, but Bahuguna and Axt remained hard at work.

I couldn't forget Harsh's promise to 'show the world that we're equal to any of these European climbers'. What he had overlooked was that climbers like Axt, with easy access to the Alps, could hone their mountaineering skills every weekend, should they wish. Harsh's only climbing experience had been in the Himalayas, just four expeditions in a lifetime. He was certainly no match for Axt – either physically or technically.

I shared these concerns with Dyhrenfurth. If climbers of the calibre of Whillans and Haston felt that ten days in the lead was enough, the same should apply to Bahuguna and Axt. Surely the time had come to call them down.

Dyhrenfurth shook his head. It was not up to him to give orders to world-class climbers like Bahuguna and Axt. They had to make their own decisions.

The next day, the weather worsened and the support climbers and Sherpas on both routes returned to Advanced Base, but Bahuguna and Axt kept working.

The third day started well. The skies were clear and Dyhrenfurth was delighted to tell me that Axt had radioed in to say that he and Harsh were finally coming down, but sadly for them another storm was brewing, and by early afternoon it was in full force.

By that time, all the climbers at Advanced Base had withdrawn to their tents, which were flapping furiously in the storm. I couldn't settle down but kept my boots and jacket on and was constantly popping my head out to see whether there was any sign of someone approaching camp from the direction of the Ridge climb. Finally, at about 4.00pm, I caught a glimpse of a single figure battling towards me through the storm, and immediately went out to meet him. It was Wolfgang Axt. Ice was clinging to his beard and eyebrows, and he was exhausted.

'Where's Harsh?'

'Oh. He's just behind me.'

Axt went straight to his tent and zipped himself in. Seconds later, I heard a faint, muffled sound through the storm. It was a distant scream.

As quickly as I could, I spread the news around the camp, and a rescue party was assembled. By the time they departed, night in the Cwm was not far off. Whillans shouted at the others to grab as many ski poles as possible so that they could mark out the route, otherwise they would never find their way back to camp in the dark through driving snow.

All of them climbed as quickly as they could, but it required lung-tearing effort, made so much worse by the storm. Perhaps because they knew the route better than the others, two of the Ridge climbers, Michel Vaucher and the young Norwegian, Odd Eliassen, were the first to reach Harsh.

He was motionless on the ice face, helpless with cold and exhaustion, and he had lost both gloves. Worst of all, the shirt he had started out with when the weather was fine had been scrunched up by his harness, exposing his naked torso to the full blast of the storm.

Clearly, Harsh had been in a bad way even before the storm started to build. With no one to help or support him, he lacked the strength and willpower to pull his heavy-duty jacket and headgear out of his backpack, but still he pressed on until he was within shouting distance of the camp. At that point, the effort of unclipping his carabiner with frozen fingers, passing it over an ice piton, and clipping it onto the next section of rope must have proved too much, and he gave up.

More to comfort him than anything else, Eliassen asked Harsh if he was still okay. Incredibly, he seemed to murmur that he was. Vaucher's first move was to free Harsh of his pack and throw it away. Then the two of them tried to lower him on a rope, but they had hardly begun when he turned upside down. Whillans, who had now arrived on the scene, climbed across the ice and turned Harsh the right way up. He then tried to move him sideways at considerable risk to himself, but it was an impossible task. The only remaining option was to lower him straight down the slope to a shelf of icy rock, where Peter Steele, the expedition's doctor and others who had joined the rescue party could take care of him.

Twenty feet above the rock shelf, the rope ran out. Whillans, teetering around on the steep slopes in the face of the storm without an ice axe or protective rope, took one last look at Harsh, who was now unconscious. His face was blue, but his eyes were still open. Whillans knew that Harsh would soon be dead and muttered his apologies: 'Sorry, Harsh, old son, you've had it.'

The rescuers were now in an unenviable position. Exhausted and battered by the storm, they had to fight their way back to the camp, where a small group of us, including Dyhrenfurth, was waiting for them. We were shattered to hear the news, but this was not the right time to pester the rescue party with questions. Every one of them had to get out of the storm and back to their tents, but I was so churned up with grief and anger that sleep was impossible.

The following morning, the wind was still raging, piling snow against the tents and creating drifts, several feet deep. One by one, the climbers made a dash to the mess tent, where some of them were hearing the news of Harsh's death for the first time.

Axt was the last to arrive, and as soon as he entered, all conversation stopped. After muttering a few 'Guten Morgen's, he grabbed a box of cereal and started shaking the contents into a bowl. Everyone was staring at Dyhrenfurth, silently imploring him to say something. Finally, our leader cleared his throat and whispered: 'Wolfgang, Harsh ist tot.'

In one account, there is a description of Axt breaking down in tears as soon as he hears the news. It is certainly not my memory of that moment. I still have a clear mental picture of Axt's expressionless stare as Dyhrenfurth went over the facts as gently and diplomatically as he could. All this proved too much for Pierre Mazeaud, the French deputy, who interrupted the monologue by yelling at Axt that he was guilty of murder through negligence.

We interviewed Vaucher, Whillans and Eliassen, who gave their own accounts of the rescue attempt with great sadness and dignity. For Eliassen, the young Norwegian, this tragedy was a turning point. He was haunted by the thought that they had abandoned Harsh while he was still alive, and as soon as he returned to camp, 'I said to Norman that for me is the summit finished. I never want to go on that traverse again.'

I was not allowed to interview Axt. Looking back, all these years later, I feel that was the right decision. He must have been going through hell at the time, and in the emotional state I was in, it would have made things worse had I been allowed to cross-examine him.

****

The storm continued for ten days, marooning all the climbers in their tents. It was the worst pre-monsoon season for seventy years, the worst weather ever experienced on Everest, and morale at Advanced Base Camp was plummeting. Despite

Advanced Base Camp.

the severe conditions, a party of Sherpas battled their way through the storm to retrieve Harsh's body, which stayed on the edge of the camp, wrapped in a scarlet flysheet and frozen solid for the next nine days.

During that time, most of us stayed alone in our tents, wrapped up in our sleeping bags with just the occasional dash through the storm to join the others at mealtimes or to relieve ourselves in some discreet corner of the camp. It was impossible to stay dry, even inside the tents, where a thick rime of frost, formed from frozen breath, was continually melting and dripping down.

For me, this was a time of introspection, and I began to feel that I had a lot in common with these climbers. Like them, I needed to escape from the complexities and banalities of everyday life and focus instead on a great overriding cause. Theirs was mountaineering, mine was filmmaking, but in both cases our motives were mixed. In those gentle days of the 'march in', the climbers could talk about the physical and mental challenges, the comradeship and the outstanding example of international cooperation they could give to the world, but personal ambition was also an important factor. Now that days were being lost and supplies were running low, Dyhrenfurth was under increasing pressure to abandon his idealistic aims and focus instead on the most plausible way of getting the 'climbing stars' to the summit.

My own response to these changing circumstances was rather different, but equally self-centred. The preconception of a great story of international brotherhood had developed into something very different, but it was also becoming clear that a strong film was taking shape. It would be a dramatic account of human conflict under stressful conditions, revealing the finest qualities in some and naked ambition in others.

Serious lobbying by the 'summiteers' started four or five days into the storm, when there was still no end in sight. Whillans argued that the climbers no longer had the time or the resources to tackle both routes and should work together as a single team on the *Direttissima*. A successful assault, straight up the face of Everest, would be an historic first, securing the reputation of this expedition for all time. A successful Ridge climb would not resonate in the same way.

Knowing that this would seriously reduce their chances, Mazeaud, the Vauchers, and others with strong summit ambitions suggested a compromise. The entire Ridge team should switch to the classical and far less demanding South Col route.

The arguments went back and forth, with Whillans stressing that victory via the South Col route had been achieved so many times that it was now almost worthless. Mazeaud argued, just as vehemently, that the Face climb was such an unknown quantity that they were in real danger of failing to get anyone to the summit. Could they imagine the ridicule they would face if the most expensive and highly publicised expedition in Everest history ended 'avec un score de zéro'?

Dyhrenfurth, acting as both translator and mediator in most of these discussions, made repeated appeals for calm and suggested that all decisions should be postponed until the storm was over, when we would be a position to make a full assessment. Unfortunately, that day of reckoning didn't come quickly, and on the ninth day of the storm, food and fuel had virtually run out. A party of Sherpas set out for Camp One at the top of the Icefall but were soon forced to turn back.

On the following day, the weather slowly started to clear. The Sherpas made a second attempt, and this time they were able to get through to Camp One and return with supplies, but the effects of the prolonged storm had been catastrophic. Lack of exercise, food and drink, as well as the continuous damp inside the tents had taken their toll. John Cleare and Ian Howell, our high-altitude team, and four climbers were diagnosed with pneumonia. Michel Vaucher was suffering from phlebitis, and Gary Colliver, one of the young American climbers, had haemorrhaging retinas. All of them would have to return to Base Camp as soon as possible, but the storm had made the Icefall even more unstable, with ice blocks continually shifting and falling, and progress would be slow and dangerous.

In spite of these hazards, Dyhrenfurth insisted that Harsh should receive a proper Hindu cremation. Apparently, the timing was crucial, since his religion decreed that this must take place within thirteen days of death.

Eight Sherpas were given the task of dragging the body down seven thousand feet to a point below the snowline where the cremation would take place. Ian Howell and Bill Kurban (our second team) came with me to film the descent.

A dead man is a far more ungainly, dangerous burden than essential supplies, and in the Icefall, conditions were so bad that we had to stop filming and concentrate on survival. Snow bridges had disappeared, crevasses had opened up, and seracs had toppled over. Progress was painfully slow, but even when they were passing under the most dangerous leaning ice-cliffs, the Sherpas could not hurry.

Although some climbers were opposed to this, I respected Dyhrenfurth's decision. The idea of dropping Harsh's body into a crevasse seemed unthinkable, even though this had been common practice when lives were lost at high altitudes on several expeditions. I couldn't help wondering, though, how Harsh, with his strong respect and concern for the Sherpas, would have felt about the risks they were taking on his behalf.

It was nearly dark by the time we had cleared the Icefall and reached Base Camp, where Harsh's wrapped body was placed in the care of Colonel Roberts, co-leader of the expedition. He had already issued instructions for a funeral pyre to be created at a place called Gorakshep, which was just below the snow line, but we soon learnt that there was something else on his mind.

While we had been struggling through the Icefall, Dyhrenfurth had radioed Roberts with the news that the former Ridge climbers would be switching to the South Col route. In response, Roberts insisted that we no longer had the manpower or the supplies to support two separate climbs: all resources should be concentrated on the Face.

Dyhrenfurth's reaction was typical. He would invite the climbers and senior Sherpas in every camp to vote on the issue. Roberts was appalled.

Early next morning, we left with our party of Sherpas as they carried Harsh's body to Gorakshep, which was a five-hour trek from Base Camp. I had expected that some of the climbers would have joined us to pay their last respects, but Roberts was the only expedition member present.

Harsh's cremation was a disturbing experience. There were no rituals, and no words were said in his memory. All we could do was to film the flames in silence. There was a dreadful moment when the body started to thaw and Harsh's hand, still in a near-perfect state, slowly reached out of the pyre towards us. As discreetly as he could, Roberts poked it back with his walking stick. Fortunately, we were no longer filming at that point; it was an image I never wanted to see again.

Thoroughly demoralised, we left Gorakshep at first light the following day and returned to Base Camp, where Peter Steele, the expedition doctor, had already arrived with the sick and injured. The latest news from Advanced Base was that the majority had voted in Roberts' favour and the South Col route had been abandoned.

We had hardly taken this in before another message was radioed from Advanced Base. Pierre Mazeaud, Yvette Vaucher and the Italian climber, Carlo Mauri, were so infuriated by this decision that they were already packing their things. Jerzy Surdel, the Polish climber/filmmaker originally commissioned to film the West Ridge climb, had decided to leave with them. We learnt later that Dyhrenfurth had made a final appeal to them to stay and support the Face climb, but Mazeaud's furious response was: 'You expect me, Pierre Mazeaud, member of the French Assembly, aged forty-two, to work as a Sherpa for Anglo-Saxons and Japanese? Never! This is not me, but France you have insulted'.

Michel Vaucher was already at Base Camp with the other sick and injured and made it clear that he supported Mazeaud's decision and would leave with Yvette, as soon as she and the others reached the camp.

As the time of their expected arrival drew near, the tension started to build. Roberts was sitting waiting for them at the far end of the mess tent with several young Sherpas standing, like bodyguards, on either side of him. Peter Steele, the expedition doctor, and Ian Stuart, who had filmed the cremation, were also present. Ian had been particularly close to Harsh, and since our return to Base Camp had been overcompensating with whisky.

It was late afternoon when Mazeaud stormed into the tent with the others in train. Pointing directly at me and then at Roberts, he shouted: 'Antony, dit-lui qu'il est un alcoolique et un gazon.' ('Antony, tell him he's an alcoholic and a paedophile.')

'What's he say? What's he say?'

I'm sure Roberts was not convinced when I cobbled something together about incompetence with supplies, but before he'd had a chance to respond, Mazeaud unleashed a tirade about an Anglo-Saxon plot to oust the continentals, collusion with the BBC to ensure that the summit was reserved for the Brits, allegations of drunkenness and pot smoking at Advanced Base, and distorted radio messages about a vote. He was still in mid-flow when poor Ian fell across the table, dislodging his spectacles.

'Regardez, un autre Anglais ivre!' shouted Mazeaud. 'Vous êtes tous des ivrognes et des idiots.' ('Look, another drunken Englishman! You are all drunkards and idiots.')

Roberts leaned forward and said quietly, 'Fuck off, Mazeaud.'

Sadly, the most idealistic climbing expedition ever to attempt Everest was degenerating into an ugly farce. For Dyhrenfurth, the tensions of the past weeks finally took their toll, and when he came down to Base Camp the following day, he was in an appalling state. Dr Steele diagnosed glandular fever and recommended that he be helicoptered off the mountain, but Dyhrenfurth would suffer one final humiliation shortly before his departure. As she spotted him coming towards her, Yvette Vaucher shouted 'Voici le salaud!' ('Here's the bastard!') and started pelting him with snowballs.

While all this was happening, I was having increasing problems with frostbite; fingers and toes were turning black, and I was starting to lose all feeling in my feet. Dr Steele warned me that these were the early stages of gangrene, and I should stay at Base Camp, but when Bill Kurban and Ian Stuart were ready to return to Advanced Base, I was determined to go with them.

Over the next ten days, more and more climbers were coming off the mountain, exhausted and dispirited, but our team held together. John Cleare had recovered sufficiently from pneumonia to be able to re-join us a few days later and, before long, there were more of us working on the film team than active climbers.

It was becoming clear that when people are pushed to the limits by oxygen starvation, sleeplessness and extreme cold, state of mind becomes increasingly important. As long as you believe that all this suffering has a purpose and is taking you closer and closer to an achievable goal, you are in a very different position from those who have lost all faith in a positive outcome, and by that time, we knew we had a powerful story in our grasp.

Despite all the setbacks, Whillans and Haston battled on up the Face, with only two other climbers to support them, Uemura and Ito. For days at a time, the four of them had nothing to eat, and the force of the wind was making the cold unbearable.

On 17 May they established Camp 6, just 2,000 feet (610m) below the summit. It was the highest point anyone had reached on the Face, but before they could make further progress, they had to deal with a sheer band of rock.

In Whillans's own words: 'We only had two people down below, supplying us with oxygen, which is very heavy, and rope which isn't light. It suddenly came into my head you're not going to do it. You're not going to come to any harm either. Too crafty for that!'

As much as I respected Whillans and Haston for their courage and determination, I felt that the real heroes of this expedition were the two Japanese climbers, Uemura and Ito. They had never pushed their own agendas or taken part in the angry debates during the storm, and this wasn't simply due to their poor grasp of

English. They had made it clear, by their actions rather than words, that they were there to serve the best interests of the expedition, and for three weeks they gave their unstinting support to Whillans and Haston.

Sadly, this wasn't enough, and on 20 May 1971, equipment was packed, tents were folded and the greatest, most glamorous, most idealistic climbing expedition ever to attempt Everest retreated down the Western Cwm.

My diary is a blank for the next few weeks, and I cannot recall how we all made it back to Kathmandu, but I do have vivid memories of leaving Base Camp alone and continuing, on and on, until I caught sight of the first patch of living green. I was so excited that I started running faster and faster, exulting in all the senses that were being restored: the sound of running water and bird song; the scent of wildflowers; the feel of soft breeze against my face. As the blood started to flow through hands and feet, numbed by frostbite, the pain was excruciating, but it didn't matter. I was in a state of ecstasy. I was back in the living world.

****

When *Surrender to Everest* was broadcast in October 1971, it was described as 'a masterpiece made of failure'. It was also the first of my documentaries to be nominated for a BAFTA award.

But what mattered most is that we had made a film that paid tribute to outstanding climbers like Whillans, Haston, Uemura and Ito and – most important of all – a film that honoured the memory of Harsh Bahuguna.

Chapter Ten

THE ABBOT OF HOKE KYO

Mrs Ishizaka was in her late sixties, gentle, soft-spoken and clad in a purple *kimono*, wrapped tightly round her slender body with a scarlet *obi*. As is the custom in Japan, we were both sitting on the floor of her tiny apartment in Hiroshima when she described what happened on 6 August 1945.

At 8.15 in the morning, she was already at work on her sewing machine in a clothes factory, two miles from the centre of the city, when 'Boom!', the sky suddenly brightened 'as though the sun was on fire'. The force of the blast threw her onto the factory floor. Too frightened to move, she stayed in the same position with her head in her hands for over an hour until rescuers finally dragged her free. Minutes later, the whole building collapsed and caught fire.

As Mrs Ishizaka relived those terrible moments, her gestures and every sound she made were so expressive that there was scarcely a need for an interpreter.

Once rescued, she ran home, passing the bodies of men, women and children 'with their faces already burnt to ash'. Unheeding, she rushed on, the only thing on her mind the fate of her mother and daughter.

'As soon as I reached our home I cried out to Mother, asking how she had been injured. She showed me her arms and chest, horribly burnt. Two days later, my mother died.' Mrs Ishizaka's daughter took four weeks to die of radiation sickness but continued working until the last day of her life.

We asked Mrs Ishizaka if she had any special mementoes of her daughter. From the family shrine, she pulled out a piece of paper, brittle through folding and unfolding. It was a testimonial from the Hiroshima telephone company, commending her daughter for three years' continual service without a day's loss through sickness or vacation.

That letter seemed to mean more to Mrs Ishizaka than any photograph or personal message from her daughter might have done, and at that moment, I began to understand how a nation devastated by war was able to rise from the ashes of defeat to become one of the world's leading industrial powers in less than three decades.

It was 1973, and Japan was now second only to the United Sates in the GDP ratings, with an economy twice the size of Britain's and well ahead of Germany's.

The great Japanese corporations – Toyota, Sony and Panasonic – had become major forces in the world's car and electronic markets, and half the world's ships were being built in Japanese shipyards. China at that time was still suffering the disastrous consequences of Mao's 'cultural revolution', and barely figured in the ratings.

Clearly, there was an important story to be told about Japan's dramatic recovery and the forces that were driving it, but there was something else that needed to be understood: the anger and violence that had erupted at critical moments throughout the post-war period.

Who could forget those newsreel images of hordes of young Japanese students bashing police shields with long poles and hurling firebombs at bulldozers during protests against the eviction of hundreds of peasant families to make way for the construction of a new international airport at Narita?

Even more disturbing were the scenes captured in Noriaki Tsuchimoto's stunning documentary *Minamata*, which told the story of a city where thousands had been poisoned by mercury-rich waste discharged into the sea by the Chisso Chemical Company.

The first signs of this tragedy had occurred as far back as 1953. Birds dropped from the sky. Fish rose out of the sea, flapping helplessly, and on the land, cats went mad, spitting and frothing among the garbage cans. Then the families of the fishermen were affected: children were born deformed and demented. Yet, for fifteen years the company had refused to accept responsibility, and only relented when the people of Minamata took to the streets and spread their message throughout Japan.

Scenes like these raised many questions. Yes, this was a country with the fastest growing economy in the world, but at what price?

****

My fascination with Japan really began on the Everest climb. The selflessness and dedication of the two Japanese climbers, Uemura and Ito, seemed to set them apart from the rest of the team, and although I could barely communicate with either of them, there was someone else on the climb who stirred my interest in their country: Murray Sayle, who was covering the expedition for the *Sunday Times*.

Murray had an outstanding record as a foreign correspondent, reporting on wars in Vietnam, Pakistan and the Middle East. He had also worked in Japan and was so drawn to that country that he would eventually settle there for the last thirty years of his life.

Murray was great company, and during those long mountain storms he would often invite me into his tent and share his experiences. Japan was a recurring topic, and I began to get a real sense of that country's values and the way society was structured. According to Murray, the qualities I so admired in Uemura and Ito were evident at every level. Work was an almost sacred duty, often overriding all other responsibilities, including duties to family.

During those periods of isolation and reflection on Everest, something else was also taking shape in my mind, which would eventually determine my whole approach to documentaries. The drama of high-altitude climbing in that magnificent setting was hugely important, but the most powerful moments were personal ones. The interviews with Vaucher, Eliassen and Whillans after they had failed to save Harsh had a power that I don't think we could have matched even if we had been able to film the actual rescue attempt.

Looking back at some of my earlier films, it was those personal moments that always seemed to stand out, whether it was our time with South Africa's black gold miners or the sight of young Antonio Mendes leaving his impoverished Portuguese village to fight other peasants in Africa.

Upon my return to England, I shared those thoughts with Tony Essex and suggested three films where we would try to tell the complex story of Japan through the personal experiences of people at every level of society, from the heads of giant corporations down to the poorest peasants and day labourers. I didn't want to hear from economists and political pundits. Viewers needed to experience the energy, dedication and hard work that was driving this nation forward, but at a very personal level. They also had to meet those who were violently opposed to the whole system and get a real sense of the source of their anger.

All those ambitions were wonderful in theory, but everything would depend on the willingness of ordinary Japanese to share their hopes and concerns with a complete stranger (and a Westerner at that), and to allow him to film them in their homes, at work, at play or in any situation that was relevant to their story.

Tony was prepared to give me five weeks for a thorough assessment, and if the signs were positive, I would be given the green light to film.

****

Before leaving for Japan, I engaged a freelance interpreter, recommended by NHK, the national broadcaster. Unfortunately, Murray Sayle was out of the country at the time, but he had put me in touch with Koji Nakamura, an outstanding journalist whom I had arranged to meet on arrival. Koji was intrigued by the approach I was hoping to take and had many suggestions, including a visit to a backstreet plastic surgery in one of the poorer parts of Tokyo, where he felt I would get a sense of the pressures at that level of society, and it was there that I spent my first day of research.

Most of those sitting in the waiting room were young women, working in bars and department stores, who had come here to raise their value in the market. For them, the challenge was to get as close as possible to the Japanese ideal of feminine beauty, which was (and probably still is) not far from the Western ideal.

The surgery was run like a factory production line. While Dr Morikawa was hollowing out cheeks and widening eyes, his two assistants were busy preparing the next patient on an adjacent operating table. As he switched back and forth, Morikawa chatted amiably and, at one point, boasted that many of his patients were able to double their earnings, thanks to his skills.

I had been given complete freedom to talk to the young women in the waiting room and was looking forward to hearing what they hoped to achieve by coming here. These were issues that had to be handled sensitively, but my interpreter behaved like a sergeant major, hurrying the women if they were slow to respond and ordering them to speak up when they sank into a whisper. After a couple of minutes, I told him to stop. We said our goodbyes and left.

Once outside, I tried to explain that interpreting was not just a matter of words. It was also about tone. Everything I intended to do in Japan depended on gaining the trust of ordinary people, and that meant treating them with respect. From now on, he would take the lead from me; no prompting, no interruptions or contradictions unless I had challenged something that had been said.

But nothing changed, and after two more dreadful days, I let him go. Sadly, his successor was no better, but where in this country would I find an interpreter, capable of the necessary warmth and empathy?

I discussed this with a good friend, Michael Jehu, who was Reuters' correspondent in Japan at the time, and he had a suggestion. Why not avoid the professionals altogether? He was very friendly with the Shamamuras, an 'aristocratic' family whose eldest daughter, Yukiko, had just graduated from university with a first-class degree, but had yet to decide on her future. She had travelled extensively with her parents, was very open-minded, and spoke excellent English.

We met the following day. Yukiko had all the warmth and openness that her predecessors lacked. When I told her that I wanted to reach people at every level in this society, she warned me that she had never set foot in a slum or any of the remote rural areas on my list, but if I felt I could trust her she would love to work on the project. It was high time, she said, that someone like her, who had been brought up in such a privileged environment, should come to know her own country.

Once Yukiko was on board, doors began to open, and I can honestly say that I haven't worked in many places where people were as frank and approachable as they were during those five weeks of research in Japan.

Yukiko and I started at the very top, meeting Akio Morita and Konosuke Matsushita, the founders of Sony and Panasonic, respectively. From there, we worked our way down through all the different social levels, from the small, family-owned workshops to rural communities and the slums of Tokyo and Osaka. We visited schools and universities and also met the parents of children who had been born with serious deformities as a result of industrial pollution. We even returned to Dr Morikawa's surgery, where the young women were happy to share their feelings with Yukiko.

It soon became clear that there was one group of people, active at all levels of this society, who were unlikely to be as approachable as everyone else. These were the *yakuza*, Japan's notorious gangster brotherhoods. In the very first week, I asked Koji to do everything possible to arrange a meeting with one of the leaders. He was not optimistic but promised to do his best.

The rival brotherhoods thrived on gambling, prostitution and protection as well as legitimate business. Some of them guarded government ministers and the heads of the great corporations. They even helped the police at times of civil disturbance. Paradoxically, they were also the most effective voice raised on behalf of the people of the slums.

As Police Superintendent Tadashi Watanabe of Tokyo's gangster squad explained to us, the *yakuza* saw themselves as descendants of the landless samurai who roamed medieval Japan, protecting peasants from rapacious feudal landlords and their enforcers. Kurosawa's Seven Samurai were *yakuza*.

I was completely frank about our intentions. We needed to meet them ourselves, hear their views and personal stories and eventually film their activities and ceremonies. Watanabe shook his head in disbelief. 'The *yakuza* never, never talk to outsiders and certainly not with cameras present.'

But he was proved wrong. During the third week of research, Koji Nakamura called me with news that Keizo Takei, one of the most prominent *yakuza* leaders had agreed to meet us in the Buddhist Temple of Hoke Kyo where – and this was hard to believe – he was the resident abbot. The temple was some thirty miles north of Tokyo, and Koji would be happy to drive us there.

During the journey, we were given a full briefing. Takei was not only a Buddhist abbot, he was also president of Zen-ai Kaigi, a federation of 500 right-wing organisations. Besides enjoying the unquestioning loyalty of his *yakuza* followers, Takei had powerful friends in high places. He had provided bodyguards for Eisaku Sato, Japan's previous premier, and shown his power and strength in a very public way during Eisenhower's state visit in 1960.

The American president had come in person to ratify the security treaty between Japan and the United States, but word soon spread that left-wing factions were planning massive demonstrations. The police realised that they lacked the manpower to guard the route Eisenhower would be taking from the airport to the Imperial Palace for the ceremonial signing and appealed to Keizo Takei for help. In response, he provided 47,000 of his followers, including 18,000 *yakuza*, who were ready to stand shoulder to shoulder with the police along the entire route. Thanks to Takei's contribution, the visit passed without any serious incidents.

We were well outside city limits when Koji pulled into a parking lot filled to capacity with upmarket American limousines. Men in suits, whom we assumed to be chauffeurs, were either sitting inside the vehicles with doors open or chatting together in groups. All heads turned towards us as we stepped out of Koji's humble Toyota and made our way towards the wooden archway that led to the temple grounds.

After Koji's briefing, Yukiko and I were certainly apprehensive as we walked with him in silence past shrines and a large statue of the Buddha to the sounds of distant bells, drumming and chanting.

As we followed the winding path, the Temple of Hoke Kyo gradually came into view. It was a magnificent structure built on five different levels, each topped with a tiled roof that swept down in a perfect curve.

We had barely taken this in when a young man in military uniform appeared out of nowhere. After exchanging a few words with Koji, he guided us to a building at the side of the temple. We left our shoes at the door before climbing the stairs to a large hall at the upper level, where some thirty men in suits were sitting on mats, arranged in two lines along opposite walls.

The abbot was seated on a raised dais at the far end, and as soon as we entered he beckoned us to come forward. Takei was in his late sixties, shaven-headed, massively well built, and dressed in a simple white kimono. Behind him, the flag of Japan – a crimson-red disc on a white background – hung from floor to ceiling.

After the traditional Buddhist greetings, we were beckoned to sit on either side of him, and as soon as we had settled he launched into a speech, which Yukiko translated in breathless whispers.

'We welcome any attempt to report our position seriously but have come to learn that the press and television are controlled by the

The Abbot of Hoke Kyo.

left, and for that reason we have no wish to cooperate with them, but we hope, Mr Thomas, that you will have the integrity to report truthfully on everything you see.'

Takei went on to admit that he had killed many times for 'the sake of my country'. He also boasted that he had 'the men and the money to organise a coup d'état tomorrow'. Any idea that there might be a contradiction between his dual roles as Buddhist abbot and *yakuza* leader was dismissed with a final, ringing self-endorsement. 'What would a monk be if he did not love his country?'

The men in suits applauded. Now it was my turn.

I repeated the assurances we had asked Koji to pass on – objectivity and no prejudgement, but this was not enough. Takei and the men in suits wanted to know where I stood.

It had always been a firm principle never to misrepresent my own position. When dealing with people with vastly different values from your own, you can be as quiet and tactful as you like, but you must also raise your concerns. The one thing you should never do is pretend that you share their values, and this applies to powerful figures like Keizo Takei as well as ordinary people who have entrusted you with their personal stories. But when Takei stared into my face for an answer, I had a sudden flash of memory and crossed a line I had never crossed before.

It was a story that Elsa, my grandmother, had told me about her brother, Nathan, one of the many psychological casualties of the First World War. On his return from the front, he had drifted aimlessly from job to job until Oswald Moseley's British Union of Fascists appeared on the scene. Nathan suddenly had a cause. He joined the movement and steadily rose in the ranks.

When senior members of the party were interned at the end of the phoney war, Nathan managed to evade capture and make contact with Berlin. He was issued with false identity papers and told to apply for the job of doorman at the United Services Club in London. His controllers wanted the names of all senior officers who were in the country. Apparently, this information would be helpful in working out troop movements.

Nathan continued at his post until late 1944, when he was struck on the head by a chunk of masonry during a V2 raid and suffered serious injury. He now faced two bleak alternatives. If he went to a hospital, he was sure that his identity would be revealed, but without medical help he would remain in a serious condition. To resolve his dilemma, he walked into the Serpentine and quietly drowned.

This, I have to stress, was Elsa's version. I had never researched this story or checked the facts, but in the presence of Takei and his associates, I decided to adapt it to suit present circumstances.

In the revised version, I had a great-uncle who had fought bravely for the country he loved during the First World War (when Japan was not on the opposing side!), but, as the Second World War approached, he felt passionately that his government was taking the wrong direction in opposing Germany and Japan. He spent four dangerous years serving the cause he believed in, but when the tide finally turned against the Axis powers, he took his own life rather than having to face a future in a society where, he felt, all principles had been compromised.

The story had an immediate effect on Takei and his henchmen, and, when a group of monks moved in to rearrange the room for supper, Koji, Yukiko and I were invited to stay.

Over the meal, Takei promised an interview and any help we might need during the making of the film, but he also issued a solemn warning, just as we were leaving: 'If I ever thought you were dishonourable, you wouldn't walk out of this temple alive.'

In truth, I had been dishonourable. I had won Takei's trust and friendship by misrepresenting my own position. Although I hadn't claimed to be a neo-Nazi myself, I had introduced Takei and his associates to a member of my family who was a Nazi spy and told his story with sympathy and respect.

****

Five weeks after the start of research, I returned to England and presented a written proposal to Tony Essex. A month later I was back in Japan with Peter Jackson, who had worked with me since I first started with Yorkshire Television, and Michael Donnelly, our sound recordist on the Portuguese films. There was now a third member of the team, John Willis, who had come on board as associate producer and would make an important contribution to the series. Two years later, he directed his own documentary, *Johnny Go Home*, which won the British Academy Award for best factual programme, and from that point, John rose to be Director of Programmes at Channel 4, Controller of Factual and Learning Programmes at the BBC and Chairman of BAFTA. The list goes on and on.

We started our filming in Japan with a rather different success story. Konosuke Matsushita, chairman and founder of Panasonic, had agreed to receive us in his palatial home. He was seventy-eight years old at the time and had only just retired from active management of the company.

During the war, Matsushita had been president of the *zaibatsu*, the business conglomerates of Japan. As we strolled with him through his magnificent garden, he told us that he had been indicted during the American occupation but had used that time of enforced retirement to formulate a philosophy that would give Japan a new spiritual direction. Now growth and production would replace militarism and territorial aggression.

Everything he had written down during his 'intense period of meditation' was finally consolidated in his bestselling book, *Thoughts on Man*.

For those left demoralised and directionless by defeat, Matsushita's message had the appeal and certainty that others find in the *Bible* or the 'Little Red Book', and it was no surprise that 15,000 of his former employees rallied round him and signed a petition demanding that the American occupiers reinstate him. By 1947 Matsushita was back in business.

Konosuke Matsushita has been called 'the deity of Japanese management', a claim that does not seem far-fetched. At the start of every working day, the company's employees lined up in ranks on a large parade ground in front of the factory to perform a ceremony that had the feel of a religious service. A senior executive mounted a platform and recited verses from the thoughts of Matsushita, which the congregation repeated after him, as if to draw strength from 'the Prophet's' message before the rigours of the day.

The ceremony ended with the company 'hymn'.

Like the American evangelical churches, with their special ministries for alcoholics, drug addicts, the elderly and the unmarried, Panasonic was genuinely concerned for the welfare of all its members. Employees received regular health checks and free medical treatment.

The company was also aware of the tensions that could build up on the production line, and provided special 'release rooms', where workers could laugh at themselves in distorted mirrors, bash out their frustrations on punch balls or batter a well-padded mannequin with one of the clubs provided.

In return for all this care and support, the company had high expectations. At the time we were filming, cohorts of businesspeople were coming from all over the world to study the company's methods. The speed of the production line was of particular interest, and I well remember one of the visitors standing over a young woman on the radio assembly line and shaking his head in disbelief as he timed her performance on a stopwatch.

These pressures did not ease at the higher levels. While filming at Panasonic, we made friends with the Esakas, a couple in their late thirties with a young son and daughter.

Mr Esaka was a rising star in the corporation. Office hours were from 8.00am to 6.00pm, but his responsibilities did not end there. Up to three evenings a week were spent in one of the plush nightspots in downtown Osaka, where Mr Esaka's duty was to build strong business relationships in this other world of space, luxury, soft lights and comfort. His clients on the night we were filming were two retailers, who soon softened up as the drink flowed and the scantily dressed hostesses hovered around them, smiling and flirting with exaggerated friendliness.

On these occasions, Mrs Esaka spent her evenings alone in her sitting room, knitting in front of the TV, while the children watched their favourite programmes on another set in their bedroom. Although the family home was in an upmarket suburb, there wasn't anywhere in the area where people could get together or a public space where the children could play.

****

It was becoming clear from our experiences that Japanese society was structured in a very different way from our own. There was little sense of class solidarity or even class difference. The most significant divide was between members of the 'company families' and 'outsiders'.

Those working for large corporations like Panasonic enjoyed job security and all kinds of benefits, including membership of company unions, headed by people on the company payroll.

Outside this protected zone, conditions were very different. Those employed in shops, restaurants and small family businesses seldom enjoyed the benefits the big companies could offer. It was the same story in the backstreet workshops, where the component parts of industrial products were being churned out on thousands of screaming lathes and ill-protected presses. Company unions felt no responsibility towards those working in these places, even though they were making a major contribution to company output.

There was only one way to be sure of getting on the right side of this divide – through education. Succeed in exams, and the way would be open to a top job in a prestigious corporation. Fail, and there was no knowing how far you might fall.

Every parent we interviewed recognised this, and the pressure on children was phenomenal. In one cram school where we filmed, they were preparing three-year-olds for entry to prestige kindergartens.

For those who finally made it through to university, the pressures didn't ease. Now the focus was on top-level degrees, but there was one significant change. At this level, all the resentments that must have built up over years of intensive schooling seemed to explode.

At one elite university we visited, students spoke about the injustices in their society and their opposition to the whole system, and for the first time we had a sense of the fury that had erupted in violent protests at Narita and Minamata, but the professor we interviewed brushed all this aside.

'Just a phase', he assured us. 'Part of the process of growing up.' He was confident that every student we interviewed would morph into a loyal and obedient member of a corporate family once their job was secured.

It was a broad generalisation, but not far from the truth.

There was one unforgettable experience during our time in schools and universities. We were filming in a large provincial cram school when one of the teachers took us aside and shared a harrowing story.

The previous evening, an eighteen-year-old student had thrown herself off the roof of the building. Before jumping, she had emptied her pockets and cut the name tabs off her clothes. Apparently, this institution was so overstretched and so impersonal that nobody had yet managed to identify her. The only personal item was an unsigned note she had pinned to her blouse. It read: 'I have passed the examination to heaven.'

As we would learn later, the Japanese have a special word for 'death by overwork'. They call it *karoshi*.

****

We left the cities, and ventured deep into the Japanese countryside, hoping to find tranquillity and a real sense of community. Our first destination was Iwate Prefecture on the northeastern tip of Honshu. People call this the Tibet of Japan. It is an area of outstanding natural beauty – mountains and forests, tinged with the colours of early autumn; streams of crystal-clear water cascading down to the plains below.

We spent our first evening with a peasant couple in their fifties. There was no proper road to their home, no telephone connection and no pipes to bring in water or take out waste; but somebody had installed a powerline. As the kettle boiled and charcoal smoke mixed with the smell of damp soil, a colour television brought in the world of the city and a desire for goods and fashions unheard of here a generation ago.

This was once a family home, which the couple had shared with their two daughters, their son and his wife's younger brother. Now all four of them had left the family home for good and joined the millions who had migrated from the countryside to the cities.

The effects of this mass exodus could be seen everywhere. Houses, and in some cases whole villages, had been abandoned and fields left untended. In the small country towns, stores had been closed and some schools had shut down. Those left behind were predominantly the elderly and the very young.

Although rural migrants could not compete with their urban cousins for top positions in prestige corporations, there were many opportunities in workshops, bars, restaurants, shops, department stores and domestic service, but that was not the full story, as we learnt from Keizo Takei, the Buddhist abbot.

During our first supper together, he told us about the huge numbers of rural migrants, who were coming to the cities without their families in search of casual day labour. According to him, the *yakuza* were their sole protectors, handling all negotiations with employers on their behalf.

During our research, Yukiko and I decided to test this ourselves, and took the 300-mile journey to Osaka, Japan's second city. Our plan was to visit Kamagasaki (today's Airin-chiku) which, at the time, was one of the country's largest and most notorious slums.

We had been advised to get there at 5.00am when the place would be at its busiest. By that time, groups of workers were already crowding around trucks, coaches and vans, with numbers scrawled on the windscreens – not the price of the vehicle, but the rate of pay for the day, as agreed between employers and senior *yakuza*.

While the workers waited, junior members of the brotherhood (the *kobun*) cross-questioned the drivers about working hours and conditions. Once satisfied, they gave the all-clear and the workers boarded. By 6.00am, the loaded vans and coaches had departed for the docks and construction sites, and for the next few hours, Kamagasaki was quiet and empty.

Yukiko and I walked down the narrow streets until we reached a half-acre slab of broken concrete, which locals called 'the park'. Here, the morning's rejects, the sick and the idle were hunkering down for the day. Some were stretched out on old mattresses which they had dragged with them into the park.

All around us were rooming houses. Some were substantial three- or four-storey buildings; others, just corrugated-iron sheds. At this time of day they were empty, but when she saw a front door ajar, Yukiko called out into the dark interior. Moments later, an elderly lady shuffled towards us, but stopped in her tracks as soon as she saw me. Yukiko was able to reassure her, and we were given permission to enter.

Inside the shed were two lines of windowless plywood cells, separated by a narrow passage. Each cell measured six feet by four, and was just short of four feet high, leaving enough space between the floor and ceiling to stack two rows of cells, on either side of a central passageway. There were detachable ladders for access to the upper level and, at the back of the shed, a crude shower and lavatory. Only in Africa had I seen conditions like this, and I couldn't help asking 'how the hell' people could be expected to dress and undress in these tiny cubicles. The old lady looked at me blankly. 'They use the passageway or the street outside.'

Yukiko quickly defused the tension and asked if we could return in the evening to talk to the workers, but the old lady had a better suggestion. She gave us the name of a bar, just down the street. It was closed now but would be packed with workers by the end of the day.

The evening we spent there was unforgettable. For the very first time in Japan, I felt a real sense of community. The workers who had gathered here were gentle people; they could afford to be. They were out of the competitive rat-race and there was nowhere else they could fall. When nights are spent in a ply-board cell and the working day begins with a quick haggle at the kerb, people begin to understand the value of the moment; how to spread a single drink over an evening, and to postpone the inevitable isolation that closes in at the end of every day.

We talked to those workers for hours, gaining many insights into life at this level of Japanese society and the many different paths that could finally lead someone to a place like Kamagasaki.

****

Seven weeks later, we returned to Kamagasaki with the full team, but had only been filming for a matter of minutes when the police ordered us to pack our equipment and accompany them to the local station. With great courtesy, the senior officer explained that filming in this area was likely to provoke a riot. We were released under strict orders not to return.

At that point, it struck me that there was one person who might have powers over the police and the local authorities, and I bitterly regretted my failure to contact him before we started filming.

As soon as he received my call, the Abbot of Hoke Kyo honoured his promise to give me any help I might need while making the film. He cancelled a planned trip to Taiwan and took the bullet train from Tokyo to Osaka so that he could deal with everything on a personal level.

We had booked a suite for him at our hotel, where he joined us in the early evening. When I asked if he wanted to know why it was so important for us to film in Kamagasaki, all he said was: 'Friends don't ask questions.'

At that point, he picked up the phone and called Mr Yamada, Osaka's *yakuza* boss, who was already standing by. Minutes later, we went downstairs to meet him.

A white Lincoln Continental pulled up in front of the hotel. The chauffeur rushed round to the passenger side and out stepped Mr Yamada, President of the Osaka Tile Company, President of the Osaka Entertainment Company, President of the Osaka Office Equipment Company and President of the Osaka Street Cleaning and Garbage Equipment Company.

He was a man who had sprung out of a slum to control a city.

Yamada was everybody's idea of a gangster. He was almost square, approximately 5' 4" high, with broad shoulders and a barrel of a torso. Dressed in the double-breasted suit of a senior *yakuza*, he also sported a diamond ring and a generous row of gold teeth.

We returned to Takei's suite, where Mr Yamada gave us full authority to film in Kamagasaki. His lieutenant, Mr Fuji, the local *yakuza* boss, would handle all our requirements.

His mission accomplished, Keizo Takei returned to Tokyo the following morning, while Mr Yamada, Mr Fuji, Yukiko and I met for lunch. The Kamagasaki boss was in his early forties and, before long, had edged his senior out of the conversation and taken charge of the meeting.

Fuji was impressive. Like many *yakuza*, he had been born into a peasant family. When he was just fourteen years old he joined the migration to the cities, only to be thrown against one of the harshest economic systems in the developed world. Eventually, he found sanctuary within the tribe.

There is nowhere on today's political spectrum where one could place a man like Fuji. As the Tokyo police superintendent had explained to us, the *yakuza* hark back to a pre-industrial age. In the contemporary context, everything they stand for is contradictory. They serve some of the most senior figures in the Japanese establishment, yet theirs is the only powerful voice raised on behalf of the people of the slums, threatening and bullying the casual employers for better pay and conditions. The *yakuza* were, and still are, both predators and prey.

Fuji was genuinely concerned for the people of Kamagasaki as he made clear in a passionate appeal to us to 'tell the world about Kamagasaki. Shame this government into action. My blood beats for my people. They have been neglected and cheated.'

With absolute frankness, I went through everything that Yukiko and I had experienced during research, from the conditions in the rooming houses to the early morning negotiations with the workers. Again, and again, Fuji nodded his approval, even adding some important suggestions of his own.

Before the meal was over, he had promised to be at our hotel at 4.00am the following day. He would arrive in a minivan with plenty of space for equipment and would also bring two of his own men to help us load and carry.

From my side, there was just one condition. As much I appreciated his help, I wanted him and his assistants to stand well away from us when we were filming. This was particularly important during interviews. I did not want anyone to feel coerced by their presence. Mr Fuji had to trust me to deliver what I had promised.

In response, Mr Fuji assured me that he would stand back, adding: 'But remember, no whitewashing, no exaggeration, and only if you stick to that will we keep you close to the heart of Kamagasaki.'

Mr Fuji kept to his side of the bargain. I hoped we honoured ours.

It was still dark when we set off for our first location – the rooming house – and had been there for only a few minutes when a police car drew up outside, but as soon as they spotted Mr Fuji, everything changed. From that point onwards we had no further problems.

For most of the time, Fuji left us in the care of his assistants, making occasional visits with his two small daughters. Sometimes he wore the full *yakuza* uniform – the dark pinstriped suit and polo neck – but when the weather was hot he walked the streets in his under shorts, exposing arms and torso, covered with the swirling patterns and colours of the famous *yakuza* tattoos. By stripping down like this, he felt he was making an important statement. Unlike the status-conscious middle-class suburbs, Kamagasaki was a place where men were judged by their character, not by their show of wealth.

We were able to film everything on my wish list and were even allowed to travel with a group of workers to a nineteen-storey building under construction in downtown Osaka, where we remained with them for the rest of their working day.

****

I don't believe many people, Japanese or foreign, have got as close to the *yakuza* as we did. In the process, we learnt a great deal about their protocols and the unwritten agreements between them and the police.

A gangster who killed a member of the public would be tried for murder, and the death penalty still applies in Japan today; but the sentence for killing a member of a rival brotherhood seldom exceeds two years, provided the killer gives himself up to the police immediately. This practice is known as 'paying service' and is a necessary step towards seniority within the brotherhoods. For his part, Mr Fuji had spent a total of eight years in prison after 'paying service' five times on Mr Yamada's behalf.

Another rule was that *yakuza* should never rob. They could extort protection money in the fashionable neighbourhoods, but not in the poorer areas. If owners refused to pay, violence against their property was permitted and no charges would be brought by the police, but physical violence against anyone other than a *yakuza* or a proven aggressor was forbidden; if that rule was broken, the police would take action.

There were also strict codes of conduct within the brotherhoods. Anyone who made a mistake that had negative consequences for other members had to perform an act of atonement in their presence. Usually, this meant cutting off the joint of a finger, beginning with the little finger of the left hand. Even Mr Fuji had lost two joints.

Just before we left Osaka, Mr Yamada invited us to film the *yakuza's* innermost ritual: a ceremony of initiation that would bring three young men into the brotherhood. As far as I know, this was a privilege that had never been granted to an outsider, and we regarded it as a real statement of trust.

The ceremony took place in an upstairs hall in central Osaka. Messrs Yamada and Fuji were sitting on one side of an altar with the three initiates facing them. Black-robed elders of the brotherhood lined the walls, which were draped with banners proclaiming the names and deeds of the great *yakuza* of history.

The ritual that followed was based on ancient Shinto marriage rites. A robed *kannushi* (priest) consecrated a bowl of sake, which was passed to Mr Yamada and then to the initiates. The ritual was repeated three times, followed by an exchange of vows. The contract of marriage between the initiates and the brotherhood was finally blessed by the *kannushi*.

It was already night when we eventually filed down the stairway and stepped back into the twentieth century. The elders waited on the pavement while chauffeurs collected their Lincolns and Thunderbirds from a nearby parking garage. As he said goodbye, a senior gangster pressed his card into my hand and asked for a special favour. When I returned to London, would I please send him a colour postcard of Queen Elizabeth?

****

Nearly fifty years have passed since we captured those moments in many different areas of Japanese life. Mrs Ishizaki, the lady from Hiroshima, Konosuke Matsushita, the founder of Panasonic, Keizo Takei, Mr Yamada and many others have long since passed away and a great deal has changed during the intervening years.

Japan's economy peaked in 1973. Since then, the country has experienced decades of near stagnation and China has taken its place as the world's second economic power. Much else, I am sure, has also changed since we made that series, but in every nation there are attitudes and beliefs that are deep-rooted and do not shift rapidly over time. I was reminded of this when I read a recent report on the numbers of deaths in the country through overwork – *karoshi*, as it is known in Japan. The most common medical causes are heart attacks and strokes, but the mental stress at workplaces drives some to take their own lives.

In 2020, 1918 people in Japan committed suicide due to work-related problems.

Chapter Eleven

THE ARAB EXPERIENCE

Out of the Ashes of Victory

The young military officer was holding a snake in a tight grip, just below its head. With a single swipe of his knife he decapitated the creature, letting the head fall to the ground. The writhing remains were still firmly in his grasp when he started to peel away the skin, exposing a few inches of raw flesh, which he sliced off and handed to me on the point of his knife. 'Eat it. Will do you good!'

The commandoes who had gathered around were thoroughly enjoying this performance, and now all eyes were on me, but I passed the machismo test. There was no other option.

It was January 1975, and we were filming in a military camp some thirty miles from Cairo. For the rest of that day, we would be treated to a fantastic show of military prowess: commandoes, laden with heavy backpacks, scaling vertical walls or crawling under barbed wire as machine guns fired above their heads; others abseiling at breakneck speed from a high concrete tower before dropping into a tank of water at ground level.

It was hard to believe that this was the same army that had suffered decades of humiliation and disaster. During the Second World War, Egypt's soldiers had stood impotently on the sidelines as their country became a European battleground. Betrayed by Farouk and his high command in 1948, they proved hopelessly inadequate in the first war against Israel, and in 1956 the boots they abandoned in the desert in the face of the advancing Israeli army became a source of derision for their foes. The next blow was the loss of Sinai – 23,000 square miles of Egyptian territory – after Israel's stunning victories in the Six-Day War of 1967. The sudden death of fifty-two-year-old President Nasser three years later added to the sense of national despair.

But just over a year before our filming, there was a dramatic change. On 6 October 1973, Egyptian forces broke through the Israeli front line along the east bank of the Suez Canal and penetrated deep into Sinai, while their Syrian allies launched simultaneous attacks on the Golan Heights. It was the Yom Kippur, the holiest day in the Jewish calendar, and the Israeli army had been taken by surprise on both fronts.

The United States immediately airlifted arms on a massive scale, and within days the Israeli army had regrouped and was counterattacking on both fronts. By the end of the first week their soldiers were within shelling distance of Damascus, and although progress was slower on the Egyptian front, by 25 October they had regained most of the territory lost in Sinai and crossed the Suez Canal into Egypt.

The consequences would have been disastrous for Egypt had it not been for the intervention of King Faisal of Saudi Arabia. In response to the American arms shipments, he persuaded the other OPEC leaders to join him in suspending all oil exports to the United States and its allies. It was the defining moment in Faisal's reign, gaining him lasting prestige amongst Arabs and Muslims across the world. It also put tremendous pressure on the United States to broker a whole series of withdrawal agreements between Egypt and Israel, culminating in the Camp David Accords, which eventually restored Egyptian sovereignty over the whole of Sinai.

And there were other consequences further afield. When the oil embargo was finally lifted in March 1974, it led to a fourfold increase in the price of crude, which had a profound effect on global politics and the global economy.

I had followed all these events closely and was fascinated by the changing dynamics in the Middle East and the effects they were having on all our lives. At that time, I hadn't visited a single Arab country, but based on everything I had read, felt we should concentrate on just three countries: Egypt, Lebanon and Saudi Arabia.

Colleagues who had worked in the Middle East were not encouraging. For them, the idea of telling personal stories at all levels of these societies was pure fantasy. I would be relatively free to operate in Lebanon, but Egypt was bureaucratic and restrictive, and if I was ever granted permission to film in Saudi Arabia, it would be under the strictest control. Nobody in that country would feel free to speak openly.

It was a daunting prospect, but I persevered until Tony Essex finally gave me the green light, and in December 1974 I landed in Cairo to begin research.

****

By that time, Israeli forces had withdrawn to a new front line eighteen miles inside Sinai. The Suez Canal could now be cleared and reopened, and for the first time in nearly seven years people were returning to rebuild the devastated canal cities, which were no longer within point-blank range of Israeli guns. A long chapter of humiliation was over, and Egypt seemed free to breathe.

It was a time of tremendous hope and optimism, and I soon learnt that everything I had been told about the restrictions in this country was seriously out-of-date. Censorship had eased, and the old enemies of the Nasser revolution had been released from prison or recalled from exile. Even tourists were coming back, and for the first time since Farouk was deposed in 1952, a Westerner like me was free to go virtually anywhere he wanted.

It was no surprise that the authorities were keen for us to film Egypt's elite commandoes, but that was a small part of the story I wanted to tell. My aim was to repeat everything I had done in Japan; but first I had to find an Egyptian Yukiko, someone with warmth and empathy who would gain people's trust.

I still find it extraordinary that the one person in Egypt most qualified to perform that role would step into my life, unannounced, on my second day of research.

I was trying to explain my vision of the film to Mohammed Heikal, editor of *Al Ahram*, the country's leading newspaper, when someone slipped quietly into his office through the open door behind me. I glanced round to see a rotund, bald little man who gestured me to continue before settling into a chair. For perhaps another five minutes, he listened intently to everything I was telling Heikal.

Then he stood up, eyes sparkling and a huge smile across his face. 'I like what you say. Let me show you Egypt.' He was Salah Jaheen, the country's most celebrated poet, lyricist, playwright and actor, who would soon become one of my closest friends.

Over the coming weeks, Salah took me to villages where the young had never seen a European, but they all seemed to know Salah, whose humanity, spontaneity and talent still inspire Egyptians today. Twenty-five years after his untimely death in 1986, Arab Spring protestors played and replayed his poems and lyrics on loudspeakers across Tahir Square.

Salah was unlike any celebrity I have ever met. He never spoke of his achievements or seemed conscious of his status. His usual attire – a black beret and a huge, crumpled jacket, straining at the buttons – was his way of saying that he was just an ordinary Egyptian. Of course, people recognised him and responded to him wherever he went, but it wasn't just his fame that drew them. It was his warmth and gentle sense of humour. Above all, Salah Jaheen was someone whom everybody trusted.

To my dear Antony in international year of Children. 1979
Salah Jaheen

Those days with Salah were unforgettable. We travelled the length and breadth of the country together, meeting scores of people – from the poorest peasants to former enemies of the Nasser revolution, who, in this relaxed post-war atmosphere, felt free to talk after decades under house arrest.

During all these travels, Salah never tried to steer me in a particular direction. He would listen carefully to my questions, and often take the discussion to a deeper level with his own thoughts and observations.

By the time the film team arrived, I really had met people at every level of this society, and once I had decided whom to include in the film, nobody declined. Although Salah could not be with us on all our filming days, he had found local interpreters who would stand in for him. What mattered most was that he had made all the original introductions.

We began filming in the Nile valley, where the long-suffering *fellaheen*, Egypt's peasant masses, dig, plough and hoe with tools that have hardly changed since the time of the pharaohs. The sliver of arable land they farm along the banks of the Nile covers an area only half the size of the Netherlands. Before the Nasser revolution most of this was owned by rich *pashas*, often of foreign extraction, but now the land belonged to the *fellaheen*. Yet, despite this massive redistribution there were, and still are, more landless peasants in Egypt than in the days of Farouk. However hard this country strains and whatever it achieves, progress is negated by the staggering rate of population growth – a gain of over a million people a year.

We sat with a group of landless *fellaheen* as they waited at dawn for the trucks to arrive with offers of work. 'Many things have changed', they told us. 'In the past, we were treated like slaves.' Their daily earnings had increased twelvefold since the revolution, to the equivalent of £6 in today's money. Now there were health clinics with a doctor and a dentist in nearly every village. People no longer feared disease, starvation and childbirth, but most of them had no illusions about their own futures or the futures of their children.

'We are peasants, my son and I,' one of them told us, 'and we will always be peasants.'

Yet, for others there was hope. In a crowded third-class railway carriage on its way to Cairo, we met (and later filmed) Hassan, son of illiterate parents, who was studying engineering. His friend Osman was a medical student whose father was a landless *fellah* while Gamal, a third-year student at Cairo University, was the son of a village water carrier.

With the revolution came free schooling for all children but, as with everything else, Egypt was, and still is, hamstrung by poverty and lack of resources. In the country school where we filmed, materials were in such short supply that children were sitting three to a desk, often sharing a single textbook. The lack of teachers and the over-crowded classrooms had forced the school to divide its seven hundred pupils into two shifts, with a daily changeover at noon.

As the headmaster told us, the village children were often pressured by their parents to leave school and help them work the land. To make matters worse, four teachers, out of his staff of twenty, had left in the past year to find better conditions and pay in Saudi Arabia and the Gulf.

For those who struggled through to university, conditions were equally hard. The Cairo lecture hall where we filmed was so crammed that students were standing in the aisles and perched on windowsills.

Yet, in spite of all the setbacks, there was real determination to succeed and improve during those heady months that followed the October War.

We filmed students who had volunteered to help rebuild the shattered canal city of Port Said and were shifting rocks and clearing debris with their bare hands. When I said to one of them that a single bulldozer could do the job that fifty of them had taken on, a young woman replied: 'What we have done, no bulldozer could do. We are rebuilding the spirit of Egypt'.

But the pressure on the Egyptian people was, and still is, overwhelming. At the time we were filming, the country had a population of 37 million. Today it is approaching 100 million, but the total area of arable land along the banks of the Nile remains the same.

The decades that followed have also been very difficult for the Egyptian people, who have increasingly turned to religion as their faith in political solutions has faded; but, with Salah's help, I believe we were able to capture that one brief moment of hope and convey what this meant to the Egyptian people.

The critics loved the film. Peter Jackson's 'strikingly beautiful' camerawork was commended in review after review, but there was one that was especially important to me: 'I have seen many documentaries telling me what it was like to be in Egypt, yet this was the first one to spell out both beautifully and brutally what it was like to be an Egyptian. Full marks.'

Thank you, Salah.

The Legacy of Faisal

Saudi Arabia was our next stop. In the decades to come, I would discover a great deal more about the way that country functions, but back in the 1970s I was only aware of the basic facts.

The discovery of the world's largest oil deposits in 1938 would eventually give immense wealth, power and influence to a largely illiterate tribal society that embraced an extreme form of puritanical Islam, known as Wahhabism. It was a creed that called for the imposition of strict Sharia law, relegated women to second-class status and regarded all Muslims who did not subscribe to its own brand of the faith as heretics.

From the start, I knew there was no hope of reaching people at every level of this society. Interviews with women were almost out of the question, and wherever we went, we would be accompanied by a government 'minder' who would have to approve every shot we took.

In spite of these severe limitations, I still felt there was an important, if very different film to be made about this country, one that would focus on a king, whose life story seemed to touch every issue that was important to understand about Saudi Arabia.

Faisal was born in 1906, the year his father, Abdul Aziz ibn Saud, a tribal leader, drove the Ottoman army out of territory he regarded as his own. Over the next three decades, Abdul Aziz conquered the Hashemite Kingdom of the Hijaz along the west coast of Arabia, taking control of the holy cities of Mecca and Medina. In 1932, the Kingdom of Saudi Arabia was finally established within its present borders, and just seven years later a massive oil field was discovered at Ghawar in eastern Arabia.

To a large extent, Faisal's father owed his military successes to the religious/political alliance his distant ancestor had formed with Muhammad Ibn Abd al-Wahhab, founder of the extreme form of Islam that has taken his name. Any Saudi king hoping to educate his people and modernise his country would have to tread very carefully in his dealings with a religious establishment that had helped to bring the House of Saud to power.

It was a challenge that required infinite cunning and patience, qualities Faisal had in abundance. As Crown Prince and de facto head of state, he had abolished slavery in 1962. Two years later, he was crowned King and immediately began to create Western-style bureaucracies and a welfare system.

In a move that would eventually cost him his life, he also introduced Saudi television, which was regarded by religious conservatives as a satanic innovation, violating Wahhabi prohibitions of any form of pictorial representation. The first TV broadcast in 1965 sparked riots in Riyadh, the capital, and when protestors tried to storm the television building, the police opened fire. Amongst those who died in the shootout was Prince Khalid bin Musaid, one of the King's nephews.

Even more controversial was Faisal's decision to introduce female education, an innovation which the Wahhabi establishment strongly opposed on the grounds that it would encourage women to neglect their family duties in pursuit of a career. Some on the extreme wing believed that female education was contrary to God's command.

To ease the passage of his controversial reforms, Faisal had adopted two important strategies. First, he did his utmost to prevent the appointment of known extremists to the country's top religious posts. But it was his second strategy that would have such far-reaching consequences.

As payback for the concessions he was being granted in his own country, Faisal was doing everything possible to spread the Wahhabi message worldwide. Billions of dollars were spent creating Wahhabi universities, political movements, madrassas (seminaries), mosques, and charities, as well as printing and distributing Wahhabi literature, including annotated versions of the *Qur'an*.

Faisal was, in fact, taking the dangerous fanaticism at the heart of Wahhabism and directing it outwards. It would take decades before the consequences would become horribly clear, but at the time we were filming, I had very little sense of this. All I knew was that Faisal was playing a slow and patient game to modernise his country. To tell that story properly, I needed access to him and would also have to find ways of revealing some of the challenges he faced.

After a long exchange of telexes and phone calls with the Ministry of Culture and Information in Riyadh, the Saudi capital, two of our requests were granted. We would be allowed to film the King at prayer in the Grand Mosque in Mecca and during his weekly *Majlis* (council) with senior religious advisors, but all my suggestions for scenes that would give us a sense of the challenges the King was facing were rejected. The list included a request to fly into the Empty Quarter to film the day-to-day life of a Bedouin tribe.

In the end, I decided to make do with what we had been offered in the hopes that we would find a way to complete the picture, and a date was agreed when we would set off for Saudi Arabia. Mustafa Hammuri, a Muslim cameraman, would film in Mecca, and Peter Jackson would work with me and the rest of the team.

****

The first few days of filming in Saudi Arabia were not easy. Erdem, our fixer/interpreter, was a bright young man of Turkish descent, who took his job seriously. He insisted that we concentrate our filming on everything that was flashy and modern in the country. This was, of course, an important part of the story we needed to tell. The fourfold increase in oil revenue had stimulated a massive boom in construction and consumer spending, and the stores in the country's two main cities, Riyadh and Jeddah, were overflowing with luxury products from oil-hungry nations.

But there were other realities that were just as striking. It was impossible to film on the streets without including shots of women, enveloped in their full-length black *niqabs* and, however discreet we were, Erdem was always concerned when any of them appeared in a shot. Once, when we were filming in a souk, the *Mutawwa'in* (Morality Police) appeared in their ankle-length white robes, brandishing canes. As always, they were on the lookout for breaches of Wahhabi codes of dress and behaviour. As soon as Peter turned the camera in their direction, Erdem insisted that we stop filming.

I tried to explain that any documentary about change and reform had to include scenes like these, but Erdem was not convinced. The only encouraging development in those first few days was confirmation that the authorities would honour their promise to allow us to film the King.

First on the list was the Thursday *Majlis* when Faisal conferred with his religious advisors in the royal palace in Riyadh. It was a scene that spoke volumes about the relationship between the King and the senior Wahhabi sheikhs.

As these elderly clerics entered the royal chamber, the King rose to receive them. After kissing his hand (and in several cases, his nose), they settled into heavy armchairs, arranged in a semicircle with the King at the centre.

The *Majlis* dragged on for nearly two hours. At one point, an old, blind sheikh gave a tedious dissertation on the deeds of Saladin and the crimes of the Crusaders. None of this seemed to have the slightest contemporary relevance, but Faisal, who was looking exhausted by this time, made no attempt to cut him short. In present company, it seemed that the King's time and patience were infinite.

The authorities also agreed that Mustafa, our Muslim cameraman, could film the King at prayer in the Grand Mosque at Mecca and accompany him when he made the four circuits of the Kaaba in the early hours of the morning before the mosque was crowded with pilgrims.

Looking at this footage again, I am amazed to see how close to Faisal our two cameramen were allowed to operate, even when the King was at prayer. The dark pouches under his eyes, the extended beak of his nose and every line and wrinkle were sharp and clear. We were staring into the face of a man who had experienced centuries of change in a single lifetime and seemed at least a decade older than his sixty-eight years.

Another surprise was to see how heavily Faisal was guarded. I counted fifty-four armed soldiers accompanying him and his close associates as they circled the Kaaba. Another sequence we filmed showed Faisal travelling from Mecca to

Jeddah in a black Rolls-Royce with armed outriders in front and on either side of the car. An ambulance and five armoured jeeps brought up the rear.

Clearly, the authorities were conscious of the dangers their King faced, but this didn't stop them granting us access to his two most controversial initiatives – state television and female education. Perhaps they were confident that the finished film would never be seen on Saudi TV, and of course, in this pre-internet age, there was no danger that controversial snippets might go viral in the country. What mattered to the authorities was that viewers in the rest of the world (and the film was eventually seen in over forty countries) would appreciate the progress and changes that were taking place under Faisal.

There was very little of interest at the TV studios, where they were recording an hour-long sermon when we went there to film. All the technicians and present-ers were male, and none of them seemed to feel under any threat because of the work they were doing. The violent demonstrations of 1965 now seemed a distant memory.

The radio station was more interesting. Here, a young woman was reading the evening news. In the privacy of the studio, she was unveiled, self-confident and very professional. As we would learn from our next experience, women could take any job in Faisal's Saudi Arabia provided they were unseen.

It was late in our second week that we were finally given permission to film in a large girls' school in Jeddah. This was a real surprise and an absolute first. No camera crew had ever been given that kind of access.

I felt it was important that Erdem and I should have a preliminary meeting with the headmistress before we went in with the team. A time was agreed, but, as we drew near to the school, my first thought was that Erdem had the wrong address. All I could see from the car was a high, windowless wall with a huge garage door at one end and a smaller door at the other, but Erdem assured me we were in the right place. Apparently, female education was still such a sensitive issue that any outward signs of a fully functioning girls' school were considered provocative.

I followed Erdem through the smaller door into a reception room, where a young woman took our names before phoning the headmistress's office. Minutes later, Mme Cecile Halaby appeared. She was a calm and impressive lady in her late forties who had been educated in Egypt and was fluent in English and French, as well, of course, as her native Arabic. Behind these walls, her only concession to the Wahhabi dress code was a light headscarf.

Mme Halaby promised that we would be free to film wherever we wanted with the obvious exception of changing rooms and bathrooms. Apparently, the girls already knew that we were coming and had been told to carry on as normal when we were filming and never to look at the camera! I thanked her profusely and asked if we could return at the start of the next school day, and perhaps film the girls as they arrived. She agreed but warned me that this would be very different from anything I might have experienced in schools elsewhere.

On this she was absolutely right. There was no way that Saudi girls could be allowed to walk to school, even if they were fully veiled. Their presence on the streets in large numbers would be considered a provocation, drawing unnecessary attention to the school. If that were not serious enough, every one of them had to be accompanied by a male guardian. To circumvent all these restrictions, the school provided buses that collected the girls from their homes.

The following morning, we were ready and waiting when the first bus approached. The driver hooted, and the huge metal door swung open. Through the windows, we could see that all the girls were wearing black *niqabs* that only revealed their eyes.

We followed the bus into an empty garage, and as soon as it stopped, the metal door slammed shut behind it. This was the cue for the girls to disembark and make their way through an inner door leading directly into the school grounds.

The moment the girls crossed that frontier, there was an outburst of chatter and laughter. The all-enveloping *niqabs* were quickly cast aside, revealing school uniforms of white blouses and black slacks.

We had entered another world. The classrooms here were light and airy, and all the adults – from the teachers down to the cooks and cleaners – were women.

Filming in a school like this was an extraordinary experience. We had expected a degree of shyness and embarrassment when these girls were faced with five relatively young foreign males, but there were no signs of that. These girls felt they were in a place where they had a right to be themselves. In the classrooms, they were confident and self-assured, and on the playing fields, they really let go.

We were invited to film a volleyball match between the school's top teams. Within minutes, the whole place went wild, with the players hugging each other and whooping for joy whenever a point was scored, while their supporters on the sidelines screamed with delight. It was as though all their pent-up feelings had suddenly been released.

Girls like these were, of course, the privileged few. Not many parents in this country believed in female education, and in the ten years since this was introduced by Faisal, the total number attending girls' schools had risen to only a hundred and fifty thousand, just a fraction of the total female population, which was close to three and a half million at that time.

And there was another problem, which one of the teachers shared with us in a very frank conversation. It was always hard, she explained, for girls like these to find work that matched their hopes and expectations once they had left school. Even those who went on to graduate from university faced similar difficulties. Wahhabi conservatism ran far too deep to allow a woman to be placed in a responsible position, particularly one that might give her any kind of authority over men.

****

Although I tried hard to persuade the men at the Ministry to reconsider their ban on any filming of Bedouin tribes, they remained adamant. Clearly, nothing could be included in this film that might be considered 'backward' by a Western audience. My counter-argument – that a sequence like this would help to put the current reforms in an historical context – was rejected.

This left me with only one option. I had a good friend who worked as a senior military advisor in the United Arab Emirates. When it was clear that the Saudis would not budge, I telexed him several times, and his eventual response was positive. Not only would he arrange for a helicopter to take us into the desert: he would also provide an interpreter to travel with us.

From Riyadh we flew to Dubai and the next day crossed into the 'Empty Quarter', on the look-out for Bedouin encampments. It was late afternoon before we finally spotted a cluster of a tents and reed huts with herds of camel standing by.

As soon as we landed and the cloud of wind-blown sand had settled, a group of men came out of the encampment to meet us. Our interpreter did a wonderful job, and not only secured filming permission but also an invitation for all of us to stay overnight in the camp. We offloaded our gear and arranged for the helicopter to collect us twenty-four hours later.

Our hosts were Saudis, but I had no idea whether they had crossed the unmarked frontier between their country and the UAE, or whether we had entered Saudi territory. In this remote desert, national frontiers seemed as meaningless as they had been during the centuries that preceded Sykes–Picot, the 1916 agreement between Britain and France to 'carve up' the Middle East into separate nations.

In the evening, the head of the tribe invited us for dinner in his tent. It was a disconcerting experience. While he chatted amiably through the interpreter, his three wives flitted silently in and out in their black *niqabs* until the floor was laden with plates of rice, dates and a goat that had been skinned, cleaned and roasted, but left with its head intact. Throughout this process, hardly a word passed between the husband and his wives, just a few monosyllabic commands, and when their work was completed, the women slipped away silently into the night.

It was the cue for our host to stick a long, blackened thumbnail into the eye of the goat, extract it, and pass it to me. This was not another machismo test, but an act of courtesy. The eye of the goat is regarded as an exceptional delicacy in these parts, but it is not a culinary experience I would recommend.

Much to my surprise, our host agreed that we could film wherever we wanted on the following day, and at first light we joined him and the other men in the community for the first of five daily prayers. No woman takes part in these rituals. In a tribal society like this, they are responsible to the menfolk, whose responsibility is to God.

After the dawn prayer, we were allowed to film the host's three wives in a reed hut behind the main tent, where they lived their separate lives with their younger children. In our presence, the women were veiled, but I was able to engage with one of them, who explained that the boys would have the freedom of the camp as soon as they reached puberty, but the girls would remain with her in 'purdah' until husbands were chosen for them.

In moments like these, one began to understand how a religion could be reshaped by the tribal values of those living thousands of miles from the great centres of Muslim learning in Egypt and the Levant. Although our host was proud to show me his copy of the *Qur'an*, neither he, nor anyone else in that community, could read or write. If they had been literate, they might have discovered that there is not a single verse in the *Qur'an* suggesting that women should be shrouded in all-enveloping black. A broader reading of Islamic history might also have familiarised them with women, such the Prophet's wife, Khadija, who had played a crucial role in the early years of Islam.

****

After Dubai, our next port of call was Beirut, the Lebanese capital, but we had barely settled in when news reached us that Faisal had been assassinated by his nephew, Prince Faisal bin Musaid. According to the reports, the prince was avenging the death of his older brother, Khalid, who had been shot and killed by the police during the violent protests against Saudi Television a decade earlier.

The assassination had taken place during a *Majlis*, similar to the one we had filmed in the royal palace; on this occasion, Faisal was receiving a delegation of Kuwaitis who had come to pay their respects. As they entered the royal chamber, the young prince slipped in beside them, and when his turn came for the customary kiss on the monarch's nose, he pulled a pistol out of the folds of his robe and fired two shots: the first struck the King's chin, the second went through his ear.

Remarkably, the King was still alive when they rushed him to hospital, where the doctors tried heart massage and blood transfusion but were unable to save him. During his dying moments, it was said that Faisal told all those present that his assassin should not face execution, but his wishes were ignored.

When I heard the news, I was shaken. It was not only the manner of Faisal's death that upset me, but there was also an irrational feeling of complicity. We had shaped the whole film around Faisal, his reforms and the risks he was taking. It was almost as though we had an intuitive sense that we were preparing an obituary. All that was required now was to get back to London as quickly as possible and put every hour we could muster into a rapid edit.

On 2 April, 1975, eight days after the King's death, *The Legacy of Faisal* was broadcast in Britain.

The great irony is that Faisal's most enduring legacy hadn't registered with any of us when we chose the title of the film, but in the decades that followed, the billions of dollars he and his successors spent spreading the Wahhabi message worldwide would change the very nature of Islam and unleash waves of violent extremism across the world.

Osama bin Laden, Abu Musab al-Zarqawi and their followers were passionate Wahhabis, as was Bakr al-Baghdadi, the leader of ISIS, and Mohammed Omar, the founder of the Taliban. Fifteen of the nineteen terrorists responsible for the 9/11 outrage were Saudis.

In Search of an Identity

Immediately after the broadcast, I returned to Lebanon with the team. Once again, our timing was uncanny. It was soon clear to us that we were filming in that country at a time when a long chapter of stability and prosperity was drawing to an end. For nearly three decades, most of the business generated by oil wealth had been conducted here, and at one level, Beirut, the capital, looked and functioned like any prosperous Western city. Banks had their headquarters here. Telephones and telexes worked smoothly to London, New York, Zurich and Düsseldorf, and the city's docks were the main port of entry for cargoes destined for the countries of the Arab East.

Lebanon was also a playground for the rich of the Arab world. There were six ski resorts within an hour's drive of Beirut, and in the summer months Lebanon's milder climate, its luxury hotels with their swimming pools and haute cuisine were a great draw for those wishing to escape the extreme heat back at home. Beirut's bars and gambling casinos were also an attraction to visitors with a taste for pleasures forbidden in their own countries under Sharia law.

But we soon discovered another more traditional Arab city beneath the shining glass and glitter of Beirut, a place where the unemployed stood on street corners every morning in search of work and the souks in the back alleys sold second-hand clothing, offal and dried fish. This was the other face of Beirut, a city geared to the needs of people living on the edge of subsistence: Syrians, Iraqis, Palestinians and Lebanese from the hill regions and the countryside.

It is part of the Arab paradox that underpopulated nations loaded with surplus wealth border countries hamstrung by poverty. In Beirut, those contrasts were felt on adjacent streets.

In one respect, though, Lebanon was unique in the Arab world. 'Freedom of the press' and 'freedom of opinion and belief' were, and still are, enshrined in the country's constitution. Whether researching or filming, we were free to go wherever we chose, and the easy access we had to leading political and religious figures was unlike anything I had experienced elsewhere, including the UK.

The Lebanese constitution also guarantees 'freedom of belief and religious practice'. Unlike Saudi Arabia, with its single 'religion of state', Lebanon was a country where a wide spectrum of religious faiths and allegiances was protected by law and represented in government, but we had not been in the country for long before it became clear that these principles were under tremendous strain.

We had our first sense of this when we visited the Palestinian camps. Twelve of them were on the fringes of Beirut, functioning collectively as a single state with its own police force, militias, schools and hospitals.

There were 300,000 Palestinian refugees in Lebanon at the time, and the majority were still living in camps, but this was not the result of Lebanese indifference. They were there by choice, as we would discover when talking to young Palestinians working and studying in Beirut. Samir, a young undergraduate, spoke for many of them when she said, 'Living in this camp reminds me always that I am a Palestinian girl, and there is Palestine, and there are the cities of Palestine – Jerusalem, Haifa, Ramallah. Beirut is not my city. Beirut is a Lebanese person's city.'

Palestinians had fled to Lebanon in three distinct waves: in 1948, following the creation of the State of Israel; in 1967, after Israel's occupation of the West Bank; and, finally, in 1971. It was that third phase that would have such a profound effect on Lebanon. Most of the refugees were *fedayeen* (Palestinian commandoes) and their families, who had been expelled from Jordan after violent confrontations with King Hussein's army, and it was the *fedayeen* who were keenest to show us their military prowess.

We were invited to a secret location to watch Palestinian commandoes in training. The 'highlight' of the afternoon was a parade of 'young lions': boys between the ages of eight and ten dressed in military uniform and carrying machine guns. 'Our future!' one of the commandoes told us.

Two days later we drove to Bikfaya, a town in the very heart of the Christian stronghold of Mount Lebanon. We had come here to meet Pierre Gemayel, leader of the ultra-right Phalangist militia, who claimed to have 20,000 fighters under his command. It was Palm Sunday, and his men put on a convincing display in the hills above the town, leaping from jeeps, advancing up a steep hill with guns blazing, loading and firing mortars.

These men had no national enemies they were expecting to confront. As Gemayel explained to us, they were training to combat those who threatened the integrity of Lebanon. Clearly, he was referring to the Palestinians.

We left the Maronite Christians on Mount Lebanon and travelled south, passing the mountain strongholds of the Druze, the Orthodox Christians, the Sunni and Shi'a Muslims, and experiencing the different textures and cultures that create this complex Arab society.

****

On Sunday 13 April 1975, Pierre Gemayal's Phalangists opened fire on a bus packed with Palestinians. Twenty-seven passengers were killed; many more were injured. Apparently, it was an act of retribution, following an attack by unidentified gunmen on Maronite Christian worshippers as they were leaving their church after a Sunday service.

The Palestinians took to the streets in protest, burning tyres and halting traffic. By the time we left the country, the Lebanese army had moved into the centre of Beirut in a serious attempt to keep the combatants apart. Roadblocks had been set up in all the main streets, and tanks were stationed at crossroads.

****

The finished programme was described by the press as a 'stunning finale' to 'a lovely, holy trilogy'. Peter Jackson was again commended for his 'brilliant camera-work', but there was one dissenting voice.

Immediately after the UK broadcast, I received a phone call from Sheikh Najib Alamuddin, president and chairman of MEA, Lebanon's national airline. He described the programme he had just seen as 'a disgrace'. 'Anyone watching your film,' he said, 'would think my country was on the brink of civil war.'

The sad truth is that civil war in the Lebanon continued, off and on, for another fifteen years, with alliances between the warring parties continually shifting and changing. It is estimated that 120,000 people lost their lives in this conflict and close to a million were displaced.

Two Israeli invasions were followed by thirty years of Syrian control, countless political assassinations and bombing outrages, culminating in the greatest disaster of all, an explosion in the port of Beirut on 4 August 2020 that killed at least 200 people, injured over 6,000 and destroyed almost half the city. Lebanon was finally brought to its knees.

Chapter Twelve

SIX DAYS IN SOWETO

On 16 June 1976, South African police opened fire on student demonstrators in Soweto. At least two hundred protestors were shot and killed on that single day.

The tragic consequence of police violence was captured in Sam Nzima's iconic photograph of a distraught teenager carrying the body of twelve-year-old Hector Pieterson, one of the first to die. By the following day, the Soweto demonstrations were making headline news across the world.

The students had taken to the streets to protest the Afrikaans Medium Decree, a new law requiring black schools to use Afrikaans as the medium of instruction in key subjects. 'Practical subjects' such as general housework, cooking and cleaning would be taught in English, while indigenous languages could only be used for religious instruction, music and 'physical culture' – whatever that might be.

Thirteen years earlier, in my film *Anatomy of Apartheid*, I had claimed that Verwoerd's Bantu Education Act was 'designed to give back to the Bantu their most precious raw material, language. Children who once had to learn the names of

Europe's emperors by heart now heard the stories of their own historical leaders, in the languages they spoke at home.'

But as I came to know Soweto well, the truth about Bantu education hit me hard: schools with no libraries, classrooms without electricity or desks for the children to work on, and class sizes of up to eighty students.

With this new law, any pretence of cultural sensitivity was stripped away. The message was clear. Since blacks are only fit for a subservient role in society, they should be taught in the languages of their future masters.

Enforced instruction in Afrikaans was a particularly sensitive issue. Only a small minority of black teachers and even fewer children spoke the language with any degree of fluency, and standards of education were bound to fall even further. Still more contentious was the fact that Afrikaans was the language of the policeman and the township bureaucrat – in Desmond Tutu's words, 'the language of the oppressor'.

The violence continued for a whole year, and a few courageous reporters and photographers brought chilling evidence out of Soweto; police driving through the townships and firing indiscriminately; truckloads of corpses being offloaded at a township police station; mourners attacked while attending the funeral of a young black activist.

Like everyone else, I was shocked by these images, and began to feel a personal responsibility. I knew the territory well and had friends there who were constantly in touch. There seemed to be an urgent need for a documentary that would give a voice to the people of Soweto and allow them to share their daily experiences and the conditions that had sparked this crisis.

But there was one huge uncertainty. Three years after I had been banned from filmmaking in South Africa, I had been allowed to return to make *The Gold Run* for British Television, but I would hear later that Hennie Momberg, my main contact at the Department of Information, had been severely criticised for granting permission. Was there the slightest chance that I would be allowed to make another documentary for British television?

The only way to find out was to arrange face-to-face meetings in Pretoria, but before I took that step, I had to see whether any UK broadcaster would be interested in my proposal.

Sadly, Tony Essex of Yorkshire Television had died of a heart attack. He was only forty-nine years old, and was sorely missed.

Now that he was no longer with us, I discussed the proposal with a number of senior executives at ITV, and was frank about the uncertainties. The most positive response came from Charles Denton, head of documentaries at ATV. Not only was he prepared to risk spending money on a potentially fruitless trip to South Africa, but he also felt that the situation in that country was so critical that I should think of two other subjects. If all went well in my Pretoria meetings, Charles would like to offer a South African trilogy to the network.

Without a moment's hesitation, I came up with two further suggestions.

Now was the time for the real test.

Everything would depend on a meeting I had arranged with the Department of Information in Pretoria.

Hennie Momberg and Errol Hines, my main government contacts there during the Sixties, had both retired, but their successors had plenty of information about me. The only thing in my favour was that I had been frank and open in my all my past dealings with the Department, but to make this trilogy I would have to cross a line I had never crossed before. I may have come close to it when I shared the story of my great-uncle with Keizo Takei, the *yakuza* boss, but he and his followers were given a clear idea of the films we intended to make.

On this occasion, I would have to invent the stories we intended to tell, and there was another serious issue. For the first time, I would be interviewing 'ordinary people' without giving them any idea of the context, but I could see no alternative. If I were to be completely frank with some of those in the white communities, they would have reported us to the authorities and all filming would have been stopped.

There's no other way of saying this: a commitment to make the films I had in mind was a commitment to deceive. Some readers may disagree with me, but I felt then, as I still do, that this was right decision.

I told the people at the Department that I intended to make a series of films about South African families – an Afrikaner family, an English-speaking family, a Bantu family, a 'Coloured' family and an Indian family.

Judging by the conditions imposed, this presentation was not entirely convincing. After a long discussion and many questions, I was told that I would be free to research in white, Indian and 'coloured' areas, but would need permission from the Department of Bantu Affairs whenever I intended to visit the townships.

Once research was completed and we were ready to film, conditions would be much tougher. Someone from the Department of Information would accompany us at all times, and when we were filming in the black townships, we would be saddled with a second 'minder' from the Department of Bantu Affairs.

There was no way we could make the films I was planning under these conditions. The only rational response would have been to pull out altogether and take the next flight back to London, but I have never been entirely rational! As my dear grandmother taught me, everything is possible if you set your heart on it. Somehow, I would find a way when the time came; maybe a second unit, posing as tourists and working clandestinely. What mattered now was that I had permission to stay in the country to do the necessary research.

The first priority was to find a way to tell the Soweto story. Although I had to report to the Department of Bantu Affairs in Johannesburg every time I intended to visit, nobody accompanied while I was researching. With the help of township friends and two black journalists who had covered the uprising from the start, we gathered an impressive body of witnesses, but slowly and reluctantly I began to face facts. Filmed interviews were going to be pure fantasy if two government 'minders' had to be with us at all times.

Then something remarkable happened. I was called to another meeting at the Department of Information and told that all future responsibilities for the films would be transferred to a senior member of another department.

I was handed a card with the name and contact details of someone who worked for Bantu Affairs. It was hard to understand how anyone from that department would be taking charge of the project. Most of the whites who worked there were at the lower level of the Afrikaner bureaucracy and, in many cases, close to retirement. Imagine my surprise when I was ushered into an untypically smart and spacious office where a bright, articulate young man rose to greet me.

It would be wrong to give his name, so I'll call him Willem. Hopefully, he is still alive and well, and the last thing I want is to create problems for him, particularly in his own community. I still have no idea why he helped me and any theories I have about his loyalties and motives are pure conjecture. All I can do is report these events as they happened.

Willem listened politely to my cover story about South African families, but I suspected from the start that he knew I was playing games. What followed was scarcely believable. Not only would I be free to continue my research in Soweto without any further need to report to Bantu Affairs, but those same conditions would apply during filming. We would be free to film there, unaccompanied by any government officials.

It was an incredible moment, but there was more to follow. Willem assured me that he would always be available if I needed advice or was having any problems with access. He also invited me to dinner at his home, a bright modern villa that was certainly beyond the reach of a typical Bantu Affairs bureaucrat.

We spent a relaxed evening together with his wife and their two young children. At one point, Willem invited me into his library and waved a hand across an entire shelf of banned communist literature. It was a signal that he was either a member of BOSS (the Bureau for State Security) or a committed communist who trusted me, but it is hard to imagine anyone in the second category daring to put those books and pamphlets on display.

This still remains a mystery, but thanks to Willem I now had official documents which we could present to the police if we were stopped in Soweto, either during research or filming. I was also given some important contacts. One person I was keen to meet was Mr Mzaidume, headmaster of Orlando West High School, who had witnessed the actual moment on 16 June when the police opened fire on protesting students as they marched past his school. He was a man with a reputation for integrity, but as he was not keen to speak to journalists, I decided to raise the matter with Willem.

As always, we spoke in code, and the conversation went along these lines.

'How's your research going, Antony?'

'Very well, thank you, but I'm still not sure that I've found the right Bantu family. It would be great if I could meet a professional family, perhaps one where the father is a school headmaster.'

'I think I should arrange for you to meet Mr Mzaidume, headmaster of Orlando West High School.'

Was this pure coincidence, or were the black journalists working with me also in touch with Willem?

Mzaidume was impressive, and it was clear from the frank way he spoke that he trusted Willem and anyone Willem recommended. I was given a graphic account of police violence, and not only on 16 June. Just three days before we met, the police had entered his school and ordered the children out of their classes. When they shouted at the police in defiance, tear gas canisters were fired into the classrooms.

Mzaidume was in his sixties, a man who, in his own words, 'was hoping, with the few days left in this service, that I would leave things at a higher standard [but] when we try to rebuild, then the police appear and break them down. The material damage may not be so important because it can still be rebuilt, but the child? Many of them have been ruined.'

He agreed to appear in the film and would be one of the most important witnesses.

After two months of research, I returned to London and wrote detailed treatments for the three programmes. We had a thirteen-week schedule for filming, which was generous, but I had to be frank with Charles about the risks we were taking. Although all had gone well at this point, we could not take anything for granted.

My plan was to organise the schedule so that we started with sequences that would be easy to explain should we be stopped and questioned. From there, we would move progressively towards the riskier material. There was always a chance that we might be stopped in the tenth or eleventh week, before we had got to the heart of any of these stories, and if that happened, we might be left with insufficient material to complete a single film.

Charles was prepared to take the risk; television was very different in those days. We were ready to go.

Sadly, the move from Yorkshire Television to ATV meant that I would no longer be working with the team that had been with me for eight years, but Peter Jackson's successor, Ernie Vincze, was also a fine cameraman, and his 'stunning images' would eventually be commended in several reviews.

****

During research for our first film, *Six Days in Soweto*, I had been able to talk to nearly a hundred adults and children. Although they knew the risks, they were determined to get their message out to the world and, in almost every case, they agreed to appear on film without concealing their identities. In the words of one young volunteer: 'We want the British people to see the truth in our faces.'

Our search for witnesses was not limited to student activists. People at all levels of society agreed to talk to us. These included parents, doctors and teachers, as well as ordinary Sowetans who had taken no part in the protests but had suffered the terrible consequences of random police violence. Archbishop Desmond Tutu, who was Dean of St Mary's Cathedral in Johannesburg at the time, made an important contribution, as did Mangosuthu Buthelezi, chief minister of the KwaZulu Bantustan. Although he had made serious compromises with the regime during the apartheid era, he joined the archbishop in playing a key role in negotiations to end racial conflict in South Africa and would eventually serve as Minister of Home Affairs in Nelson Mandela's government.

As already mentioned, there was a serious moral issue I had to face. The first rule of documentary filmmaking is that people accused of serious offences should be given a right of reply, but I could not offer this to police officers and government officials without disclosing the subject; once that was known we would have been ordered out of the country.

All I can say is that we did not find any contradictions in the testimonies we were given and, in many cases, these were backed by photographic evidence. If a parent, a schoolmaster, or someone of Desmond Tutu's status had said anything that appeared to contradict the testimonies of the student activists, we would have raised the matter with them immediately.

In a one-hour documentary, we could not tell the full story of an entire year of conflict. We decided, instead, to concentrate on just six days.

But this would not be a film that moved relentlessly from one violent confrontation to the next. Viewers had to understand the context. They had to share some of the experiences that had made such an impact on me when I got to know Soweto well – whether it was the dawn rush through the dust and wood smoke to catch the buses and trains for Johannesburg, or quieter moments in family homes, where children as young as twelve had to look after their siblings and take on all the responsibilities of the house during the long hours when both parents were away at work. We had to give real meaning to the words that a father had once said to me: 'These are not children. These are men. These are women.'

Viewers also had to experience the realities of Bantu education: the crammed classrooms; teachers struggling to teach mathematics in Afrikaans, which was probably their third or fourth language; young girls being taught how to scrub and wash. (To quote the teacher's words in a lesson we filmed: 'You make the water soapy, then you dip the cottons into the water and rub them in your hands. Now show me how to rub this.')

We also had to hear from parents and children who were well aware of the huge disparities in the state's funding of black and white education.

All these insights were woven into the six-day chronology.

Day One: 16 June 1976.

The first witnesses to appear in the film were three members of the Soweto Students Representative Council, which had been formed in secrecy to plan the first demonstration. They had escaped the police dragnet for a whole year and were the only people we interviewed who asked for their identities to be concealed. Special care also had to be taken to find a location where we could park and offload our equipment without attracting attention.

Our three witnesses insisted that they had planned a peaceful demonstration. If students were confronted by the police and ordered to disperse, they should do so immediately.

At 8.15 in the morning and precisely according to plan, students simultaneously marched out of five schools in Soweto, intending to converge on the Orlando football stadium, where they had planned a mass meeting to protest the Afrikaans Medium Decree. By the time the march had reached Orlando West High School, four thousand students were involved.

When we interviewed Mr Mzaidume, the school headmaster, nearly a year later, he stood at the exact spot where he had witnessed the first outbreak of violence. His testimony would be supported by ten other witnesses.

Suddenly, and without warning, the police fired tear gas canisters and live rounds into the crowd. One of the first casualties was twelve-year-old Hector Pieterson, who had been shot in the mouth. He was rushed to a local clinic but died on the way.

As the police continued firing, the crowd responded with a mix of panic and fury. Some rushed to find shelter in nearby homes, but when they did, the police fired tear gas canisters through the windows. Others stood their ground, throwing the gas canisters back at the police before they exploded. Some even charged the police, using dustbin lids as shields, and were shot, again and again, before they fell.

In the words of one witness: 'We had reached saturation point where we could no longer take anything without retaliating.'

By mid-afternoon, the student demonstration had been fanned into a full-scale riot. All cars entering Soweto were stopped at student roadblocks, and drivers forced to make the black power salute before they could proceed. As students attacked the beer halls, symbols of their parents' humiliation, thugs and looters joined in. Soweto was in chaos, and everywhere, the police were firing indiscriminately.

During that first day, Melville Eddlestein, a Bantu Affairs official, was murdered. The precise number of black victims is not known, and their names are not recorded.

Our final witness to the events in Soweto of 16 June was a fifteen-year-old girl who had been shot in the back as she was crossing the street to visit her uncle, five miles from the scene of the first student/police encounter. Now paralysed from the waist down, she was struggling to continue her education at home through a correspondence course. She told us that many of the mothers who lost their children that day had no idea where the bodies were taken. She could only thank the Lord that she had been spared and was still able to study and have the use of her hands.

Day Two: 17 June 1976

As the new day broke, heavy police and military reinforcements were taking positions throughout Soweto, and the Hippo made its first dramatic appearance. An armoured vehicle designed with an exceptionally high clearance as protection from guerrilla landmines, the Hippo was to become a new symbol of white power in Soweto.

Dr Nthato Motlana, a good friend of mine, described how he saw one of the Hippos moving across the stretch of open ground in front of his house where 'little kids, no more than eight years old', were playing. Suddenly, the police inside the Hippo started 'taking pot shots at the little kids'. Motlana rushed out, shouting, 'What do you think you're doing? You're actually shooting at children, playing in an open field!' The shooting stopped, and the Hippo withdrew in shame, but this was a rare response. Right across Soweto, the police were shooting indiscriminately.

The consequences for some families were catastrophic. One father told us that his daughter had been shot on her way home from school. His wife had a weak heart, and before their child was released from hospital, she died from strain and worry. To attend his wife's funeral and visit his daughter in hospital, he took three days off work and was sacked. Since then, he had not received any unemployment money or compensation for his daughter's injury. He couldn't even afford to pay what he owed for his daughter's wheelchair. We left him with enough to solve that problem. It was the one and only time a Soweto witness received any payment from us.

Throughout that second day, Orlando Police Station was one of the main dumping grounds of dead and injured. One of the journalists who was working with us had recorded a statement from Desmond Tutu. It was a graphic account of the scenes he had witnessed at the police station on the afternoon of 17 June and was given to us on the strict understanding that the source would not be disclosed. Even then, Tutu was taking risks. His is one of the most recognisable voices of any person I know.

In this testimony, Tutu described the moment when a large truck pulled up in front of the police station. He couldn't see what was inside, but he could hear people 'crying and in deep pain':

> I then went inside the police station where I saw people who were injured, were shot. Some of them you could see that they were in great pain, but the police seemed not to bother about them. There was no medical attention given to them. There were about eighty dead and over a hundred injured.
>
> In the evening more bodies were coming in. Among the corpses was an elderly man, who was not dead at the time. You could see him struggling among the corpses. Then I heard one white policeman coming in and saying that others should come and see black power in action. Everything was just humorous to them.
>
> Later on, when I went out, that person was dead.
>
> Corpses were taken away in the government mortuary van. They were thrown in just like bags of potatoes. It shows how life has become cheap in our country. When you are black, you are nothing.

To back Tutu's testimony, we acquired chilling photographs of bodies being loaded into the trucks. We also managed to film in the actual police station, which was quiet and empty on the day we were there. As the camera panned across the open space in front of the desks, it wasn't hard to visualise the scene that night, when nearly two hundred dead and injured men, women and children were heaped together on the concrete floor.

Days Three, Four and Five: 23, 24 & 25 August 1976

If the residents of Soweto had second-class status during the apartheid era, Soweto's hostel dwellers belonged to a third class. These were migrant workers, mostly recruited from black homelands. Many of them were uneducated, desperately poor, and only permitted in urban areas as and when white-owned industry required them. They had no security beyond their short-term contracts and were housed in barracks or 'hostels', as they were officially known, where they lived separated from their wives and children for periods of up to two years.

When Soweto parents stayed away from work in sympathy with the students, the hostel dwellers did not strike, and were harassed when they returned at the end of the day.

According to Mangosuthu Buthelezi: 'The police thought that this was a golden opportunity to create division in the black community. They took advantage of the bitterness of the hostel dwellers to urge them to attack the residents of Soweto. They were clutching at anything to ensure that they broke down the solidarity and resistance of the people at that time.'

On the evening of 23 August, Zulus armed with pangas, knives and clubs burst out of their hostel and entered the Soweto district of Meadowlands. One of their first victims was the elderly lady who received us in a spotless front room decorated with a few simple tokens of her Roman Catholic faith – a crucifix and a framed picture of the Sacred Heart of Jesus.

In broken English, she described how the hostel dwellers smashed doors and windows with their axes, before forcing their way into all the houses along the street. The eldest of her three sons was hacked to death in front of her. Her two other sons, Arthur and Gideon, ran into the street and were butchered there. 'Now I was running outside, crying. I didn't know if they are dead. I asked the people about my children. They say: "All dead."'

According to the old lady and her neighbours, the police did not intervene. No ambulances were sent, and the bodies lay in the street until the following day.

Pro-government press and broadcasting were now able to report to the world that blacks were killing blacks in Soweto. Issues had been confused, and the student movement partially discredited.

On 24 August, the hostel dwellers were once more out in force. According to witnesses, including black journalists who gave us photographic evidence, the police were now openly involved on the side of the hostel dwellers.

On the third day, the hostel riots were subsiding, but the police continued to drive through Soweto, firing indiscriminately from unmarked vehicles.

Day Six: 24 October 1976

On that day, a large crowd had converged on Doornkop Cemetery in Soweto to pay their respects to Jake Mashubani, a student who had allegedly hanged himself in prison. But this would not be a conventional funeral service. Those present sang freedom songs and 'raised our clenched fists in salute of our dead black brother, who had died for the cause'.

As they stood around the grave, they noticed police cars drawing up along the borders of the cemetery, but the service continued 'as if nothing was happening'. Then a single shot was fired, and a police officer ordered them to disperse. 'People started shouting "Peace! Peace!" and making the peace sign to the police.' More shots were fired, and now they were aimed at the mourners.

According to two witnesses: 'People started panicking, running helter-skelter in all directions. There was just pandemonium in the cemetery, people stumbling, some jumping into open graves. I saw someone fall, but I couldn't just wait, and I ran. The police were just shooting indiscriminately. It was like shooting buck, running wild.'

A young woman told us how she was trying to save two little girls by carrying one on her shoulder and holding the other by the hand as she ran beside her. The first child was shot and fell to the ground. The second child lost her grip and disappeared in the melee.

Another witness, a girl in her teens, had lost consciousness when she was hit in the leg. Hours later, she woke up in hospital to be told that the wound was so severe they would have to amputate. Her first response was to beg them to let her die, but finally she found the strength to carry on:

'Now I can't move, but I will continue with the struggle. I can get an artificial leg and walk, and again, I can struggle until I die. Yes, they will kill us, but not all of us. We'll still struggle until we die. Another one will be born. He will struggle and die until we get freedom.'

Chapter Thirteen

THE SEARCH FOR SANDRA LAING

Sandra Laing with her parents, Abraham and Sannie.

The second subject made headline news at a time when I was in turmoil over the decision whether to leave South Africa or stay.

In February 1966, ten-year-old Sandra Laing had been expelled from a white school in the Afrikaner town of Piet Retief on grounds of 'racial impurity'. Over the previous three years, complaints from teachers, parents and fellow pupils about her darker skin and tightly curled black hair had reached such a pitch that the school board finally launched an appeal to the Department of the Interior to have her reclassified as a 'Coloured'. Once this was granted, the school was free to expel her.

The threat of 'reclassification' hung over many South African families during the apartheid era, but what made this case exceptional was the response of Sandra's parents. Abraham and Sannie were white Afrikaners and staunch supporters of the Nationalist Government that had framed South Africa's race laws but, unlike others in a similar crisis, they did not hang their heads in shame, but fought hard for Sandra's right to be white again. As well as launching an appeal to the South African Supreme Court, they encouraged the press to tell their story.

As soon as I read the first reports, I made the impulsive decision to drive two hundred miles to the family home in a remote corner of the Eastern Transvaal where the Laings had built a stone cottage and a trading store/post office, where they served an all-black clientele from a nearby 'Bantu homeland'.

On that day, the space between the two buildings was crowded with reporters, photographers and a film unit. Sandra's parents welcomed this attention and made sure that the cameramen took shots of their daughter posing with them, and even chasing a goose into the veldt.

But the atmosphere suddenly changed when one of the reporters referred to rumours of an affair between Mrs Laing and a black lover.

Abraham's response was immediate and passionate. This was an outrageous slur. Sandra was their child. 'If her appearance is due to some coloured blood in either of us, then it must be very far back among our forebears and neither of us is aware of it.'

Historically, Abraham was absolutely right. During the early years of white settlement, sexual relations, particularly between masters and slaves, were common. The irony, of course, was that the Laings and many other Afrikaners from long-established families did not take the next logical step and reject apartheid as an absurdity.

In May the following year, the Laings' appeal to the Supreme Court was rejected. Once again, I returned to the family home and also visited a second 'native trading store' which Abraham Laing ran in a place called Panbult, some twelve miles from their home. Sandra was there, helping her father sell blankets and cheap plastic shoes to their black clientele.

By now, letters were pouring in from England, the United States, Scandinavia, the Netherlands, New Zealand and even Iran with offers to adopt Sandra, but the Laings had no intention of giving up their daughter.

Two months later, a new law was passed, decreeing that children could not be classified differently from their parents. Within days, Abraham Laing received a courteous letter from the Minister of Home Affairs, confirming that his daughter's reclassification had been reversed.

Others were less fortunate. The new law could also be used to force people who had been passing as whites into a less privileged racial group, simply on the evidence of the colour of one of their parents, but Sandra was white again, and her case was no longer an international embarrassment.

Several years later, a South African friend who knew my interest in the story sent me an article from the *Rand Daily Mail*, the country's most influential anti-apartheid newspaper. Apparently, Sandra had absconded from an all-white school and eloped to Swaziland with her black lover. She was fifteen years old at the time.

After that, I received no further news of Sandra.

When sharing this with Charles, I felt there were two priorities. First, I had to find Sandra and get her permission to tell her story. If she agreed, I would have to embed myself in the Afrikaans community that had rejected her. We had to learn how these people thought and offer a perspective on apartheid at a very personal level.

Once I was back in South Africa, my first port of call was the Laings' family home, where I had first seen Sandra, but much had changed in eleven years. The whole area had now been incorporated into the neighbouring 'bantustan', and the stone cottage and the store opposite were occupied by black families. Abraham's second trading store in Panbult had been abandoned.

The new residents told me that Abraham and Sannie had moved to a place called Pongola, but none of them seemed to know anything about their daughter Sandra.

After a long search I traced her and her husband Petrus, who were living in 'Tjakastad', a black 'homeland' close to the Swazi border. Sandra was touched by my interest in her story, and for several hours I sat with her and Petrus in their rondavel while their two children, Henry and Elsie, continually popped in and out. Before the day was over, Sandra and Petrus had agreed to appear in the film. Like Sandra's parents when they were fighting for their daughter's right to be white, they felt that publicity was a form of protection.

In Piet Retief, the town that had rejected Sandra, I used my fictional quest for an Afrikaans family as an excuse to meet people at all levels of white society, paying particular attention to the teaching staff and Sandra's contemporaries at the school that had expelled her.

****

For me, the absurdity and cruelty of apartheid were expressed in a single image which Ernie captured on the second day of filming. While we were in the home of an Afrikaans farming family, we heard sounds of laughter coming from the nursery and followed it to the source. The farmer's four-year-old son was sitting, stark naked, on the folded arms of his black nanny. He had one arm around her neck and was continually touching her face with his other hand. Both were laughing, and our sudden arrival with the camera caused no embarrassment to either of them.

Even in the apartheid era, young Afrikaans children were allowed to develop a casual love and physical familiarity with their black nannies, who were sometimes closer to them than their own mothers. If they lived in rural areas, as Sandra did, they might have had no other playmates except the children of black servants and labourers, but as soon as those white children reached school age, there was a sudden change.

Such was Sandra's fate when her parents delivered her to the boarding hostel for primary school children in the town of Piet Retief. She was just seven years old.

As we would discover when Mr Koch, the man from Bantu Administration, took us to a hilltop overlooking the town, Piet Retief was apartheid South Africa in microcosm. Immediately below us were the tin and breeze block shacks that housed black South Africans. Beyond that was a low hill which screened the black township from white Piet Retief.

Far behind us, a row of houses had been dropped into the empty veldt. These were for 'coloureds', who had been expelled from their previous homes in white Piet Retief. Separated from the 'coloureds' by a decent stretch of no-man's-land was the Indian township; the homes of shopkeepers, also barred from trading or living in white Piet Retief.

The boarding hostel Sandra entered on that afternoon in January 1963 was firmly located in white Piet Retief. From the moment she crossed that threshold, the blurred lines that had hitherto distinguished the races would be firmly drawn, and a little girl who called herself a white Afrikaner would be teased, taunted and eventually expelled.

They had a special name for the system of education in white schools like this: 'Christian National Education' (CNE). There was certainly a strong emphasis on religion, with no fewer than seven periods of worship and religious study every day, but was this really Christianity?

Somehow the teachers here and, indeed, most of the whites in Piet Retief, had managed to reconcile the gospel message with apartheid by drawing the boundaries of their Christian compassion around their own tribe. 'Love thy neighbour as thyself', as long as he or she is white.

Johannes van Tonder, the principal of the hostel where Sandra boarded, was very clear about the limits of his Christian responsibilities. 'We accept the black man', he told us. 'We accept him for what he is, and the day when he reaches the same point of development as what we are, we'll accept him on the same level.'

When I asked how long this process might take, he shook his head and waited for the next question. It was only when the camera was switched off that he said: 'To be honest with you, Antony, I think it will take them about four thousand years.' (I am afraid you only have my word for that!)

There were fourteen churches in Piet Retief to satisfy the spiritual needs of the town's four and a half thousand whites. The largest and most influential was the Dutch Reformed Church. The building, with its soaring spire and magnificent Cape Dutch gables, dominated the town. On Sundays the place was packed.

As Pastor Gerber mounted the pulpit, Mr van Tonder and the other elders and deacons made their ceremonial entry, dressed identically in black suits and white ties.

In his sermon, the pastor seemed to suggest that South Africa's apartheid laws were enacted in obedience to God's Word, and that those who opposed them would finally come to recognise the truth and follow South Africa's example.

He concluded his sermon with an appeal to God to 'bless our guns'. Presumably, he was referring to South Africa's military involvements in Southwest Africa (today's Namibia) and Angola. He might even have been thinking of the actions the police were still taking in Soweto.

A couple of miles away in the township, there was another Dutch Reformed church, roughly built out of corrugated iron and breeze block, where some thirty black worshippers had come together. This was one of three 'daughter churches'. There was another one for 'coloureds' and a third for Asians. In this brand of the faith, congregations were segregated before God.

Lessons about racial difference and racial superiority were also a key part of the CNE curriculum in white schools funded by the government.

When we asked to film a history class at Sandra's former school, the teacher chose to tell the story of Piet Retief, the Boer leader after whom the town was named. In 1838 he had come in peace to negotiate a land deal with Dingaan, King of the Zulus, but as soon as he and his followers had laid down their arms, the Zulu king ordered his warriors to bludgeon them to death. It was a story of black treachery that should be an example to all of us.

Even more chilling was the class where children, as young as seven, were being taught about racial differences. Behind the teacher was a photo display, showing blacks ploughing fields and driving cattle, and whites teaching and nursing. There was even a photo of a young white woman loading a washing machine in an ultra-modern kitchen. Below is a translation of the actual exchange between the Afrikaans teacher and her young pupils:

Q What does our skin look like? What colour is it?
A A light skin.
Q And our eyes, what are they like?
A We have light eyes.
Q And now the black people, what's their skin like?
A Dark skin.
Q There's a difference in the eyes and the noses and the mouths. Their hair is crinkly, and their noses are …?
A Flat.
Q What are their mouths like, their lips?
A Thick lips.
Q Where do these black people work?

A On the farm.

Q What do they plant?

A Mealies.

Q With their animals, yes. And now we come to the whites. What do we see here?

A A teacher.

Q That's right, and a nursing sister. What else do we see? This lady, what does she do?

A She works in the house.

Q Yes. There are many kinds of work that we whites do. Think of your own fathers.

So much for 'Christian National Education'. Little Sandra Laing didn't stand a chance.

****

Mr van Tonder, her housemaster, was one of the main speakers at the teachers' meeting where they decided to refer Sandra's case to the Department of the Interior.

Two months later, Sandra was called out of class and told to pack her things. It was van Tonder who drove her to her father's store in Panbult, and although she asked him, again and again, why he was taking her away from school, he refused to give an answer.

When they arrived at the store, van Tonder took her father aside. Sandra couldn't hear what passed between them, but when Abraham came back to the car, he was in tears. Together, they offloaded Sandra's bags and van Tonder drove away.

Sandra stayed at the store with her father until he closed for lunch and drove her home. When her mother, Sannie, heard that Sandra had been expelled from school, she also broke down in tears.

Both parents realised they were in a vulnerable position. A 'coloured' child was not permitted to reside in a white home except as a servant. There had also been several cases when a 'coloured' child born to a white mother had been taken from her and placed in a 'coloured' orphanage. The other great concern was that Sandra would slip further and further behind her white contemporaries during her many months out of school while the family waited for the court's decision. For Abraham, the option of sending her to a 'coloured' school was unthinkable. He would have to do his best to tutor his daughter in all key subjects.

Even when Sandra's reclassification was finally reversed, the family's problems were not over. Nine white schools refused to accept Sandra before a place was finally secured for her in St Dominic's Academy, a Catholic convent in the largely English-speaking province of Natal. St Dominic's did not follow the CNE curriculum or believe that apartheid was their Christian duty. For the first time, we were able to talk frankly about Sandra to her former teachers and tell them about the film we were making.

Sister Flora and Sister Jordana remembered her well. Sandra was twelve years old when she entered the school and, despite her father's efforts, she had fallen far behind children her own age. There was also the problem of language. St Dominic's was an English-speaking school; Sandra was an Afrikaner. The nuns decided that Sandra would only be able to cope if they placed her in the same class as children two or three years younger. They knew this would be humiliating but felt they had no alternative.

'Sandra,' they told us, 'was very shy and retiring as far the staff and other children were concerned.' Unsurprisingly, 'she was also happier with black people than with whites. Joseph – he's our driver – he just remembered her as a very friendly little girl.'

Joseph not only remembered Sandra with affection, but he also opened the next chapter of her story. 'She left one term and she never came back, and I heard that she met Petrus Zwane, an African. They went to Swaziland; then they were pushed over to the Transvaal, and since then I've never heard anything of them.'

Petrus Zwane was a handsome young man in his mid-twenties who made regular visits to both the Laings' trading stores, unloading fruit and vegetables from the back of his truck. As Sandra reached her teens, a strong mutual attraction developed between them. Although she knew that Petrus had a wife and three children, Sandra couldn't hold back, and when she was just fourteen, the couple made love for the first time.

They both knew the risks they were taking. If they were found out, not only would they face the wrath of Sandra's parents and Petrus's wife, Lisa, they would both be guilty of a criminal offence. Sexual relations between a white – as Sandra now was – and a black were forbidden by law. To make matters worse, Sandra was below the legal age of consent.

Everything suddenly came to a head in June 1970 at the start of Sandra's winter holiday. Early one morning she spotted Lisa, sitting outside under a tree. She seemed to be waiting for Sannie to open the store.

Sandra had a sudden premonition and ran across to Lisa, who produced a photograph of her in school uniform which she had found in Petrus's jacket pocket. Without a moment's hesitation, Sandra blurted out the truth. Yes, Petrus was her boyfriend, but she promised Lisa that she had no intention of taking him away from her and begged her not to show the photo to her parents. But Lisa had other ideas. Immediately Sannie arrived, she not only showed her the photograph but, ignoring the pleas of mother and daughter, announced that she was on her way to Panbult to share this evidence with Sandra's father.

When Abraham stormed into the house that evening, Sandra insisted that her relationship with Petrus was just a friendship, but Abraham suspected otherwise, and the shouting continued late into the night. For four years he had fought to maintain Sandra's white status and struggled to give her the best education possible, and now she was heartlessly throwing everything away.

For the whole of that six-week holiday, Abraham barely spoke to his daughter, and when she returned for the Christmas break, nothing had changed. Sandra was so distressed that she begged Petrus to run away with her, and during the Easter holiday, the couple quietly slipped out in Petrus's truck and headed for Swaziland.

The former British protectorate of Swaziland was now an independent African state, where whites and blacks could cohabit without the risk of prosecution, but the couple were still taking risks. Sandra had entered the country illegally. She had no passport or even an identity card, as these were not required in South Africa until a child reached the age of sixteen.

They headed for Mbabane, the capital, where Petrus rented a room and continued to earn a living buying fruit and vegetables from farmers and selling them in the city.

Just as they were beginning to feel settled, they were woken at dawn by a mighty banging on the door. Two black policemen walked in and accused Petrus of 'stealing a Boer child'. When Sandra protested that she was here of her own free will, they told her that she was also in serious trouble for entering the country illegally.

Petrus was given a one-month sentence and Sandra was escorted to the border, where South African police were waiting to arrest her and take her to a local jail. Within a week, she was summoned to appear before a magistrate, to be told that Petrus was in prison in Swaziland and she would never see him again. Her only option was to return to her parents. If she refused, she would be sent back to jail, but Sandra was defiant. She would wait for her boyfriend, even if this meant spending the rest of her life behind bars.

Towards the end of her second month in prison, she was summoned before the magistrate again, this time with Petrus in attendance. Once again, she was ordered to return to her parents. Once again, she refused. Finally, the magistrate admitted defeat and simply told Petrus to take Sandra home.

Fortunately for Petrus and Sandra, the government was more concerned about black people lingering in white areas than they were about a white girl with brown skin living in a black township, but Sandra never lost her fear that the law might eventually catch up with them.

In November 1971, Sandra turned sixteen and was now at an age when she could apply for an identity card. She was three months pregnant at the time and knew that as long as she was classified white, there was a real danger that her children would be taken away from her. The face-saving law the government had introduced to solve the original problem now worked against her. She was white. Petrus was black. The only way she could be sure to keep her children was to register as a 'Coloured'.

The Department of Home Affairs referred her request to her father, who sent a short, sharp reply: 'Since Sandra's natural parents are white, the race she submitted is incorrect. No such permission can be granted.'

Very wisely, Sandra decided not to attract further attention with more applications, and the couple moved to Kromkrans, a black community surrounded by white towns and farms. Here Petrus built a solid four-room brick house and, for the very first time, he and Sandra felt settled.

Blacks had lived in Kromkrans since 1912, but in 1976 the residents were given two weeks to leave before the bulldozers moved in. In government parlance, places like this were known as 'black spots', and the plan was to eliminate them entirely.

Like millions of South Africans before them, Petrus and Sandra were now forced to take the road to an ethnic 'homeland', where blacks had the right to own their homes, vote for their tribal leaders and enjoy self-determination.

In reality, these 'Bantustans' were dumps for surplus people; for the old, the women and the children. Most of the men were away, working in white industries and farms, but Petrus was an exception. He and Sandra set up a shop with a counter, and with the help of the locals built a rondavel with a corrugated iron kitchen next to it.

The day before returning to film Sandra and Petrus, we stopped in the little town of Pongola, where I had been told we would find Sandra's parents.

At the town centre was a row of brand-new white shops. Hidden behind them was a parallel row of native trading stores, linked to the main road by a discreet alleyway. At the largest and newest, we found Abraham and Sannie serving an all-black clientele.

Without giving them any idea of the film we were making, I asked if we could take a few shots in the store, and Abraham agreed. Once the camera was rolling, I told him that his face was familiar, and then, after a suitable pause, suddenly asked:

'Of course, aren't you related to Sandra Laing?'

'Yes.' Abraham replied. 'She's our child.'

As the questions continued, Abraham never once raised his voice in anger. What came across from both of them was a sense of profound sadness:

Q Do you still feel as strongly for her as you did eleven years ago?
A Yes. That is natural.
Q Where is she living? Do you have any idea?
A No, I am not discussing her any further with you.
Q Do you ever hear from her, Mrs Laing?
A Yes, I hear from her.
Q Does she ever come and visit you?
A [With a sideways glance to Abraham.] No. She doesn't. My husband doesn't want to see her.
Q Why?
A I don't know.

I will never forget the uncomprehending, pained expressions on both their faces as they answered these questions, and for the very first time I felt that they, too, were apartheid's victims.

The following day, we were with Sandra and Petrus at their home in Tjakastad. Sandra had surrounded herself with the trappings of her Afrikaans childhood and heritage. On the wall was a tapestry featuring windmills and tulips along a Dutch canal, and a few precious family photographs – Sandra in the uniform of the school in Piet Retief; Sandra with her mother; and a snapshot of her parents during some long-forgotten holiday by the sea when Abraham was in his prime.

Sandra had remained in regular contact with her mother after she and Petrus fled to Swaziland, but all communication stopped when they finally moved to Tjakastad. Since then, five of Sandra's letters had been unanswered.

The conversation turned to the past, to her memories of nuns and bureaucrats, teachers and pupils, her few friends and many tormentors. In contrast to her treatment by whites, Sandra had never been rejected by blacks. Here in Tjakastad, the local people had not only helped Petrus build their home, they had also taught Sandra how to manage without tap water or sanitation and how to cope with childbirth and illness without the benefit of a local doctor.

As Sandra looked back, what were her feelings towards the community that had rejected her? 'People,' I added, 'who think they live by the *Bible* and the Lord's commandments.'

It was Petrus who answered that. 'What they did was bad, but that's not my business. All I can say to them is: "Thank you for giving me my wife."'

It was an appropriate place to end the film.

The Search for Sandra Laing was seen in over fifty countries, and I was delighted that Ernie Vincze, our cameraman, and Barry Reynolds, our editor, received special mention in the reviews. But the response that meant the most to me appeared in two South African papers – the *Cape Times* and the *Daily Dispatch*.

The film had been seen by Stanley Uys, political editor of Johannesburg's *Sunday Times*, who was in England at the time of the broadcast. In his review, he wrote: 'I have never seen such a powerful indictment of apartheid on the television screen. The punch line in the film is overpowering. After this film, the South African Department of Information and all its associated publicists and propagandists might as well fold their tents and steal away.'

I hoped I had repaid a debt.

Chapter Fourteen

WORKING FOR BRITAIN

In virtually all the reviews, *The Search for Sandra Laing* was seen as a shattering indictment of Afrikaners. They had come across as 'dreadful people, pious, sanctimonious, hypocritical, racist and callous'. The film had taken viewers 'inside the Afrikaner mind', and 'laid bare, with cruel economy, that blend of racial bigotry and religious self-righteousness which made them the world's most unattractive people'.

In short, *The Search for Sandra Laing* had exposed an alien culture that was almost beyond our understanding, but as we gathered more and more evidence of the violence against the people of Soweto, I began to have serious concerns about the values of the people they served; Johannesburg's largely English-speaking community to which I had once belonged.

The city's white suburbs were as familiarly British as Tonbridge or Bude; Anglican Church on a Sunday; a Roedean school for girls and a King Edward's school for boys; Rotary dinners; Scout jamborees and charities for the most deserving causes.

White Johannesburg appeared to function in accordance with all the decent British middle-class norms, but barely ten miles away in Soweto, the people who enabled this city to function were being brutally oppressed. And yet most English-speaking whites we interviewed seemed completely detached from everything that was happening there. And there another serious issue.

At the time of the Soweto uprising, Britain was South Africa's most important trading partner, contributing more to the South African economy than all the other countries in the world put together. There had been sports boycotts since the early Sixties, which significantly affected white morale in South Africa but did not deter British investment. Serious economic sanctions were not imposed until 1986, with far-reaching consequences. Within four years, Mandela was released from prison and negotiations were under way to end apartheid and introduce majority rule.

But until that crucial step was taken, South Africa continued to be a haven for the foreign investor. During the apartheid era, employers had no legal obligation to recognise black unions or to provide pensions, medical aid or severance pay. In some cases, black workers were being paid as little as a tenth of the rate for the same job in Europe. Under these conditions, the rewards for investment in South Africa were huge: a return of over 20 per cent per annum, as against 8 per cent in the United Kingdom.

The violence in Soweto may have taken off some of the gloss, but at the time we were filming, there were still more than two thousand enterprises either owned by Britain or controlled through a majority shareholding. It was estimated that over a quarter of a million black South Africans were *Working for Britain*, which was the title we chose for the third film in the series.

As always, we wanted to avoid interviews with political pundits and economic experts. Our aim was to get as close as possible to the workers themselves and allow these important issues to emerge through their lives and experiences. We also had to be fair in our choice of companies, and finally settled on Leyland International, which was doing its best to develop the skills of its black workers. At the opposite extreme was the sugar company Tate & Lyle, which had a very different record. To complete the picture, we also felt it was important to look at the consequences for black employees when a British company pulled out of South Africa.

Leyland had a troubled history in the early Seventies and was saved from collapse when Harold Wilson's Labour Government agreed to nationalise the company in 1975. In a real sense, those who were now working in Leyland International's assembly plants and repair shops in South Africa were servants of the British government. Another controversial issue was Leyland's role as one of the chief suppliers for the South African Defence Force, providing trucks, Land Rovers and armoured personnel carriers.

We approached the company with a simple request. Would they give us permission to build a major part of our film around the lives of two of their employees: one black, one white? Leyland was proud of the working conditions in all its plants, and the request was granted.

The two candidates they selected could not have been more interesting choices. Both were experienced mechanics in their mid-thirties, working in Leyland's large repair shop at Elandsfontein, twelve miles from central Johannesburg.

Charles Malote was a black South African. Jeff was a recent immigrant from Sheffield who had come to South Africa with his wife, Lesley, and their three children, and was planning to settle permanently. For reasons that will become clear, I do not think it would be fair to give the family name.

The two men worked in the same repair shop, but while Jeff was recognised as a qualified mechanic, Charles was known as a repair shop assistant, and his hourly rate was less than a fifth of Jeff's.

On our first day at the Elandsfontein plant, we filmed Charles as he disconnected a prop shaft and removed a gearbox and clutch from a large truck.

Assistant or not, he neither required nor received any supervision. In our amateur judgement, there was no distinction between the work done by Charles and the white mechanics on either side of him.

It didn't take long for one of the whites to understand the implications of the scene we were filming. The supervisor was consulted, and a special charade was organised for the benefit of the British viewer.

On cue, one of the white mechanics walked over to Charles to inspect the clutch plate he had removed. 'You'll have to get a new one, Charlie.'

The intention, of course, was to illustrate the different responsibilities of blacks and whites and make some sense of that five-to-one pay ratio, but the young mechanic was an unconvincing and embarrassed actor, and Charles assured us later that it was the first time he had ever taken part in a performance like this. The decision to replace a clutch or any other engine part was his, and his alone.

Charles was a gentle person. He didn't rant about injustices; he quietly gave us the facts. He had been born in a 'Bantu Homeland', and under the laws of apartheid had no rights to reside in an industrial area for more than 72 hours. Against all odds, he was able to find employers who were willing to take him on and allow him to develop his skills to a high level, which was probably why the company had suggested him. Seven years as a garage mechanic had been followed by two years on a car assembly line and six months' special training in diesel mechanics. In his opinion, he was as well qualified for the job as any of the whites who worked alongside him.

His situation was just one example of the way 'job reservation' worked in apartheid South Africa. The motor industry had white mechanics and black 'repair shop assistants'; the railways had white shunters and black 'train compilers'. The list goes on and on, and no matter how much black workers developed their skills, they had no chance of promotion to the top levels, which were reserved for whites.

As a result, men who might be working side by side and doing the same job lived in separate worlds that seldom touched. At the Leyland assembly plant, blacks and whites were served out of different windows during the morning tea break. Canteens and washrooms were segregated.

Outside the factory, those contrasts were even more striking. Charles lived in Tembisa, a black township a ten-mile train ride from the Leyland works.

Jeff and his family lived in a spacious three-bedroom house in the white suburb of Maryland. It had a swimming pool, a large garden and was only a few minutes' walk from the Leyland repair shop.

When we interviewed them, Lesley enthused about the way Leyland had treated them from the moment they had arrived in South Africa.

'They met us at the airport, and took us straight to a furnished apartment, provided a car for us, which was thoughtful, because you can't get around on public transport.'

When it came to finding a home, they were spoilt for choice. Lesley, again:

You've only got to let an estate agent get a little whiff that you might be interested in property, and they're round you like bees round a honey pot. Oh! We saw so many houses. I was baffled. But we picked this one because of its nearness to Jeff's work, near enough to schools. We liked the area, liked the pool. So, we moved in. Never looked back!

We travelled in a crowded train with Charles, following him and scores of other workers as they returned to their homes in Tembisa. It was late evening, and smoke poured out of the chimneys of row upon row of small breeze block houses, packed so tightly together that there was no space for anything resembling a garden.

Although Charles had been working in the Johannesburg area for twenty years, his situation was still precarious. He couldn't own or rent a property in Tembisa or any of the other black townships serving the city.

In his own words: 'To have a home in Johannesburg [people like me] have got to work for one employer for more than ten years, regardless whether the conditions are bad or good. You've got to tolerate whatever harsh approaches are made to you. Even then, you would still be on the waiting list.'

In effect, the law bound Charlie to Leyland. If he lost his job at any stage, there could be serious consequences.

'I've got to be very, very careful what I do, what I say, because if I happen to lose my job, then the worst thing is that I would not be allowed to stay here. I would be forced to separate from my wife and child, because they are allowed here, but I'm from the homeland. There's no alternative except to go back to the homeland.'

Until he had served a ten-year term with one employer, Charles and his wife Julie had to rely on the kindness of friends. At the time we were filming, they were temporary lodgers in the home of Ezekiel, Doris and their five children. Space was so tight that the children had to eat their supper on the floor. Charles and Julie knew that this was only a temporary solution and were fully prepared for a life continually on the move.

'That's why we don't even have a wardrobe, a table, a chair, because any day we may have to move. That's why I don't even have a bed because it would be very heavy. I only use a stretcher, which at least my wife can carry, and I can carry, and that's all.'

There was one precious item that Charles and Julie also took with them wherever they went – a framed photograph of their two-year old son, Thabo (the Sesotho word for happiness). Because they were determined not to expose their child to all the changes and uncertainties they were facing, they had agreed to leave him in the care of Julie's mother, who had a permanent home in Soweto. It had not been an easy decision.

'We would like to be with my child every night, every day, but unfortunately there is nothing we can do. When his mother sees other children, she thinks of her own child, and I also. I'm really not happy without seeing my child, the only son I have.'

For Jeff and Lesley, conditions in South Africa were very different and a significant improvement on anything they had known in England. For the first time in their lives, they had a maid to work for them. The food was cheaper, taxes were lower, the working week was shorter and there were many exciting options for their children. 'Ballet or cubs or brownies or the soccer team or tennis or netball. There's always something going on.'

Neither of them had any sense of the huge disparities between their lifestyles and those of Jeff's black co-workers, and when I raised the subject, I was shocked that a couple, straight out of England, were already parroting the same clichés and excuses I had heard again and again from hard-core racists in South Africa's white community:

Lesley: In England they've got the wrong idea altogether about the blacks. They're not ill-treated. In fact, in a lot of ways, they're pampered. They've got the opportunities, the same as we have.

Jeff: But they're just not interested. They've got no sense of responsibility at all, and while the white man will shoulder responsibility, they're quite happy … as long as they've got the food and cigarettes.

Lesley: (laughing) The beer on Friday!

Jeff: The beer on Friday, yeah. They're happy, just greasing vehicles and washing them. As long as they can get the money, they're not bothered.

Lesley: They've no sense of responsibility at all. You can't trust them to do a job properly.

Jeff: They're called repair shop assistants, and I think that is about their limit, and then you've got to keep a watchful eye on them.

Lesley: They're kleptomaniacs, a lot of them, and they don't know right from wrong. But that's their nature, you know. It's a different civilisation to ours.

＊＊＊＊

Three weeks before the broadcast, we screened the film for Michael Edwardes, the chief executive of British Leyland. His only complaint was that his company would be featured in the same film as Tate & Lyle, but he did contact us later with a request to insert the following paragraph in the commentary.

'Leyland International told us last week that they have already advised all interested parties that the company will negotiate on the basis of a formal agreement with a black union as soon as fifty percent of their black labour force has joined such a union.'

I can only hope that our film helped to contribute to this change, but it must be said that under the laws of apartheid black unions had no legal clout.

****

At the time we were filming, it was estimated that 30 per cent of South Africa's black labour force – close to two million people – were out of work. Those who spoke out against economic sanctions argued, quite rightly, that blacks would be the first to suffer if and when foreign manufacturers pulled out of the country. What they failed to acknowledge was that this suffering was made considerably worse by the way those companies had been allowed to operate in South Africa during the apartheid era.

For fourteen years, Mathilda Quebeca had worked at the Sirdar textile factory, a wholly-owned subsidiary of Sirdar Ltd, Wakefield, England.

In June 1974, Sirdar sold their South African business to an Anglo-French consortium, which resold to a local company within a year.

When we first met Mrs Quebeca, she was returning from work at her usual time of eight in the evening. She was a softly spoken, gentle woman in her mid-forties, who shared her cramped terraced house in Meadowlands, Soweto, with her husband, their four children and an elderly aunt.

When Sirdar was under British ownership, Mrs Quebeca was being paid seven rand (equivalent to £35 in today's money) for a sixty-hour week. She was also eligible for a bonus of five rand provided she clocked in on time every day. So great was her fear of losing this bonus that she got up every morning at 4.00am to be sure to catch a train that left Meadowlands just after 5.00am.

Conditions improved slightly after the British left, and her basic salary increased by four rand, but even when her husband's earnings were included, there was still barely enough to cover rent, food and heating, as well as books, school fees and uniforms for the children.

Mrs Quebeca spent fifteen hours away from home every working day. On Saturdays, she shopped, washed clothes and caught up with all the household chores. There were no parks, cinemas or social centres in Meadowlands, but during the few precious moments when she was able to step off the treadmill, there was one place where she and her family could gather together and enjoy the company of others: their local Roman Catholic church.

Two months after our first meeting with Mrs Quebeca, she was sacked by Sirdar without notice. The original British owners had made no provisions for pensions or severance pay. Under South African law and the terms of the sale, those who took over were free to carry on without any obligations. Mrs Quebeca's fourteen years of service to a British company was considered irrelevant.

****

At the opposite extreme from Leyland was the Illovo group of companies, which had three large sugar estates in Natal. Tate & Lyle were the principal shareholders.

In 1973, Tate & Lyle's affairs were examined by a parliamentary select committee. They were found to be paying their field labourers the minimum wages required by South African law, sixty-three South African cents a day, equivalent to £2.59 a day in today's money. This was just below Charles Malote's hourly rate at Leyland.

The following year, Tate & Lyle was one of the few British companies in South Africa to refuse to participate in an inquiry set up by Christian Concern for South Africa. However, they agreed to take part in another inquiry in April 1975. This happened to be the same month that one of their subsidiaries was awarded a £92 million contract in the Ivory Coast (in black Africa). Tate & Lyle's record in white Africa was now a matter of concern.

When we asked to film cane cutters in action on the company's Noodsberg estate, permission was granted, but under close scrutiny. We were not permitted to interview any of the workers or to see their living quarters.

We persisted with our requests and were finally escorted to one of five compounds on the Illovo group's principal estate. Mr Wardle, the man in charge, explained that this was for factory personnel, who were, of course, the elite among black workers.

The compound consisted of a large dormitory and scores of breeze block cabins, each housing eight workers. Even here, we were not permitted to conduct any interviews or enter the living quarters, but Peter Magubane, a well-known South African photographer, did manage to slip into the dormitory with a stills camera when the occupants were out at work. The beds were crammed so closely together that there was no room for any other furniture. Clothes and other personal belongings had to be stored behind a covering of wire mesh, which ran along one of the walls.

Mr Wardle laid on a tribal dance for our benefit, but the feature he was keenest to promote was the compound's new tennis court. At his bidding, four workers appeared in neat white shorts and T-shirts, and we were asked to film them walking towards the court. As none of them was carrying a racket, I suggested they might like to go back to collect these, and perhaps give us a chance to film them in action.

Only then did the truth emerge: the court was merely a cosmetic addition, and none of these men owned a racket or knew how to play tennis. Nevertheless, we gave Mr Wardle the shot he requested.

After these experiences, we gave up all attempts to film with official permission. The company had another estate, Doornkop, with three compounds. Two of them, B and C, were guarded, but Compound A was accessible, and we slipped in there late one afternoon.

Workers chose to live in this largely unsupervised compound so that they could be with girlfriends or wives and children, but the conditions were deplorable. There was no sanitation, and all the water had to be carried in buckets from a stream. Several of the children had swollen bellies, symptomatic of kwashiorkor, a serious form of malnutrition.

I don't doubt that Tate & Lyle were telling the truth when they said that living conditions were better in Compounds B and C, but sadly, Compound A was the only place where we were free to talk to cane cutters and labourers.

The male cane cutters told us they were paid the equivalent of £9.50 a week (£56 at today's rate). According to one of them, they left the compound every morning in the dark to start work in the fields at 6.00am.

We conducted separate interviews with two female labourers, who both gave us the same figure for their daily wage: one rand. In today's money, that's equivalent to £23.60 for a six-day week. Out of this, they had to pay for food and all other necessities. One of them, who worked as a weeder, claimed that people like her received no sick payment when they were too ill to work, and no compensation if they were injured on the job.

A male labourer, who was probably in his sixties, told us that he had 'worked here for many years, too many to remember'. For most of that time, he had been employed in the sugar mill 'pulling chains on the railway truck'. When he was no longer capable of hard physical labour, he was transferred to B Compound where he was given the job of a sweeper, but now that he was not fit to work, he claimed that he no longer received any benefits from the company. 'Even money for food, I don't earn. When I go to the hospital, I use my own money.'

I had been back in England for only a couple of weeks when I received a call from Lord Windlesham, managing director of ATV. Apparently, Tate & Lyle had told him that an ATV film unit had entered a compound that was 'no longer used to house our field-labourers and has been taken over by squatters'. We were accused of paying these squatters to make false statements about rates of pay and working conditions on the Illovo estates.

It was clear from their tone that Lord Windlesham was expected to sort out the problem by simply cancelling the documentary, but his lordship was not one of those establishment figures who could be won over with a nod and a wink. He told them that he did not believe I was capable of anything like that but promised to look into the matter.

During my entire career, I have never conducted an interview with anyone who has requested payment before agreeing to take part. People have appeared in my films because they had experiences and opinions they wished to share. However, once filming had been completed, I felt I had a right to support those who were really struggling. This was certainly true in the case of Sandra and Petrus; before leaving them for the final time, we had offered a gift that we felt was appropriate. Life in the Tjakastad 'homeland' was tough for them both, and there would have been no filming without their willing cooperation. And, except on one occasion, described earlier, no contributor to the Soweto film received any kind of payment.

However, conditions in the Tate & Lyle compound had been so distressing that we could not drive away without leaving money for people in dire need. The claim that those who spoke to us about their pay and working conditions were performers 'paid to make false statements' was a gross insult to all of them. Payment was our decision, and it was not mentioned to anybody until filming was over.

Editing hadn't started at the time Tate & Lyle made their complaint, and I suggested that we invite their representatives to a special screening so they could see everything we had filmed in that compound 'from clapperboard to clapperboard'. As all the interviews had been conducted through an interpreter, I also felt we should invite an independent academic, fluent in Zulu and Xhosa, to watch the footage with us. He or she would then be in a position tell us if there had been any prompting or retakes to achieve better 'performances'; anything, in fact, that might suggest that these were not genuine interviews.

The screening was attended by Sir Henry Saxon Tate, the managing director of Tate & Lyle at the time, and several of his senior colleagues. Also present was an expert in Southern African languages from the University of London.

When the lights came back on, I believe I was the first to break the silence. Could the linguist please give us his impressions?

He told us it was clear that these were spontaneous interviews, not performances.

Tate & Lyle now needed to look for other ways to discredit this material, and I'm afraid I gave them the opportunity. When I was asked who we had used as interpreter, I told them he was a legal clerk for David Naidoo, a highly respected Durban lawyer and the brother of a close friend of mine.

Passing on that information was a serious mistake, and it didn't take long for Tate & Lyle's local people to find the name of our interpreter, Simeon Gobo. The next thing we were told was that Simeon was 'a former employee of the Illovo Group, who had been fired for dishonesty'. According to Tate & Lyle, we had engaged an interpreter who held a grudge against the company.

It was hard to believe that someone who had worked so closely with us throughout that day had never mentioned this connection, but we took Tate & Lyle at their word. It was the second serious mistake.

Lord Windlesham asked me if Simeon had selected any of the fourteen people we had interviewed. Strictly speaking, he hadn't, but at one point I had spotted two men and a boy approaching the compound from a distance and asked Simeon to go up the hill to meet them. They were cane cutters, and once they had reached the compound, they agreed to talk to us. To remove any possible doubts, Lord Windlesham suggested that we should not use those interviews, and informed Tate & Lyle of his decision.

The next day, large advertisements appeared in all the leading British newspapers, accusing us of giving 'a totally unrepresentative picture of the company in South Africa' and claiming that 'already ATV has withdrawn three sequences after they were proved by us to be faked'. On that same day, I also managed to get through to David Naidoo, who assured me that Simeon was 'a very, very, honest guy', who had worked exclusively for him for many years. He had never been employed by the Illovo group.

Not only were Tate & Lyle putting my career in jeopardy with these false accusations but, much more importantly, their efforts to discredit the series were a terrible insult to all those black South Africans who had agreed to be interviewed in the series without hiding their identities so that the British people could 'see the truth in our faces'.

In spite of the way Tate & Lyle had behaved, Lord Windlesham remained true to his principles and insisted we be fair and open in all our dealings with them. They were sent transcripts of all the interviews, with the original Xhosa and Zulu texts in capital letters and English translations beneath. For this task, we had engaged two translators, who worked independently so that we could double-check for accuracy. If nothing else, these transcripts certainly confirmed that Simeon had translated my questions faithfully and had made no attempt to influence the answers.

The legal battle continued right up to the day of the broadcast, and well into the following year to prevent ATV from repeating the programme or releasing it in foreign countries that were showing the other two programmes in the series. The legal costs spiralled, and finally ATV decided that they could not continue. Lord

Windlesham had honoured his original promise that *Working for Britain* would be broadcast in the UK, whatever that took, but the film was not seen in any other country.

In response to the broadcast, the critics made it very clear where they stood on the Tate & Lyle issue: 'Antony Thomas demonstrates the extent to which the white regime is shored up by British collaboration in brutal economic suppression … A numbing, shaming film, particularly in its now-famous intelligence on Tate & Lyle.' (*Observer*)

'*Working for Britain* raised major questions about Britain's morality … Mr Thomas would have to be the greatest faker in history if he had fabricated the sights and sounds of people, suffering in last night's film.' (*Daily Express*)

According to an editorial in the *Times*: 'It is particularly unfortunate that Mr Thomas's powerful series, which raised vital issues and deserved and required serious examination, should be treated in this way.'

Two months after the broadcast, Tate & Lyle sold its share in the Illovo Group.

In March of the following year, the South African trilogy received the British Academy Award for the best factual television series of 1977.

Chapter Fifteen

DEATH OF A PRINCESS

In January 1978, when the *Daily Express* published its graphic front-page photo of an executioner's sword striking the neck of a kneeling figure, there was an accompanying article, providing the basic 'facts':

'The victims were Princess Misha'al, granddaughter of King Khalid's elder brother and a young student with whom she had eloped. Their crime: he was a commoner, and their marriage defied the Islamic family code.'

Different versions of the story soon appeared in magazines and newspapers across the world. In one account it was claimed that Princess Misha'al had actually married her lover in a secret ceremony conducted by 'a friendly sheikh'. Apparently, the couple were planning to flee the country together with the help of 'two Armenian air hostesses' but had been arrested in the attempt. Prince Muhammad, the King's elder brother, was so incensed by his granddaughter's decision to marry a commoner that he had insisted on this double execution.

Within a few days the *Daily Express* had revised its original version, on the basis of testimony given by Rosemarie Buschow, a German nanny who had been in Saudi Arabia at the time of the execution, looking after 'little Susu', the princess's baby cousin.

Buschow claimed to have had a close friendship with Misha'al and insisted that she had not been condemned to death for marrying a commoner. She was guilty of adultery. When Misha'al was in her early teens, the family had arranged a marriage between her and a royal cousin. It was a loveless match, but her husband refused to grant a divorce and, according to Buschow, 'the laws of Islam are clear. The lovers must die.'

In this version, the King and his elder brother, Prince Muhammad, were 'wise and fair leaders'. As soon as they heard that Misha'al had been arrested with her lover, they were 'heartbroken' and 'in tears', but 'they could not make an exception for one of their own family. They had to administer the law.'

For reasons which will become clear, I won't give the names of those who drew me deeper into this story, but a few weeks after the execution had made headlines, I was visiting an Arab friend who resides in Britain and has had a very successful career here. He had also given me support and advice when I was making the Arab trilogy in 1975.

The previous evening, he had been invited to dinner at the London home of one of the most powerful and influential figures within the Saudi establishment. After the ladies had retired to another room, his host launched an attack on the British media, which he accused of being heavily biased against Saudi Arabia. To give his guests a sense of the way the facts were being distorted, he offered to tell 'the true story' of this double execution.

Apparently, Princess Misha'al was a privileged member of the Saudi royal family and the favourite granddaughter of Prince Muhammad. When she was the right age, the family had chosen a suitable husband for her, but she had refused to fulfil the marriage contract. She already had the benefit of a good education in a Saudi school, and as soon as she reached university age, she had insisted on continuing her studies in Beirut.

In this environment, Misha'al was exposed to many different influences: radical Arab politics, women's liberation, Western values – all pulling in different directions. To make matters worse, she fell in love with a boy from her own country and made no attempt to conceal this relationship. When her studies were over, she persuaded her lover to return with her to Saudi Arabia, where they intended to challenge traditional values by living in an adulterous relationship.

The host assured his guests that executions for adultery were very rare in his country. Under Sharia law there must be four independent and honourable male witnesses, or eight independent and honourable female witnesses, to the sexual act before a guilty verdict can be passed. The only other way the accused can be condemned is out of his or her own mouth, by saying three times before the court: 'I have committed adultery.'

Apparently, the princess admitted her guilt at the very start of the trial, and the king immediately stopped the proceedings. He loved Misha'al and summoned her to his private rooms. Didn't she understand that if she admitted her guilt for a second and third time, he couldn't save her – her grandfather couldn't save her? All she had to do was to go back and promise never to see that boy again.

The princess returned to the court and repeated for a second and third time: 'I have committed adultery. I have committed adultery.' In a matter of seconds, she had condemned herself and the boy.

I was stunned by this version, which seemed to touch so many of the predicaments facing those in an extremely conservative Arab society, but the only way I could tell this story would be through drama. It would be a huge step for me, and before going any further, I needed some second opinions.

When working on the Arab trilogy, I had formed close friendships in Lebanon, Egypt and London, and my first impulse was to share the story with an Arab diplomat I respected and trusted. Did he believe the version I had been given, and if he did, could he understand why I felt such a strong commitment to the story?

He not only answered both questions in the affirmative, but went much further. In his opinion, it was a story 'that gets to the heart of the Arab predicament'.

'In Arab culture,' he explained, 'the family is everything, but how do you maintain that respect when you are separated from your parents by a gap of centuries? As I have already told you, my father never travelled more than ten kilometres on a donkey, and I am here, a serving diplomat.'

At this point, I stopped him. When doing documentary research, I always record important meetings. Would he mind if I used this little gadget on the understanding that nothing he said would be attributed to him? He was happy to proceed.

'To survive as an Arab,' he continued, 'you have to live in two different worlds at once. For some, it's difficult; for others it's impossible, like your princess. When she was forced back into the desert matrix again, she said: "No. No. No." She would rather destroy herself and the boy she loved. She could be any Arab girl in any Arab country. If you could tell that story …'

A Lebanese friend I met later that day was equally passionate. When I told her that I found it hard to understand how the princess could have stood before the court and condemned herself to death, her immediate response was: 'Then you don't understand the Arab character, the intense dedication to a cause, something uncompromising, something you Europeans don't have. We follow it to the death if necessary.'

That night, I sat down and wrote a proposal for a drama, which at that stage was based closely on the version of the princess's story I had been given. Looking at the document now, I can scarcely believe my naivety!

In my view, this version turns an ugly tale of Arab barbarism into one of the most moving accounts of a woman's predicament and eventual self-sacrifice that I have ever heard. It is no exaggeration to say that the final meeting between Misha'al and King Khalid stands on the level of some of the greatest moral confrontations in recorded history – Christ before Pilate, Saint Joan before a church court. It is also one of those rare combinations; a powerful love story that touches crucial political and social issues. Above all, it is true.

I presented the document to Charles Denton, who had given me such strong support with the South African trilogy. He not only agreed to provide initial research funding but was also confident that I could cope with the switch from documentary to drama and named a number of directors who had taken that route.

The next priority was to find a writer, and we chose Penelope Mortimer, a well-established journalist and novelist. Her semi-autobiographical book, *The Pumpkin Eater*, had also been the basis for a successful film, but before we could make a final commitment, I had to check the basic facts. The top priorities were meetings with the two witnesses who had already given their accounts to the press.

Barry Milner, the British carpenter, who had taken the enormous risk of photographing the execution, was in his mid-twenties, and was happy to welcome me to the terraced house in Yorkshire which he shared with his mother. His time in Saudi Arabia had been a life-changing experience, and not only on account of the execution. In that country, he was earning five times as much as he was paid in England, and now had enough money to put down a deposit on a new home. He and his fiancée were already house-hunting and were free to marry whenever they chose.

Like everyone else, Milner allowed me to record the meeting, and we started at the very beginning. How did he hear about the execution in the first place?

He told me he knew something serious was about to take place when he and his mates were returning from work at the end of their Friday shift. All traffic on the road to their hotel had been stopped, and they had to walk the rest of the way. When he asked 'the little Lebanese guy' at the hotel reception what was happening, he was told that 'some guy was up for the chop. He didn't say nowt about a princess. I thought it was one guy who was gonna get it.'

Milner went up to his room, which overlooked a stretch of wasteland where cars and trucks occasionally parked, but on this particular day he could see a number of vehicles and officials, protected from the gathering crowd by a ring of armed police.

Milner had never seen an execution, and after a quick shower and change, he decided to go out with his Instamatic hidden in a cigarette packet, 'with a little window cut out for the lens'.

When he left the hotel, crowds were continuing to build. 'They were coming out of the mosques. Funny, isn't it? Straight out of church and off to see a bloke get chopped.'

Barry pushed and shoved his way forward to get a better view, and finally caught a glimpse of a veiled woman and a young man being led out of two different vehicles.

'The guy's hands were tied behind his back. He looked as though he'd been drugged or beaten up. He was wobbling all over the pace. He wasn't resisting.'

'They led the girl off to the right-hand side, as I was looking at it. She was veiled, I didn't see her face. Then they knelt her down by this pile of sand. It's daft, but I had no idea what was going to happen to her. As far as I knew, there was just one guy who was going to get done.'

At that point, Milner decided to get a better view.

'There were these big iron wheels at the back, and all these Arab lads were perched on the wheels like vultures. So, I ran round the back of the crowd and made towards them. I was about halfway there when the shooting started.'

By the time Barry had climbed one of the wheels, the girl was already dead, 'just a black heap', but he was a first-hand witness to all that followed.

'Then they blindfolded the boy.'

'You mean they had made him watch the girl die?'

'Aye.'

'What did he do?'

'He hadn't got a lot about him. I don't think I would have been in his boots. They practically had to carry him to the middle of the square, and then they made him kneel. I tell you I was shaking. I've never seen anything like that before. They chopped him round the neck, both sides, and then at the back. Six blows.'

'And the crowd? How did they react?'

'Just the odd clap as it were being done, and then the bodies were loaded onto stretchers and chucked into the back of the trucks. The crowd pissed off, and that were it.'

Clearly, the description in the *Express* of 'thousands in the square, some of them children, throwing up their arms and cheering' was a case of creative journalism, but that was not my main concern. The savagery of this double execution did not fit well with Buschow's descriptions of a loving and caring grandfather, who, like his brother, the King, was 'heartbroken' and 'in tears' when they heard about Misha'al's transgression.

There was something else I didn't understand. When I was in Jeddah, working on *The Legacy of Faisal*, I was shown a courtyard in the old Turkish port where all executions were said to take place. Why was an exception made in this case?

I decided to raise these issues with Rosemary Buschow, who had left Saudi Arabia immediately after the execution and was now settled in London.

There is a curious contradiction here. As I had learnt to my cost, a documentary filmmaker who makes any kind of payment to those who give their testimony risks being accused of 'bribing them to make false statements', even if payment isn't mentioned until filming has finished, and the people concerned are in desperate need.

In drama, the rules are different. Buschow had been close to Misha'al and her testimony was vital. I was sure that she could provide important insights into the princess's character and help me resolve some of the contradictions that were emerging, but she wouldn't say a word until her agent had negotiated a fee with ATV and a contract had been signed.

I went to see Buschow on several occasions, but whenever I raised my queries about the execution, she always gave the same response: 'You tell your story, and I'll tell mine.' She wouldn't even answer the most basic question of all: 'Please tell me if the story I have been given is true – at least in its essentials.'

But there was one tantalising moment when she did open up. 'There she is! That's her!' She had produced a photograph of a slender girl in a white shirt and checked skirt, dancing solo to the delight of several young women who had gathered around her.

'She was so beautiful, slim; something of a wild animal.'

At that point, Buschow loaded a cassette. 'I always play this when I'm upset.' It was the pop song *Save Your Kisses for Me*, apparently one of Misha'al's favourites. Pressing two fingers together, Buschow whispered: 'She and I were just like that.'

****

I'm afraid patience is not one of my qualities. I was desperate to meet people who might have known Misha'al personally and decided to make a quick trip to Beirut. If I could discover which university she had attended, there was every chance I would be able to trace some of her contemporaries and get a real sense of the princess during her student years.

It was my first visit to Beirut since 1975, and I was shocked to see how much the city had suffered from three years of civil war. The beautiful Bab Idriss Square at the heart of the city was in ruins and, although fighting in the area had stopped, I could still hear the distant sounds of shelling and gunfire. As the taxi drove took me past the shattered ruins, I felt embarrassed to be here in pursuit of a love story which, at that stage, seemed to have no connection with the tragedy that was unfolding all around me.

On the following day, I had arranged separate meetings with two leading journalists, hoping that they would know which universities the princess and her lover had attended. One of them was sure that she would have been at the Beirut Women's College, but both warned me to be as discreet as possible with my inquiries. To stress the point, one of them produced a copy of a weekly magazine which had devoted a two-page spread to the princess's story, under the headline: THEY MET IN BEIRUT. Apparently, the people in internal security were so angry that they forced the magazine to shut down.

My version of the princess's story was broadly accepted by both journalists, but one of them insisted that I should not overlook the role that Misha'al's grandfather, Prince Muhammad, had played in this tragedy.

'A very notorious person. He was one of those who swept out of the desert, sword in hand, at his father's side. Ironically, he was also one of the original Arab playboys. In the early Fifties, he used to go abroad every year, drink, gamble, women. Although he is the oldest surviving son of Abdul Aziz and should by rights be king, he was passed over twice.'

According to this source, Prince Muhammad was known as 'the father of two evils'. 'Not just one evil; doubly evil', and when he heard what his favourite granddaughter had done, he flew into a rage. To save his honour publicly, he had to prove to everyone that 'he had the balls to take away her life'.

I questioned this. Surely the princess was responsible for her own death? 'If she had pleaded not guilty in court and there were no witnesses to the sexual act, she would be free, and the grandfather would have been powerless.'

'Absolutely right, but instead they were both set on this collision course. She carried the old man's seeds, as they say. She was also fiery-tempered, a bit wild. She acted first and thought afterwards. I quite agree. She brought it on herself.'

****

My days were spent visiting the universities and colleges, my evenings with friends. At that stage, I still believed the version of the princess's story that had sent me on this quest, and when I repeated it to friends, I was astonished how passionately some of them responded. The women, in particular, identified with Misha'al, and a Palestinian family I was close to immediately adopted her to their cause.

Their daughter Samia told me: 'I love that girl and understand why she chose to die.' Her mother also identified with Misha'al:

As a Palestinian, when I was deprived of my homeland and everything
that belonged to me, I had this feeling of revolt. I wanted to express it, but
nobody would give me an ear. I felt sometimes I was going to explode. I am

sure she came to that point herself. She had no other expression, except to die.

But you're identifying with someone from a highly privileged society, with every material possession; a princess.

But they contained her, like they've tried to contain the Palestinian revolution. They gave her all the material comforts of life, but she refused. She didn't want them. She wanted to *be* and not to have.

A close friend, whom I'll call Mona, also felt an immediate connection. Like the Princess, she had been born into a very conservative Arab family, but in her case, in Jordan. One of her earliest memories as a child was the moment when she stepped into the courtyard of the family home to see a servant girl dousing her clothes with petrol before setting herself alight. Little Mona screamed for help, but by the time this came, it was too late.

When Mona was several years older, her mother gave her the bare facts. It was shame that had driven that girl to take her life. She was pregnant, and as an unmarried woman, she would have been a social pariah once her secret was known.

As Mona traced her early life, there seemed to be so many parallels between her own experiences and Misha'al's. After a long, hard battle for the right to go to university, Mona finally succeeded, and left for the United States at the age of nineteen. As soon as she graduated, she returned to Jordan, where she found the family atmosphere insufferable. 'It was so claustrophobic – uncles, aunts – the whole extended family. Although I had been to university, I wasn't allowed to eat in the dining room: that was men's territory.'

Mona moved into a hotel, but the family soon traced her. 'They walked in and said: "We are the family", and they checked me out.' Eventually, Mona escaped to Beirut and, within a year, married the man of her choice. Fortunately, the family had given up by that time and, unlike Misha'al, Mona never confronted them with the man she loved.

These insights were completely unexpected. I was meeting people I had known for several years who were inspired by my version of Misha'al's story to reveal inner feelings and past experiences they had never shared with me before. Evening after evening was the same, but the daytime search for Misha'al's university was a different experience.

The war was having a serious effect on every institution I visited. Although none of them had been under attack, there were days, and sometimes whole weeks, when most of the students and staff felt it was unsafe to make the journey. Once again, I felt guilty to be focusing on Misha'al, and every time I discreetly mentioned her name there was always the same blank stare.

'No. She was never a student here.'

I never sensed that the truth was being hidden. Indeed, on two occasions, I was invited to check the college records.

****

'University! Of course, she was never at university. I could have told you that if you had waited for the contract to be signed before all this flying about. University! Her mind was like a fifteen-year-old. But her instincts, her feelings, those were very different. In those things, she was a woman.'

I was back in London. Rosemarie Buschow had finally signed her contract, the money had been paid, and she was ready to answer any questions about Misha'al. Penelope Mortimer was now with me, and we were ready for a long session in Buschow's London apartment.

She told us she had left for Saudi Arabia in February 1976, to look after little Susu, Misha'al's baby cousin. During her time there, she lived with his mother, Princess Moudi, 'in a palace full of women'. Misha'al lived in another palace with her parents. Susu's grandfather, Prince Muhammad, had a palace of his own.

'Three palaces in all?'

'No. Nine palaces. Everyone had a palace in Riyadh, the capital, a palace in Jeddah and a palace in the mountains.'

Buschow had a clear memory of her first meeting with Misha'al.

It was about three weeks after I arrived. We were all in the Riyadh palace. One morning I woke up and the whole place was full of rubbish, a mess. There had been a big party the night before, and all the princesses were sleeping. No one moved all day, except the servants. Then, at about five o'clock in the afternoon – I remember it so well – she was literally like a child. She started calling the baby 'my husband, my husband' – these royals all marry their cousins – and she told me she was just going to wait until little Susu was old enough to marry her.

Although Buschow and Misha'al barely understood a word of the other's language, they seemed to have an immediate connection, and from that moment, Misha'al became a regular visitor to the palace where Buschow lived.

As Buschow responded to our questions, a vivid picture emerged of the indulgent and vacuous lives of these largely uneducated princesses. When they eventually stirred, late in the day, the servants would lay out 'eleven costumes for them to choose from or go round to the boutiques and bring back the latest Paris fashions, all on approval, and when a princess has a bath, the servant runs the water and talks to her to cheer her up'.

'TV was the big thing. Not the local programmes, they were rubbish. But cassettes. We were always getting films and TV programmes. We saw *The Sound of Music* a dozen times. They knew every scene by heart. *Top of the Pops* used to come in every week, fresh from London.'

'But apart from partying and watching TV, what did these princesses actually do?'

'Nothing. Nothing.'

'Did they ever take any exercise?'

(With a giggle) 'Only, hopefully, making love.'

But Buschow was not going to be drawn out any further. As she reminded me, her contract was to talk to us about Misha'al, not the others.

She was certain that the princess had never been to Lebanon. As far as she knew, the family's visit to London in October 1976 was Misha'al's first trip abroad. In the early weeks, she stayed with her grandfather, mother and sisters in the family home in The Boltons, while Buschow and Susu were booked into a suite at the Park Royal Hotel, but she and Misha'al managed to see each other regularly.

Apparently, this visit had a profound effect on Misha'al, who was enchanted with the high-end shops in London's West End. On one occasion, she was coming out of a Bond Street jeweller's when she bumped into the man who had been chosen as her husband, all those years ago. For a moment, the two of them stared at each other in silence before he dived into a waiting car and was driven away.

One of Misha'al's early decisions was to have plastic surgery. She said she wanted a 'European nose so that she could be English, American, German, any nationality'. Except, presumably, Saudi Arabian.

In November, the family returned home, but Misha'al was allowed to stay in London, and moved into a suite next to Buschow's at the Park Royal. One evening, when the two women were alone together, Misha'al removed her necklace of black worry beads, which had a gold locket at the centre. She opened it to reveal a photo of a young man. 'Habibi, habibi. My darling, my darling. The beads are from my darling.'

Buschow had never met the young man, nor was she given his name. She wasn't even sure whether the romance was reality or fantasy.

In late December 1976, Misha'al, Buschow and Susu returned to Saudi Arabia. Another London holiday had been planned for the following summer, but Prince Muhammad suddenly cancelled all arrangements. A short while later, Buschow was given a solemn warning by an expatriate friend with close links to the royal family.

'There's trouble gathering around Misha'al, and if you get anywhere near her, you'll be caught too.'

'What has she done?'

'There's no need for you to know anything. Just keep off Misha'al's path.'

Everything came to a head in early July 1977, when Buschow was staying with Princess Moudi and her family in their Riyadh palace. After spending her day off at the home of her expatriate friend, she returned to the palace to discover that the place was almost empty. Only her personal servant and little Susu remained.

'I said to her: "What's happened? Where is everybody?" And [the servant] said: "Everybody go to Jeddah. Misha'al has drowned."'

Buschow was frantic. She tried to call the Jeddah palace, but the line was always engaged. Then, in the middle of the night, the phone rang. It was her employer, Princess Moudi. 'She said that Misha'al went for a midnight swim. She got drowned, and they found her clothes on the beach. The police and everyone are out on the water.'

Buschow could hardly believe this. A midnight plunge into the sea was not the sport of Arabian princesses, whose main concern was their coiffure, and the conditions along the stretch of coast where Misha'al's clothes had been found were challenging, even for an experienced swimmer.

> I said out loud: 'She's alive! I'm sure she's alive.'
>
> A week went by, maybe more. Then at last, a phone call. 'How's the baby?' It was his mother. I said: 'Never mind the baby, what's with the Princess?' And she said: 'She knew exactly what she was doing and the shame she brought on our family, and they had to be killed, both of them.'
>
> Can you imagine? The last thing I heard was that she had drowned. I said: 'What do you mean?' And she said, 'This is our law, and this is our country's habit; and if she had thought properly about it, she wouldn't have done it, but there was no choice.' And I said, 'What happened? What did they do to her?' And she said, 'They hurt her until she died.'

As she recalled this conversation, Buschow was close to tears, but I'm afraid I submitted her to a barrage of questions. There was so much that needed clarification.

Q Did anyone talk to you about a trial?

A There has to be a trial.

Q Yes, but if there was a trial, there must be four independent witnesses to the sexual act.

A What's wrong with that?

Q Nothing, except that it's practically impossible, or there must have been an admission of guilt. Was the girl you knew the type who could stand up before a court and condemn herself to death?

A A religious person is very loyal. They can't fiddle and make lies like we do.

Q But the princess? Was she the type who could die for her religion?

A I told you. None of us is going to know what happened in that court.

Q But why was she condemned to death? You implied that all the other women were having affairs.

A She had brought public shame. Everyone knew what she was doing. It was public.

Q So, it was public. It wasn't the immorality; it was the indiscretion?

****

So many unanswered questions.

It's hard to imagine any programme controller in today's television giving a producer the resources to continue an investigation when it was clear that the basic 'facts' in the original proposal were dubious, but Charles Denton still had faith in the project.

He had read the transcripts of the London and Beirut interviews and agreed that these took us far beyond a single graphic love story. We both felt that the drama should be shaped around the search for the truth about Misha'al. Those who had already talked to me, and others I would meet if we extended the research into Saudi Arabia, should be treated as characters in their own right; people who had been inspired by my original version of Misha'al's story to offer insights into their own lives and experiences they had never shared with me before. Above all, they would have a context, whether they were living through civil war in Lebanon, or coping with conditions in ultra-conservative Saudi Arabia.

In normal circumstances, the search for the truth about Misha'al would have been an ideal subject for a documentary, but the situation we were dealing with was far from normal. Only five of the many people we interviewed agreed that their identities could be revealed: Buschow, Milner and the Palestinian family in Lebanon.

At that stage, we still had no clear idea of the overall structure or the final conclusions, but in spite of all the uncertainties, Charles agreed to fund further research in Saudi Arabia, and this time Penelope would join me.

My documentary *The Legacy of Faisal* had been reasonably well received by the authorities, and they were happy to issue visas on the understanding that this visit would only be for research. For the second time in my career, I gave the authorities no idea of the subject we were investigating.

In October 1978, Penelope and I left for Saudi Arabia.

Our principal aim was to find out whether there really had been a trial and, if so, to learn as much as we could about the actual proceedings, but it was also important to give Penelope a real 'feel' of the country. We visited souks, fashionable boutiques and shops laden with electronic goods and expensive furniture. We took a good look at the palace where Buschow had lived – only from the outside, of course – and also located Milner's hotel and the actual site of the double execution.

Interviews had to be discreet. The only journalists we trusted were outsiders – one British and one American. Both of them were doubtful about the trial, but as far as they were concerned, Misha'al's story was yesterday's news, and neither of them had investigated the matter further.

Penelope and I had to be particularly careful when talking to Saudi journalists and local people. When we felt it was safe to raise the issue, most of them assured us that there had been a trial, but it was amazing how many different versions of a story can circulate in a country where news is heavily censored. One Saudi journalist told us that Barry Milner was 'a CIA plant', another that Misha'al had made the appalling mistake of returning to Saudi Arabia with the illegitimate child she had given birth to in France, but the most insane version was the one we heard at an evening gathering of expatriates. Apparently, there was a rumour doing the rounds that Princess Misha'al was still alive. To save his favourite granddaughter, Prince Muhammad had paid a vast sum to a Bedouin family for one of their daughters, who was substituted for Misha'al on the day of the execution.

If facts were in short supply, we did have an unforgettable experience on our first Friday in Saudi Arabia. We had hired a car and driver to take us to the historical city of Taif in the mountains east of Jeddah. As we drew close to the centre, crowds were gathering in the streets, forcing the driver to slow down to walking pace. Suddenly, he turned to us with a broad smile, drew a finger across his throat and whispered: 'Execution!'

It was a difficult decision, but I felt we had to witness this. If our project went ahead, we would have to recreate a public execution, and it was important to get a true sense of the crowd reaction. Would it be the chilling indifference Barry Milner had described in his interview – 'Just the odd clap as it were being done' – or would we see 'crowds, including children, throwing up their arms and cheering', as reported by the *Daily Express*?

After our driver found a parking space, we followed the crowds into an open square where three young men were awaiting execution. There was a strong police presence, but what immediately caught our attention was a group of men, clearly of European origin, standing close to a line of ambulances.

I asked the driver to find out what crimes the condemned men had committed, but all he could gather from those standing nearby were vague references to an orgy. It is well known that homosexuality is rife in Saudi Arabia because of the strict segregation of the sexes, and since no women had been condemned, I assumed these were gay men who had pushed the boundaries too far.

It is not easy to stay calm and dispassionate when faced with a scene like this, and I couldn't help looking away every time the executioner raised his sword, but one thing was certain. Each man was decapitated with a single stroke. Barbaric this certainly was, but it didn't match the horror that Barry Milner described when he witnessed the execution of Misha'al's lover: 'They chopped him round the neck, both sides, and then at the back. Six blows.'

But there was one important connection between Milner's experience and ours: the casual indifference of the crowd. There was no cheering, no applause, no 'jumping up and down', just a dull murmur every time the sword struck.

After the executions, the Europeans made quick examinations of the bodies before giving the all-clear for stretchers to be loaded into the waiting ambulances. If these men really were qualified doctors, it made their complicity even more shocking.

By this time, the spectators were already drifting away, and I cannot improve on Milner's description of those final moments: 'They just pissed off and that were it.'

****

Our top priority was to find out all we could about Misha'al's trial. We had told the authorities that we were anxious to learn as much as possible about the application of Sharia law. Would it be possible to visit the courts in Jeddah and perhaps talk to some of the Islamic lawyers and judges? We were assured that permission would be granted but, day after day, my calls and occasional visits to the Ministry were met with the same response: 'Perhaps tomorrow.'

One of the first people we contacted during that second week was a young lady I'll call Samira. Her uncle, a good friend of mine in Beirut, had put us in touch.

In her interview, Samira gave voice to those millions of Muslims who regard Wahhabism as a perversion of their faith. She spoke passionately about 'the democratic values of Islam' and the days 'when women led armies of the faithful into battle and were equal partners in marriage'. She also insisted that there was nothing in the *Qur'an* to suggest that women should be hidden beneath the veil, only that they should show modesty.

Like my Palestinian friends in Beirut and many others we had spoken to, Samira had adopted Princess Misha'al to her cause. 'By her actions she was saying: "Look at this blasphemy. Look what is being done to our women." She couldn't mix with like-minded people, as I do. She had to die to make her point.'

Another important outcome of that meeting was Samira's promise to put us in touch with a Saudi Arabian princess who was 'well-informed, someone we respect very much'.

The process took time, but it was worth the wait. Altogether, there were two interviews with this princess. Penelope was present during the first one but had already returned to London when I had a second and much longer meeting and was shown some very revealing 16mm footage she had taken. For obvious reasons, I cannot give her name or describe how and where we were able to meet. All I can say is that she was impressive and, unlike most of her kind, an educated woman, whom we called the Emira in the film.

During our interview with Rosemarie Buschow, she had hinted that the princesses 'caged up in those palaces' played dangerous sexual games but had refused to be drawn out any further. The Emira came straight to the point.

'To relieve their boredom, these princesses live the most intricate and busy sex lives. Very little romance. Quick liaisons. Sometimes cruel, always dangerous.'

'But how do they make contact with men?'

'The chauffeur and personal maid. They make the contacts and have the secrets. Of course, they're bribed, heavily bribed. The irony is that it's the women who choose the men. In a society as strict and tight as this, women are the predators. Men cannot choose, because of the veil.'

The Emira described some of the ways women made their choices. Apparently, there was a particular road in the desert, where men drove by slowly at dusk while the women watched from their cars. If they found a man attractive, they noted his number and told their chauffeur to make contact.

The sword dances on national days offered another opportunity. 'At night, in the desert; the women sitting in their cars in the dark, watching men, selecting their men. The men know that they are being watched, so they excel themselves.'

But if this kind of behaviour was commonplace, why, I asked, was Misha'al singled out? Did she and her lover flaunt their relationship?

'Not in that sense.' Like the other princesses, Misha'al had had several brief liaisons, but everything changed when she found someone she really loved.

According to the Emira, she had spotted him on a TV programme and felt an immediate attraction. Her chauffeur was then sent to trace him and deliver the message that an important letter was waiting for him in a boutique.

'It's an old trick, but he wasn't a prince or someone accustomed to these games … And there she was, waiting for him. A royal princess.'

'But wasn't he aware of the dangers?'

'Of course, he was. He was very frightened at first, but she was a powerful little thing.'

'They planned to run away together when she was on her next holiday in London, but her grandfather had received reports about the women's behaviour on the previous visit and gave the orders: "No more trips abroad."'

Misha'al rebelled. She adopted a role. She became an actress, playing a part in a half-understood world of picture magazines, movies and tragic love songs, and when her family moved to their beachside villa, she devised a dangerous and complicated way to escape with her lover.

'She persuaded her mother to let her go for a midnight swim. The boy was waiting for her. She left a set of clothes on the beach to fake a drowning, and off she went with him.'

Two people we met claimed they had caught sight of the couple in the days that followed, but in entirely different locations – a fashionable seaside resort and an isolated and rather run-down beach hotel – but one fact was indisputable. If Misha'al and her lover were serious about leaving the country together, they were wasting valuable time. Four days had elapsed since Misha'al left her clothes on the beach, and there was still no sign of a body despite an extensive search by boat and helicopter. By now the family was suspicious, and all airports were put on alert.

The Emira was not prepared to dismiss this as mere stupidity. She understood how much those four days of physical intimacy with a man she loved must have meant to Misha'al, but she also believed that she would have known there was no future in this relationship. He was educated; she could barely read and write. She even lacked the most basic domestic skills, and if they managed to escape together, there was always the risk that the family would track them down.

According to the Emira, Misha'al had insisted that the two of them should check in separately at the airport – for his safety. Since a Saudi woman is not permitted to travel unaccompanied by a male, she disguised herself as a boy. It was a desperate ploy; in the Emira's view, Misha'al would have known this from the start.

'We have a saying in Arabic: "A thief isn't caught unless he wants to be caught."'

Misha'al was spotted very quickly and arrested. To her great distress, the police went off in search of the boy, who was waiting for her in the departure lounge. The couple were then driven away in separate vans.

****

By the time I met the Emira, I had already been to the Islamic Courts in Jeddah and knew the tragic sequel. The Ministry had provided me with a 'translator/ minder', and I spent an entire morning attending a trial and speaking to several lawyers, one of whom really stood out. He spoke excellent English, and when he invited me to his office to continue our discussion I accepted immediately. Happily, the minder did not think it was necessary to join us.

As soon as we were alone together, I posed the crucial question. 'The princess who was tried for adultery? It's hard to imagine the King going to one of the courts I've seen today. Where was she actually tried?'

He answered without a moment's hesitation:

> There was no trial. The couple were taken straight from the airport to Prince Muhammad's palace. On the following Friday they were executed by his own bodyguards. The King was against it, but the Prince is outside the law. Honour! 'He who gives life has the right to take it away.' That's not the law of Islam, it's the law of the tribe.

Everything fell into place, including the unusual choice for the site of the execution, but there was something else I found particularly shocking. Under Sharia law, as practiced in Saudi Arabia, six is the maximum number of blows permitted in an execution and is reserved for those found guilty of a particularly heinous offence. The usual punishment for an unmarried man who has had sexual intercourse with a married woman is a hundred lashes, but to avenge the gross dishonour to his family, the 'Father of Two Evils' had subjected the boy who had eloped with his granddaughter to the cruellest punishment permitted under Sharia law.

Chapter Sixteen

ACTION AND REACTION

The princess who had drawn me into this story was a self-confident university graduate who dared to live in an open relationship with the boy she loved and had chosen to condemn herself to death rather than compromise her principles.

The real Misha'al was a nineteen-year-old who could barely read and write and was totally unprepared for the realities of life; someone – to quote Rosemarie Buschow – 'with the mind of a fifteen-year-old, but the instincts and feelings of a woman'. Yet, in her own immature way, she had challenged the system. She had refused the husband the family had chosen for her and made one desperate attempt to break free with the boy she loved.

The original version of Misha'al's story had inspired Arab friends to give me extraordinary insights into their lives and express feelings they had never shared with me before. She was the one who had given this journey meaning, and I was now more determined than ever to try and describe the whole experience on film.

It would be an expensive project, with a budget far in excess of anything required for a standard documentary. To fund this film we would have to involve a number of foreign broadcasters, but before we could make the first approaches, we needed a final script, a budget and a schedule. Most important of all, we had to find an Arab country where we would be allowed to film.

Charles Denton had already given me generous support, but to take us through all these additional stages we needed another backer, one who would be prepared to share the costs and risks involved.

The one person who immediately came to mind was David Fanning, executive producer of WGBH WORLD, the leading documentary arm of the Public Broadcasting Service in the United States. We first met when he came to London to view the Japanese trilogy, which was subsequently broadcast in the US under the WORLD banner. Since then, we had remained in close contact.

I sent David a synopsis outlining the shape of the film as I saw it, as well as transcripts of the key interviews. His initial response was positive, and after a number of phone calls, he came to London for a meeting with Penelope and me.

The rules that David and I had agreed were now clear. At one level, this would be a dramatisation of my journey from Britain to Lebanon and Saudi Arabia in search of the truth about the princess. To protect the identities of those we interviewed, all names would be changed; for consistency those included Buschow and Milner, who became Grüber and Jackson, while the investigator would be called Christopher Ryder. For added protection, the occupations and ages of all the Arabs I interviewed would be changed. My friend the senior diplomat became a university lecturer, and as already explained, the woman who had dared to describe Wahhabism as 'a perversion of Islam' would be given a completely different name and background. She became Samira, a teacher in a Saudi girls' school.

While identities would be fictionalised, the content of the original interviews had to be respected in the strictest way. As is perfectly acceptable in the documentary tradition, these interviews would be edited, but no opinion would be expressed, or statement made, unless it came from an original source.

To follow Christopher's journey, we would need to film in Lebanon, but Saudi Arabia was not an option. In part, we would have to rely on material we had shot when making the documentary on King Faisal – establishing shots of the streets, the souks, the boutiques and upmarket stores, as well as our coverage of the girls' school in Jeddah, which would provide a context for Samira.

The biggest challenges were dramatisations of key incidents recalled by witnesses whose testimony we trusted. These included the executions of Misha'al and her lover, the first meeting between Buschow and Misha'al, and the arrests at the airport. Here the settings had to be as authentic as possible, and any dialogue would have to be in Arabic. While we would be able to film the first stage of Ryder's journey in the authentic Beirut settings, any attempt to stage a public execution in a country in the throes of civil war was out of the question. Apart from that, the Lebanese landscape was unsuitable for some of the key scenes we needed. Somehow, we would have to find another Arab country where we would be permitted to film key moments in this story, including the double execution.

While David returned to Boston and Penelope settled down to write the script, I set off on a tour of North African countries – Algeria, Tunisia and finally Egypt, where my timing could not have been better. A month before I arrived, Egypt had signed the Camp David Accord with Israel. Saudi Arabia's furious response had pushed that country's relationship with Egypt to an all-time low. I also had many friends in Egypt, including Youssef Chaheen, the leading film producer/director in the Arab world at that time, and dear Salah Jaheen, who had done so much to help me when I made *Out of the Ashes of Victory* in Egypt in 1974.

Salah was with me when I presented synopses of the film to the Censorship Department, the Ministry of Culture, and the Foreign Film Department. Within a week, filming permission was granted, but on one condition. No mention should be made of Saudi Arabia. We all knew this was a game and that the main incidents and the characters involved – even the way they were dressed – would make the setting very clear, but I stuck to my word. King Khalid, Prince Muhammad and Princess Misha'al were never mentioned by name. They were simply the King, the old Prince and the Princess, while the main cities in the story – Jeddah and Riyadh – were not identified.

Once filming permission was granted, I spent several weeks looking for locations and going through all the costs with Youssef before returning to London.

Penelope Mortimer was now ready to present the first draft of her script. It was a huge disappointment. She had strayed far away from the original interviews, and invented palace scenes, including one in which the old Prince and the princesses spoke to each other in English. David insisted that she start again and stick closely to the transcripts, but Penelope would not accept this. In her words, it would reduce her status to that of a 'highly-priced copy-typist', and she withdrew from the project.

In spite of his responsibilities as head of a major documentary department, David was willing to set aside all the time needed to prepare the script. We spent an initial week at his house in Massachusetts, cutting up sections of the transcripts and pasting them on sheets of paper as we tried to work out a final structure.

Once we had a version that we were both happy with, I took this to Charles for his approval and also had it checked by experts, Arab and British, whom we trusted. Charles then appointed a co-producer, Martin McKeand, who worked with me on a schedule and a final budget. It was now time to pull out all the stops in the search for co-funding.

It was a long process, but by the summer of 1979, we had firm commitments from broadcasters in Germany, Canada, the Netherlands, Australia and New Zealand, as well as an agreement with a New York distributor who was granted residual rights in all other countries.

Without a doubt, the actual filming was the most satisfying part of the process. I had a fine cameraman in Ivan Strasburg and two outstanding actors in the main roles – Judy Parfitt as Buschow/Grüber and Paul Freeman as Christopher Ryder, the investigator. Paul played the role with subtlety and conviction, and it would come as no surprise that he was snapped up by Hollywood shortly after the US broadcast and given a major role in *Raiders of the Lost Ark*. A very successful career followed.

When it came to casting the Arab roles, my initial concern was finding actors capable of giving us the feeling of an authentic, spontaneous interview. From all I had seen on Arab TV, there seemed to be a strong tendency to overdramatise, but I need not have worried. All the Arab actors we cast understood the importance of toning everything down to a convincing, conversational level. Interestingly, three people interviewed during research asked to appear in the film, and it was impossible to distinguish their spontaneous interviews from the scripted statements delivered by the Arab actors, many of whom felt equally strongly about the issues we were dealing with.

Last, but certainly not least, was the lovely Suzanne Abou Taleb, a second-year student at a Cairo drama school, who played the role of Princess Misha'al with such warmth and spontaneity.

Six weeks before *Death of a Princess* was broadcast, I arranged special screenings of the programme in London, Beirut and Cairo.

In the light of all that would happen later, it's extraordinary to look back at the letter I wrote to Lord Windlesham, managing director of ATV, three weeks before the UK broadcast of *Death of a Princess*. To quote the opening paragraph:

> I have just returned from a trip to Beirut and Cairo. As I mentioned to you, I was afraid of all sorts of reactions under Saudi Government pressure – actors claiming that they had not fully understood the implications of the script, the Egyptian Censorship department alleging that I had bribed the lady censor who had been present during all the filming.
>
> My imagination was, I'm afraid, running wild. After the horrible series of 'dirty tricks' that followed the showing of *The South African Experience*, I am happy to report that all these fears were groundless.

In the letter, I listed the names of all the government officials who had attended special screenings of the film in Lebanon and Egypt together with all the Arab actors who took part, and assured Lord Windlesham that the response was very positive at both events:

> Habin Latif, the Director General of Information and Tourism in Lebanon was so moved by *Death of a Princess* that he invited me to make a film about 'the Pain of the Lebanon' with the full support of his government and with absolute freedom of interpretation, and when I asked his Egyptian equivalent whether he had any concerns about the Saudi response, he replied: 'They know that if they attack the film, they will only help to publicise it, and they are far too intelligent to do that.'

Out of all the actors, there was only one who asked not to be given a credit. Apparently, he had business links with a Saudi company.

I ended my letter to Lord Windlesham with the following assurance: 'After this trip to Egypt and Lebanon, I feel that we will be spared any of the unpleasantness that followed the broadcast of *The South African Experience*.'

How wrong I was!

****

What all of us had possibly overlooked was a crucial event that took place while we were editing *Death of a Princess*.

In November 1979, some five hundred heavily armed Wahhabi extremists, led by Imam Juhayman al-Otaybi, occupied the Grand Mosque in Mecca, Islam's holiest shrine.

After taking the worshippers hostage, the invaders chained the gates shut and broadcast their demands through the mosque's loudspeakers. The House of Saud must be overthrown, they demanded, 'because it is corrupt, ostentatious and has destroyed Saudi culture by an aggressive policy of Westernisation'. Oil exports to the United States should be stopped. Non-Muslims should be expelled from the country, television abolished, and female education brought to an immediate end.

The siege of Mecca lasted for over two weeks and was finally broken when Saudi forces, working under the direction of three members of the French intelligence service, drilled holes into the courtyard of the mosque and dropped grenades into the rooms below, indiscriminately killing hostages and driving the remaining rebels into open areas where they could be picked off by sharpshooters.

Juhayman and sixty-seven of his fellow rebels finally surrendered. Sixty-three of them, including Juhayman, were publicly executed in the squares of eight Saudi cities.

King Khalid decided that the safest way to cope with this challenge was not to fight extremism but to concede. For a while, women were forbidden to perform any further role in television, either as announcers, interviewees or characters in drama. Cinemas and music shops were shut down, and the religious police were encouraged to become more assertive. School curricula were changed to provide many more hours of religious studies, and gender segregation was extended 'to the humblest coffee shop'.

At a sensitive time like this, a film in which one character describes Wahhabism as 'a perversion of Islam' and another claims that royal princesses lived 'intricate and busy sex lives' was likely to be highly inflammatory.

The Saudi authorities were alerted to the film by the pre-publicity in the week preceding the UK broadcast. *Death of a Princess* was described as 'a stunning two-hour film' (*Daily Express*), which 'unearths a mass of contradictions and extraordinary insights into the moral and political dilemmas of Arabs in the modern world' (*Observer*). The *Sunday Times* reviewer wrote that 'a dramatised film has to be very good to tell a greater truth than a documentary. This is such a film. It should in time win all the awards going.'

The UK broadcast on 9 April 1980 set off a firestorm. One journalist described it as 'probably the biggest single incident on an international scale, involving a television film, since television was created'.

The British ambassador was expelled and four hundred members of the Saudi royal family, living or holidaying in Britain, were recalled. The Saudis also threatened to impose sanctions on British business interests in their country and to break formal ties with the United Kingdom.

All this was happening at a time when the Saudis were planning to spend 120 billion dollars on a five-year plan that offered many opportunities to British companies. The Saudi Air Force was largely equipped with British fighters and some two thousand employees of the British Aircraft Corporation were running the air defence system. Altogether, thirty thousand Britons were working in that country, and Britain was also heavily dependent on Saudi oil.

Death of a Princess prompted an intense debate in the media on questions of economic responsibility versus freedom of expression, but nine days after the broadcast there was no longer any need to wrestle with these difficult issues. Those who opposed the film could dismiss *Death of a Princess* as a work of fiction, thanks to a letter from Penelope Mortimer which was published in the *New Statesman* on 18 April 1980.

In it she wrote:

With the exception of Barry Milner, the British carpenter, who had already sold his story to the *Daily Express* [and] Rosemarie Buschow … every interview and every character in the film is fabricated. The 'revelation' of the domestic lives of the Saudi princesses – man-hunting in the desert, rendezvous in boutiques – was taken entirely on the evidence of an ex-patriate divorcee, as was the story of the princess first seeing her lover on Saudi television. No real effort was made to check up on such information. Rumour and opinion somehow came to be presented as fact.

Thomas says that this is the most honest film he has ever made (presumably including the much-awarded *South African Experience*) and fabrication isn't necessarily dishonest: it simply means that the audience, foolishly believing it to be authentic, is conned.

I have no idea what prompted Penelope to write that letter. She had seen the film six weeks before the broadcast, was full of praise and wanted confirmation that she would receive a credit.

She was not present when I had my main interview with the Emira, which included the screening of 16mm film footage she had taken in Saudi Arabia, nor was she involved when David and I worked hard to get sufficient evidence to support the Emira's testimony.

I wrote to Penelope immediately and received a jocular reply in which she described her original letter as 'a fairly light-hearted statement in the *New Statesman* which one assumes is read by friends'.

In a letter the journal published the following week, David Fanning challenged Mortimer's claim that 'every interview and every character is fabricated':

> For a writer of Ms Mortimer's reputation and skill, this is a careless and misleading phrase. It implies that *Death of a Princess* is a work of fiction. In fact, the dialogue is a careful assembly of research and transcriptions of actual interviews. I have read those transcripts and assisted in corroborating the controversial facts in the film. It is, however, the identity of the characters who speak these words that has been 'fabricated', in a conscious effort to disguise their source. The hysteria of the official Saudi reaction to the film only confirms that this was a wise and legitimate decision.

The following week, the *New Statesman* published a second letter from Penelope Mortimer in which she wrote: 'By fabricated I meant manufactured or constructed; if I had meant invented or forged, I would have said so.'

Yes, we edited the interviews, just as we do when working on any documentary, and if that is what Penelope meant by 'manufactured and constructed', she should have stated it clearly in her original letter. But nobody took any notice of her later qualification.

Instead, there was a furious reaction to *Death of a Princess*, solely on the basis of the first letter. In a Parliamentary debate on 24 April, Sir Ian Gilmour, the Lord Privy Seal, told the House that:

> There were undoubtedly incidents in the film, as we know from Mrs. Penelope Mortimer, that had virtually no factual basis at all, and were based on innuendo and rumour. They should not have been shown. The dressing up of alleged fact in fiction is not only objectionable to our foreign relations, but strongly objectionable in films relating to this country.

During that debate, the attacks became increasingly personal. One MP who sounded off was Nicholas Winterton. He had failed miserably in his attempt to defend the South African government during the discussion programme that followed the broadcast of the South African trilogy, and was now taking his revenge.

'Is my honourable friend aware that some of us on the Government benches would wish to apologise to the Saudi Arabian Government for the insult and discourtesy shown to them in this film? Is he further aware that the producer of the film, Antony Thomas, has a history of producing inaccurate and biased films?'

Perhaps he was thinking of the Tate & Lyle controversy, but he didn't offer any examples.

Penelope's letter also set off a number of personal attacks in the press. A particularly vicious article appeared in the satirical weekly *Private Eye*. The seventeen-year gap that separated *Anatomy of Apartheid* from the three-part *South African Experience* was ignored, and the impression given that the films were made simultaneously. 'He was paid by the South Africans to make the first one and British television to make the second.' *Private Eye* had also been in touch with Chris van der Walt, the director of information at the South African embassy. Like Nicholas Winterton, he had come off badly in the discussion programme that followed the screening of the South African trilogy, and now took his revenge by claiming that *Anatomy* 'was too pro-apartheid to be used. It was embarrassing and could not be shown.'

Lies, lies and more lies. Until the early Seventies, the government used *Anatomy* as a major propaganda tool to spread the message across Europe and the United States that apartheid had evolved into a system respectful of black culture and black rights to independence in self-governing homelands. I had also been present on the one occasion when the film was shown to an all-white cinema audience in South Africa. The response had been so hostile that it was never shown in the country again.

But all these attacks paled in comparison to the treatment of the Arab actors who had been credited in the film. The Saudis did everything in their power to end their careers, and when Salah Jaheen called me about this, I told him they shouldn't hesitate to claim that they had never seen the full script or the finished film if that would help the situation.

When diplomatic cables were released thirty years later, they provided an astonishing record of the pressure the Saudi Government had put on countries across the world (including the co-producing countries) not to show the film.

Fortunately for the governments involved, there was no longer any need to wrestle with difficult issues of freedom of speech versus economic responsibility. Penelope had given them an easy way out. 'Every interview and every character' were 'fabricated'. This was clearly not a film that should be shown in their country. Even ITV finally caved in, refusing to enter *Death of a Princess* in any film festival.

Meanwhile, the pressure on PBS was phenomenal. The programme was scheduled to air in the US on 19 May 1980, giving all those who opposed the broadcast plenty of time to mount their attacks. Warren Christopher, the Acting Secretary of State, urged PBS not to show the film. Mobil Oil, which had extensive interests in Saudi Arabia and was also a significant PBS funder, ran advertisements in five leading newspapers, including the *New York Times*, claiming that *Death of a Princess* was a work of fiction: 'A New Fairy Tale.' They based their case for suppression solely on the evidence of the Mortimer letter, which was quoted in full without, of course, any reference to her later qualifications or David's letter of reply.

To add to the furore, a class action lawsuit was instituted by a Muslim group in California on behalf of:

- 'More than six hundred million followers of the Islamic faith throughout the world.
- More than 3 million followers of the Islamic faith in the United States.
- More than 500,000 followers of the Islamic faith in Canada.
- American employees working in Saudi Arabia.
- Americans who are committed to a respect for world and Islamic traditions.'

The plaintiffs described *Death of a Princess* as:

… part of an international conspiracy to insult, ridicule, discredit and abuse followers of Islam throughout the world and the kingdom of Saudi Arabia.

The conspirators are committed to prevent the orderly spread of Islam, because they believe Islam constitutes a major barrier to their planned illegal acquisition of Arab lands, including Jerusalem and the preservation of apartheid practices in South Africa.

The exact monetary damages to the class of plaintiffs cannot be completely ascertained, however it might well exceed $20 billion.

The action was dismissed by the Californian court as 'bordering on the frivolous'.

In spite of all this pressure, Lawrence Grossman, the president of PBS, stood firm. 'We plan to schedule the program. We have great faith in the program. It's a program of integrity. It was made responsibly, and we intend to broadcast it.'

When *Death of a Princess* was finally shown, it garnered the largest audience public television had ever achieved up to that time, and the reviews were outstanding. 'It was Public Television's finest hour … not only because of the quality of the film itself – which was as remarkable to read as it was fascinating to watch – but also because of public television's seeming resistance to almost impossible pressures from government and corporate backers alike to supress the film.'

In 2005, on the twenty-fifth anniversary of the first broadcast, *Death of a Princess* was shown again on the PBS network. In Britain, ITV was too frightened to do the same, but on this occasion the Saudis were silent. Perhaps they had learnt from past experience.

There was an interesting comment in the *New York Times* review, pointing out how little had changed in Saudi Arabia during the years between the two broadcasts.

Twenty-seven documentaries followed *Death of a Princess*, and in all that time there was never a suggestion of faking or misrepresentation, except on one occasion. A member of a Shi'a group in London claimed that my interpreter had mistranslated a question I had put to a senior ayatollah I interviewed in our 2008 film *The Qur'an*.

Other than that, I had a clear run!

Chapter Seventeen

TRADERS IN DEATH AND DESTRUCTION

On the morning of 22 December 1979, eight detectives were on standby in a suite on the 27th floor of a New York hotel. Two of them were surveillance experts, who had been taking it in turns to record all conversations in the adjacent suite for nearly three days. The others were armed and ready for immediate action.

All their attention was focused on a series of business meetings taking place in the next-door suite. Two of those involved were major players in the illegal arms trade. Their 'clients' were Jose Raad and Jimmy Rodriguez, working undercover for the New York City police.

Following a tip-off, the two Spanish-speaking detectives had contacted the suspects, posing as leading players in a far-right terrorist group operating in South America. Jose Raad played the part of *el padrone*, the 'big boss', who had no understanding of English, while Jimmy Rodriguez acted as translator and weapons expert, a role he was well qualified to play.

Their performances were so convincing that the suspects had already introduced them to their main weapons suppliers, and it was now time for both parties to draw up a final contract, specifying the weapons that would be provided. The final list included ten thousand machine guns, poisons, explosives and a silenced sniper rifle.

As soon as both parties had signed, Rodriguez handed over a down payment of $56,000 in cash. At that point, he picked up the hotel telephone, dialled a blank line and ordered 'coffee, doughnuts and a French cruller'.

It was the signal the squad next door had been waiting for, and within seconds, detectives stormed the suite, weapons at the ready.

The two suspects were handcuffed and driven under armed guard to the criminal courts at 100 Center Street, where they were fingerprinted and photographed in the squad room on the ninth floor.

In New York police records, they are listed as:

Terpil, Frank Edward. Date of Birth: November 2nd, 1939. Place of Birth: Brooklyn, New York. Height: 5' 11". Weight: 215 lbs. Hair: Brown. Race: White.

Korkola, George Gregory, nickname Gary. Date of Birth: February 9th 1942. Place of Birth: Detroit, Michigan. Height: 5' 11". Weight:175 lbs. Hair: blond. Race: White.

It was clear to all involved that Terpil was the leading figure in this partnership, and he was certainly a man with an interesting history. After joining the army at the age of nineteen, he had been recruited by the CIA.

In 1972, according to the official version, Terpil left the agency and went into 'private practice', selling weapons and assassination devices to anyone who was prepared to pay. Apart from the machine guns and a silenced sniper rifle, he had offered the undercover detectives poisons, exploding briefcases and a pen that fired a poison dart through a Teflon barrel, which was recommended for discreet assassinations on aeroplanes.

During the many hours they had spent together, Rodriguez had secretly recorded twenty-five hours of conversation in which Terpil boasted of his links with the CIA and Scotland Yard as well as an astonishing assortment of dictators and terrorists, including Colonel Gaddafi, the Libyan head of state, Ilich Ramírez Sánchez, known as Carlos the Jackal, Idi Amin, the former president of Uganda, and Amin's competitor in terror, the self-styled Emperor Bokassa.

Shortly before midnight on the day of their arrest, Terpil and Korkola were arraigned in court, but in spite of the serous changes against them, they were released on bail after each had posted bonds of $100,000.

Four months later, Frank Terpil was arrested again. This time, he and another former CIA agent, Edwin P. Wilson, were indicted by the federal authorities in Washington DC on charges including 'acting as an agent for a foreign power' – to wit, Libya – 'transportation of explosives in foreign commerce and conspiracy to commit murder', but once again both defendants were released on bail.

In September 1980, just days before the start of the New York trial, Wilson, Terpil and Korkola fled the country. Terpil flew out of Washington DC on a forged passport and headed for the Middle East, abandoning his wife, Marilyn, his two boys and a lavish home barely a mile away from CIA headquarters in Langley, Virginia.

Both court cases proceeded without them, and on 5 May 1981, Terpil and Korkola were found guilty in absentia of all eleven charges against them in the New York indictment. Acting judge Thomas P. Gallagan recommended that both men serve the maximum term the law allowed: 53 years.

In court, he said: 'These men trade in death and destruction. They have no allegiance to any flag. They prosper in a world at war. Wherever terrorism and torture are, they are.'

****

At the time of the Terpil trials, David Fanning and I were working together on a very different project. Shortly after the broadcast of *Death of a Princess*, Twentieth Century-Fox invited us to Hollywood to discuss ideas for a feature film. Our first proposal was *Surrender to Everest*. We wanted to build on everything we had learnt from *Death of a Princess* and offer another dramatisation based on real events.

Our proposal was accepted at the first meeting, and David and I signed on for membership of the Writers Guild of America, but we had barely finished the first draft of the script when the WGA called a strike. All meetings and discussions had to stop, and it was predicted that this was likely to be a long-term dispute.

Apart from the frustration of having to set the work aside, there were serious financial implications. Fortunately for David, he had been able to stay with his wife Karen in her parents' home in Laguna beach, but I was in expensive accommodation, courtesy of Twentieth Century-Fox. The monthly rent would now be my responsibility.

After several more weeks had passed with no end in sight, David was contacted by Jim Hougan, an investigative journalist with an impressive record. Apparently, Frank Terpil had phoned him on an open line from Beirut, asking for his help to 'present the defence side of my case via TV and cine media'.

David and I both felt that we should take this opportunity, even if it meant putting our current work aside and returning to it later. The Terpil case touched many important issues that Jim had raised in his highly acclaimed book published a year before Terpil's arrest. *Spooks: The Haunting of America* gives a chilling account of the way thousands of 'spooks', trained by the CIA, the FBI and other key agencies, retire from government service to sell their skills in wiretapping, computer penetration and industrial espionage to large corporations and wealthy individuals. Some take their clandestine crafts even further, 'arranging coup d'états and selling murderous devices to fugitive millionaires and Third World fascists alike'.

Terpil was not on Jim's radar when *Spooks* was written, but during his time on bail he had called Jim to say that he had read his book and knew many of the principal players. Why didn't the two of them get together for a drink? Several meetings followed, and when Terpil fled the country, Jim was one of the first people he contacted.

While I agreed with David that this was an important subject, it would mark a turning point for me. For the very first time, I would be focusing on one man, and if the accounts I had read about Terpil were correct, I could no longer perform the role of sympathetic listener. I would have to be an interrogator.

The first priority was to meet Terpil and find out how he would deal with some of the toughest charges against him. Would he give us real insights into his character and the way he operated, or would we get nothing more than a series of monosyllabic denials?

After several messages back and forth, Terpil agreed to meet Jim and me in the Sheraton Hotel, Damascus.

'Trader in death and destruction.'

I'll never forget my feelings as the elevator moved us slowly upwards towards Terpil's room on the fourth floor. Jim was surprisingly relaxed, but phrases like 'trader in death and destruction, terrorism and torture' and 'major supplier of assassination devices' kept resonating in my mind.

Finally, we reached Terpil's room. The door opened, and we received a warm greeting from a jovial middle-aged man dressed in a crumpled safari jacket. He was bald, overweight and sported a thick black moustache; nothing about him or his manner seemed threatening. He immediately introduced us to his partner, Ruth Broca, a lovely Filipina in her early thirties who clearly adored him.

As soon as we had settled down, and without any prompting from Jim or me, Terpil launched into stories about Gaddafi and the other tyrants he had served. As he laughed and joked about Idi Amin's secret passion for Princess Margaret and the evenings he spent in the dictator's massage parlour, listening to records of Scottish pipe bands, I began to feel that we hadn't been invited here to deal with questions of innocence or guilt, but to join Terpil in a world with no moral coordinates. Some people – people like Terpil – were a lot smarter (and wittier) than others, and that was the only distinction that mattered.

When I raised some of the most serious allegations, there were no denials, and no offence was taken. Terpil was happy to deal with every question on his own terms. 'Was it true that you supplied interrogation equipment and torture equipment to Idi Amin?'

'What's torture equipment? The Chinese used slow water-drip treatment, but I don't feel that all water exports should be controlled by license!' (Laughter.)

'You seem to make a complete distinction between what you supply and what it might be used for. Do you ever stop to think of the consequences for ordinary human beings?'

'I'm sure the people from Dow Chemicals didn't think of the consequences of selling napalm. I doubt if they feel any more responsible for the ultimate use than I did for my equipment.'

This was not my first encounter with evil. The Abbot of Hoke Kyo admitted to multiple murders 'for the sake of my country'. Those who banished Sandra Laing from their community and asked God to bless their guns were also secure in their belief that they were following His command, but Terpil didn't need any ideological cover. Life, all of life, was a joke.

But my interest in the subject went beyond character. Terpil's actions and experiences raised some crucial questions. How was it possible for someone like him to acquire and sell vast quantities of lethal equipment to dictators and tyrants across the world? How did he manage to slip so easily out of the United States, just days before the start of a federal trial that had attracted serious media attention? (Terpil actually showed us the forged passport he used when he jumped bail, and it was hard to imagine any border control officer being fooled by it.)

Above all, there was the issue of his relationship with the CIA. Was Terpil really discharged from the Agency in 1972, or was he chosen to play the role of 'a trader in death and destruction' to gain the trust of terrorists and other enemies of the United States so that he could feed valuable information back to the Agency?

Or was the truth somewhere in between – that this was a man who had genuinely gone out on his own, and had been allowed to continue his lethal trade for seven years because of the occasional snippets of crucial information he was able to pass back to the CIA?

****

Two months after that first meeting, David, Jim and I flew to Beirut with the team, which included Ivan Strasburg, the director of photography who had made such an important contribution to *Death of Princess*.

By that time, we had interviewed people at all levels in the intelligence communities and confronted one of Terpil's main suppliers. We had also met those who had known him personally during the different chapters of his life, including his mother, his two sisters and several childhood friends in Brooklyn. It was there that we began to get a real sense of the influences and experiences that had shaped a man like Frank Terpil, and once we had settled down with him and Ruth in their Beirut apartment, it was where I chose to start.

As Terpil looked back over his early years, what were his feelings towards the people he had grown up with?

With Frank and Ruth in Beirut.

'Quite honestly, the people of Brooklyn are kind of like the Archie Bunkers on TV. If I would have stayed there, I wouldn't have known anything different. I'd be in the same situation as they are.'

I asked Terpil what his father did for a living. After a moment's hesitation, he said: 'He was basically in the military all the time. He got called up in World War II. Then Korea broke out, so I don't remember too much about him, except that he was in uniform most of the time.'

Terpil's mother, Viola, was a wonderfully expressive women, then in her mid-sixties. When we interviewed her in her Brooklyn home, she preferred to tell the truth. 'Frank's father worked for Western Electric. He was a sprayer, working in a spray booth, spraying phones.'

Frank was twelve years old when his father died, 'and I said to him, now that Daddy has gone, how do you feel, and he just looked at me and said: "I would rather you didn't ask that because I don't want to discuss it." So, we never, ever discussed his father. Never! To this day.'

'Was Frank afraid of emotions?'

'I think Frank has blanked out a lot about his life, and I think that's why he is the personality that he is, but it's an art, believe me. It's an art to blank things out. It's not that easy.'

'And Frank has developed that art?'

'I'm glad. I'm glad. I think it's wonderful because it makes your life so much easier.'

Had Frank given her any trouble as a child? Viola paused for a moment, and then asked: 'Did I tell you about the machine gun?'

An astonishing story unfolded. Apparently, fifteen-year-old Frank had bought a machine gun from a corrupt policeman and sold it at a profit to the son of his headmaster.

Viola was at work when the police called to tell her that Frank had been arrested. She rushed to the station, but they refused to let her see him. Just as she was leaving, she caught sight of Frank, sitting alone in a room with the door slightly ajar. After making sure no one was in earshot, Viola gave him some sound maternal advice: 'Frank, whatever your story is, stick to it.'

Viola wasn't angry with Frank for buying and selling a machine gun. On the contrary, she was proud of him. 'He was creative. It was a big thing to put this together. That was Frank. He always had great imagination.'

'You weren't worried that Frank had a machine gun?'

'No. No. Not at all. Not at all.'

Terpil confirmed the story. As he saw it, he was simply conforming to the values of those around him.

'The morality of New York is my morality. It's how I was brought up. I certainly learned at a very early age that a dollar placed in the right hands could do wonders.'

I asked Viola whether she felt this was a fair comment – that corruption in New York, and particularly Brooklyn, was almost a way of life.

She could scarcely believe the question. 'Antony, where have you been? You mean you haven't heard of corruption in New York? I think all the big cities are so corrupt. Even the small towns are so corrupt. New York City especially is corrupt, corrupt, corrupt.'

Viola was not the only one who shared Frank's views on life and morality. His two sisters, Adele and Lorraine, were also proud of their brother and felt that a great injustice had been done to him. They believed in him and would always stick by him. 'If he feels what he is doing is right, then it's right.'

It is understandable that close family members would be loyal to Frank, but it was a shock to discover that those views were shared in the wider community. We met a number of Frank's childhood friends in Farrell's Bar, Brooklyn, and their approval was unanimous. To quote one of them: 'Frank was an accredited international arms dealer. It was a business he created. He became successful. He raised a family; something done within the structure of our society. In some ways, he deserves a medal for what he has done.'

****

When he was nineteen years old, Frank Terpil found a way out of Brooklyn. He joined the army. Seven years later, he was recruited by the CIA and trained in the Technical Services Division, in his words, 'the Dirty Tricks Brigade, dealing with everything from bugging and technical surveillance through to assassinations'.

Brooklyn morality and a great deal more were now legitimate.

In 1970, Terpil was posted to India, and soon showed signs of his taste for the good life. He rented a large house in New Delhi with 'a staff of thirteen to fifteen servants' and bought himself a Cadillac. To fund this lifestyle, he had to supplement his modest federal salary, and soon found a solution.

Banks in neighbouring Afghanistan were mistakenly overvaluing the Indian rupee. Terpil would fly planeloads of hard currency to Kabul, change them into rupees, then re-exchange them at a vast profit back in Delhi. 'It was so easy,' he told us.

Sadly for him, his career was cut short in 1971 when he was stranded in Afghanistan with his black-market money by the unexpected outbreak of the India–Pakistan war. His employers were not impressed, and he was recalled to

CIA headquarters in Langley, Virginia, where, according to his account, they have a particular punishment for renegade agents.

'They have this euphemism of "walking the halls". You're not given a desk. You don't have an assignment, and consequently, you end up going to the cafeteria every day, where you see other people in this position.'

Fed up with these conditions, Terpil 'resigned' from the CIA in July 1972 to work freelance, taking with him the skills he had learnt there. That is the official version. It was also Terpil's version, but others had a very different story to tell.

In 1974, two years after Terpil had supposedly left the agency, he paid a surprise visit to Marty Keyser, a master craftsman known in his day as 'the Michelangelo of the bugging business'. At the time, Keyser was working under contract to supply the CIA with equipment for Egyptian intelligence. It was supposed to be a secret deal, but Terpil knew the exact specifications as well as the price and quantity of every item on the list. On his second visit, Terpil asked for modifications, but Keyser was sure that Terpil no longer worked for the CIA and stuck to the terms of the original contract.

Once it was confirmed that all the equipment had reached its destination, Keyser flew to Cairo, where Terpil was waiting to meet him and introduce their CIA contact. The next day, the three of them had a long session with a group of Egyptian generals, who examined every item in their presence. Keyser told us that he was 'absolutely baffled' when the generals asked him why he hadn't made the modifications Terpil had requested.

We discussed Keyser's concerns with William Colby, director of the CIA at the time. How had Terpil manoeuvred himself into this position, two years after he had supposedly left the agency?

Colby was evasive. 'That's the function of agents, to manoeuvre themselves into a situation by their own wits and so forth. Not abnormal at all, but to be frank, I really don't know the facts of this case.'

I persevered. 'Has it ever been the practice to appear to fire people from the CIA in order to put them into deep cover?'

'It's possible, sure. Those kinds of things used to be done years ago, but not anymore.'

Terpil's subsequent activities in Libya were even more 'baffling'. Egypt may have been a US ally, but the Libyan dictator, Muammar Gaddafi, was regarded as America's arch-enemy.

This was the issue that troubled Master Sergeant Luke F. Thompson when he was asked to recruit a team of five Green Beret commandoes to fly with him to Libya, where they would train members of Ghaddafi's militia. Thompson immediately contacted counterintelligence and was assured that the whole operation was 'completely legal and above board.'

On arrival, Thompson's team was escorted to a desert palace, where people of unknown nationalities were being taught how to make booby traps – 'ashtrays, books, desks that would explode as soon as they were moved'.

Frank Terpil was in charge of the whole operation.

It was obvious to Thompson that these were not devices that would be used in conventional warfare, and he decided to pull out immediately. On his return to the United States, he reported everything he had seen to his commanding officer and to the members of counterintelligence who had given him the original clearance, but there was no follow-up.

The ring of silence might have held, had it not been for the New York undercover operation and the two trials that followed when some of Terpil's former associates came forward to give evidence.

Among them was Kevin Mulcahy, a former CIA agent, who had been invited by Terpil to join him as one of his partners in ICT (Intercontinental Technology), a company registered in Washington DC in 1976.

When Mulcahy discovered that Muammar Gaddafi was one of ICT's principal customers, he assumed that this was a covert CIA operation. But once he saw that the equipment being sent to Libya included tons of explosives, hundreds of classified night-vision devices and half a million detonators, he gave detailed reports to the CIA and the FBI. No action was taken.

We approached the CIA, the FBI and the Justice Department for comments on Terpil's activities in Libya, but all requests were refused.

A CIA study, published shortly before we were filming, described Gaddafi as 'the most prominent state sponsor and participant in international terrorism'.

'Wasn't there some irony,' I asked Terpil, 'that you were using CIA suppliers, shippers, and members of US Special Forces to work for Gaddafi?'

But Terpil would not be drawn. He insisted that 'the leading powers were well aware of what was going on. If they deny and say they were not cognizant of this, then where are their intelligence services?'

The implications of the Libyan operation extended far beyond Washington. As there were no direct flights between the United States and Libya, Terpil needed reliable transfer points in Europe.

According to Mulcahy, London's Heathrow Airport was the most important link in the supply chain. With the help of 'some associates within the British government', Terpil was able to arrange for lethal material and armed personnel to be switched to Libyan flights without any need to leave the international zone and pass through British customs and passport control.

Off the record, Mulcahy named one of Terpil's high-level contacts in British intelligence. Terpil confirmed the name and claimed that the man in question had done a great deal more than smooth the way with the British authorities.

'In some cases, when we needed some material that wasn't available from one of our sources, he freely gave us some other sources of possible supply … I'm sure he is still on active duty. We regarded him as our professional babysitter.'

Using an unlisted number Terpil had provided, I phoned the 'babysitter', and a meeting was arranged in a London hotel. The man confirmed his association with Terpil but denied that he had been involved in any unsanctioned operation. He went on to suggest that Terpil's Libyan operation was in the best long-term interests of the Western powers. He also warned me that if I was secretly recording the meeting or ever mentioned his name to anyone, I would end up 'under a bush in Surrey'.

****

When the Libyan operation was finally shut down in 1977, Terpil decided to offer his services to Idi Amin, the Ugandan dictator, who was responsible for rampant human rights abuses, ethnic persecution, extrajudicial killings, corruption and gross economic mismanagement. After six years in power, Amin was now losing his vicious grip on the nation in the face of widespread dissent and needed outside help.

It didn't take long for Terpil to work his way into the dictator's inner circle, sidelining Bob Astles, the former British Colonial Officer who had acted as Amin's *éminence grise* for several years.

But it wasn't just charm that gave Terpil his special status. It was the hardware he could offer a dictator who felt under threat: machine guns, explosives, poisons, surveillance equipment and tasers, which could be used for torture as well as crowd control.

During Amin's bloody reign, Ugandans were being picked up day and night by snatch squads and taken to State Research, a grim, three-storey building in Kampala, the Ugandan capital, where thousands were tortured, starved and slaughtered.

The dictator's official residence stood next door, confirming his direct involvement in the killings, but Terpil had an even closer association with State Research. He operated out of an office on the third floor.

When the time came to raise these issues with Terpil, I began with the same questions I had asked during our first meeting in Damascus. Did he supply interrogation equipment and torture equipment to Amin? Did he ever think of the consequences for ordinary human beings?

His answers hadn't changed. He was just the supplier and took no responsibility for the way his equipment was used. He had never taken part in torture or visited the basement where prisoners were kept. His office was on the third floor, 'purely an administrative area'.

'But you knew that torture was going on?'

'It was hard to miss when you walked out of State Research across the courtyard.'

It would indeed have been hard to miss. In testimony obtained from survivors after the fall of Amin, we were given graphic accounts of prisoners being beaten to death in the basement and their bodies thrown into the courtyard. One witness was actually held in a room on Terpil's floor, where he and other prisoners were denied food and water for days at a time. The place was so cramped that some died of suffocation.

Even if Terpil had never entered the basement or any of the rooms on his floor where prisoners were kept, he must have heard what was going on.

After a long pause, he answered: 'Yes. At times you could hear sounds emitting.'

'Screams?'

'Screams. Yeah.'

As he talked about his Ugandan years, Terpil revealed his closeness to a dictator, who had rewarded him with the nickname 'Waraggi' (White Lightning).

When the regime finally collapsed, it was Frank Terpil who sat at Amin's side on the last plane out of Uganda on the night of 13 April 1979. In the hold beneath them were steel trunks which Amin's lackeys had loaded with gold bars.

Tripoli, the Libyan capital, was the first stop, but from there the two of them went their separate ways. Terpil joined his wife Marilyn and their two sons in their lavish home in Langley, Virginia, while Amin was given sanctuary in Saudi Arabia. In a recorded telephone conversation that Terpil played for us, we heard Amin tell his former henchman that he had 'decided just to be now a religious man'.

****

Terpil's exploits raised so many questions. If sworn evidence given in court by Mulcahy, Thompson, Keyser and others is to be believed, Terpil maintained his links with the CIA when operating in Egypt and Libya. It is certainly possible that he was feeding back useful information from both countries, but it is hard to imagine that the agency would have had any interest in the activities of Idi Amin. All the evidence suggests that Terpil was operating in Uganda as a freelance weapons salesman, but he was still able to supply all the lethal equipment the dictator had required.

Among the grisly relics discovered at State Research was a contract, listing the supplies that Terpil's company, Intercontinental Technology, had shipped to the

Ugandan dictator at an agreed price of $3,343,000 (nearly fourteen million dollars in today's money). The most startling revelation was the number of British and American companies that seemed willing to provide their hardware without any concerns about the destination or the ultimate use.

The evidence obtained from the New York undercover operation brought the whole question of Terpil's suppliers to the fore. Rodriguez and Raad had made it clear from the start that they were key figures in a far-right terrorist group, yet Terpil was able to assure them that he could supply all the weapons they required and deliver them to any destination they specified.

Apparently, there were two weapons manufacturers in England he could rely on to supply the ten thousand machine guns Rodriguez had requested, but there was another reason why the UK was such a good option. Over the years, Terpil had cultivated important contacts in British intelligence and the military, people he could rely on to provide an end-user's certificate, the key document required for an export licence. In this case, the certificate would show that the machine guns had been ordered by the government of the Philippines, but once clearance had been granted and the shipment was on its way, it would be delivered to a destination in the Caribbean that Rodriguez had specified. All that was required to set everything into motion was an advance of $56,000 to cover the bribes Terpil would have to pay in Britain and the Philippines.

Before agreeing to this, Rodriguez had set down two conditions. First, he would have to visit the supplier and test-fire some of the machine guns on offer. He would also need to meet and question all those involved in the illegal shipment to be sure that they had a foolproof procedure in place.

On 17 December 1979, Rodriguez flew into Heathrow Airport and went straight to a London hotel, where seven people were waiting for him in a conference room on the ground floor. When he entered, Terpil was already typing the final contract but quickly broke off to introduce the detective to his associates. Among them was Colonel Warren, a former marine, now 'in retirement'. His responsibility was to organise the fake end-user's certificate. Also present were Sam Urik, the shipper, who was subsequently arrested for drug-running, and Robin Braid-Taylor, who agreed to take Rodriguez to the Interarms warehouse in Manchester to test-fire their weapons.

In sworn testimony during the New York trial, Rodriguez made it clear that Braid-Taylor understood all the implications of the deal, including the use of a phoney end-user's certificate.

'He was in it for the money, period. He wasn't interested whether I was from the right or the left. If I had said I was a communist, I'm sure he would have given me the same deal.'

When we interviewed Braid-Taylor, he dismissed this as 'an absolute lie'. Colonel Warren refused to see us.

I asked Rodriguez if he felt that England was one of those countries where it was relatively easy for terrorists to acquire weapons; much easier, for instance, than the United States.

'Definitely, much easier. But the British government is where the fault is. If they could supply an export license on the basis of an end-user's certificate for the Philippines without checking with the Philippines and making sure these weapons were, in fact, due there, they are at fault'.

****

After we left Beirut, Terpil had a number of narrow escapes before he was finally given sanctuary in Cuba, where Jim Hougan visited him on several occasions. Ruth had originally joined him there, but by the time Jim paid his final visit, Terpil was living with Nurys, his much younger Cuban girlfriend, in a simple bungalow overlooking the Playas del Este, a string of white sandy beaches, close to Havana.

Over the years, Terpil gradually fell off the radar and lost his place on the FBI's most wanted list. According to Nurys, he died peacefully of heart failure in their seaside home on 1 March 2016. He was 76 years old.

****

Shortly after Terpil's death, I was having a confidential discussion with the Interior Minister of a small country that was surrounded by dangerous neighbours. He surprised me with his scathing comments about intelligence agencies, describing them as 'snake pits of competing factions and divided loyalties'. According to him, people who are trained to deceive cannot be expected to hold moral values or resist the temptation to use their skills and inside knowledge for their own advantage.

I shared the question that had troubled us throughout our time on the Terpil film: 'Where does intelligence stop, and crime actually begin?'

'It's a seamless border', he replied.

****

The finished film won the US Emmy Award for documentary of the year, but by then David and I had lost any opportunity we might have had to work together on a feature film. In that world, timing is everything and, by now, our two main contacts had left Twentieth Century-Fox, but I have few regrets. Documentaries were giving me so many rich and, in some cases, life-changing experiences that I would keep the focus there for the rest of my working life.

Chapter Eighteen

TRUTH, LIES AND CONSEQUENCES

Between *Death of a Princess* and my retirement in 2016, there was a continual flow of documentaries on all kinds of subjects from sexual identity (*Middle Sexes*) to our treatment of animals (*Man and Animal*) and *The Tank Man*, our 2006 film about conditions in China which was inspired by one of the most iconic photographs of the twentieth century.

It was a process of inquiry and discovery that I wanted to share with as many people as possible, and I owe a huge debt to those who gave me the resources and the freedom to do this as well as to the outstanding colleagues who worked with me on these projects.

Of all the subjects we covered, one was especially important to me: religious faith. Nine films were devoted to this, and in many ways, they were stages in a very personal journey that would have life-changing consequences.

As a young man, I was a committed Christian, inspired by the Gospels and their clear message about our responsibilities towards the poor and the disadvantaged, about compassion, forgiveness and the dangers of wealth and privilege. Although I repeatedly failed to live up to those standards, they were, and still are, a strong influence on my life and thinking.

Unlike many Christians, I did not believe in the literal truth of the *Bible* but accepted the theory of evolution and all that science has revealed about the age and scale of the universe and our insignificant place within it. I was also keenly aware of the many crimes committed in the name of religion but held firmly to the belief that there was an irrefutable truth at the core of my Christian faith. Perhaps this showed lack of imagination and insight, but it was only when I had first-hand experience of how some of the most powerful and influential religious movements operate that I began to call everything into question.

One of the first to come under scrutiny was the evangelical Church in the United States, where belief in the literal truth of the *Bible* is the dominant doctrine. It was a brand of the faith that was going from strength to strength while my own Anglican Church was in crisis with shrinking congregations and as many as a hundred church closures in a single year.

But it wasn't just church membership and attendance that I found so striking. By the early 1980s, evangelical Christianity was becoming a political force in the United States. One of the key moments was Ronald Reagan's famous campaign speech to a large gathering of (mainly) Southern Baptists in Dallas, Texas, in August 1980. His opening words would reverberate throughout the decade and beyond. 'I know that you cannot endorse me, but I only brought that up because I want you to know that I endorse you and what you're doing.'

What followed was a call to the American people to 'uphold traditional Judeo–Christian values' and to look to the *Bible* for all the answers to 'the complex and horrendous questions confronting us at home and worldwide.' It was music to the ears of this particular audience, and Reagan received thunderous applause, but he was not alone in stirring fundamentalist Christians into political action. A whole clique of TV evangelists – Pat Robertson, Jerry Falwell, James Robison and Jim Bakker, to mention a few – were telling God's people that they were 'sick and tired of hearing about all the radicals and the perverts and the liberals and the communists coming out of the closet'. Now was the time for God's people 'to come out of the closet, out of the churches and change America'.

By 1984, the year of the next presidential election, this campaign had gathered such momentum that Reagan was returned to office with an even greater share of the popular vote.

The Republicans had reached out to a form of Christianity that has its roots in the folk religion of the American frontier. As well as emphasising the literal truth of the *Bible*, it stresses the importance of a direct personal relationship between the individual and God. Many followers believe in a defining moment of personal salvation – the 'born again' experience when all sins are forgiven and the faithful secure their place in Paradise.

This alliance between religion and politics would change the political landscape of America forever, drawing blue-collar workers, who had previously either supported the Democrats or felt detached from politics, into the Republican fold. In time, it would transform the party of Abraham Lincoln into the party of Donald Trump.

****

I had been following these events closely, and in 1987, we set out to make two films, *Thy Kingdom Come* and *Thy Will be Done*, hoping to find out why this brand of Christianity was taking such a powerful hold in the United States and how the political right was managing to attract so many members to its cause.

Twenty-six years later, we returned to the subject with the film *Questioning Darwin*.

Our first port of call was Dallas, Texas, the so-called 'Buckle of the Bible belt'. It had the largest quota of millionaires, one of the highest crime rates and severest poverty rates of any American city. Yet Dallas could also be described as one of the most Christian places on earth. It had the highest proportion of paid-up church members of any large metropolitan area, and the majority embraced the most conservative form of Christianity.

If anyone had the right to be called the vicar of Dallas, it was Dr Criswell, pastor of The First Baptist Church. He had officiated at that famous gathering in August 1980 and was chosen to give the welcoming address to Ronald Reagan.

As we were guided into his office, Dr Criswell rose to greet us from behind a huge, gilded desk. He was a pugnacious man, then in his seventies, and as soon as the camera began turning, he launched into a description of his church in language one would have expected from a successful entrepreneur, rather than a man of God.

'Our church has five blocks in the downtown heart of this city and in this priceless portion of downtown Dallas. There is not another corporation that has as much property in the heart of this city, and I use it for the Kingdom of God, and love doing it. It's like this office in which you now stand. This is no poor man's place, as you can see.'

It certainly wasn't a poor man's place. Large Persian rugs and expensive reproductions of Louis Quinze sofas and chairs were scattered across the vast interior. There were antique cabinets with displays of Meissen plates and vases, and one entire wall was dominated by a classical landscape set in a huge, gilded frame.

Very quietly, I said to him: 'I'd like to share something personal. I believe the Gospels are telling me to let go of all my material possessions before I can really call myself a Christian. I am incapable of making that commitment and it sets up a conflict. Do you ever experience a similar conflict?'

Criswell was appalled at the suggestion. 'You have a completely wrong idea of the Gospels. There is no virtue in being poor. A man who is a Christian will have a tendency to be prosperous. I tell the young men who are capable in the church: "Make money, succeed."'

There is no other way of saying this. Criswell and the many millions who think like him have inverted Christ's message and created their own man-made 'gospel of wealth'.

****

The First Baptist Church of Dallas is a city within a city. It has its own nurseries, gymnasium, primary school, secondary school and university.

We filmed classes where children were being taught that the universe was created in six twenty-four-hour days, and that if they followed the genealogies set down in Genesis, they would see that creation occurred four thousand years before the birth of Christ, 'not millions of years ago as evolutionists say.'

At the pinnacle of this educational establishment was the Criswell College, which groomed more graduates for the ministry than any other university or college within the fifteen-million strong Southern Baptist community. Dr Patterson, the college principal, was regarded as the main force behind the re-emergence of fundamentalism in America, but his ambitions were not limited to his own country. Graduates from this college were being sent out to missionise the world.

When it came to issues of race, First Baptist brought back distressing memories of the Dutch Reformed Church in Piet Retief, the Afrikaner town that had rejected Sandra Laing. In all the services we attended, we didn't see a single black face and would soon discover that Criswell's church had funded separate 'ethnic' churches in the poorer parts of the city.

I asked Criswell, 'Why can't you worship together as one community?'

Criswell's response was chilling: 'Birds of a feather flock together. People of like backgrounds gravitate towards each other, and they don't mix very well.'

If birds of a feather flock together, leopards certainly don't change their spots. When the Supreme Court introduced the first anti-segregation rulings in 1954, Criswell urged state legislators to resist. 'Integrationists', he told them, were 'infidels, dead from the neck up. In our churches, negroes could never excel, and it's a kindness to send them to churches of their own.'

It was against this background that Criswell started pouring money into separate ethnic churches.

In return for desperately needed buildings, furnishing, car parks and salaries, the black and Hispanic preachers chosen to lead these churches dutifully spread the Criswell message. During a service we filmed, the black preacher actually spoke out against black aspiration and, by implication, against integration.

'Secular humanists would have you believe that this world is set up for you to do your own thing. God says: "No. No." If you get caught lifting yourself up, God says: "I'll cut you down."'

Criswell held out against black membership of the 'mother church' until 1968, and although he and his followers no longer had the power to stop black families attending services there, I doubt if any of them would have been made to feel welcome.

First Baptist also had an inner-city chapel that ministered to the street people of Dallas, but Criswell showed little respect or compassion for the people who came there for help. They were, in his words: 'the flotsam and jetsam of humanity, who have found themselves cast out of society because they are drug addicts, they are drunks, they are prostitutes, they are pickpockets. They are everything that belongs to a lower level of life.'

If wealth and prosperity are signs of God's approval, it clearly follows that sickness and poverty are signs of his disapproval, for which the poor must pay the price.

We filmed in the inner-city chapel on a cold winter's evening. Street people, huddled together on benches, were subjected to an hour-long sermon before they were offered any food or drink. As he preached, the pastor paced back and forth, literally screaming meaningless abuse at his 'flock'.

'I wonder how many people today are burning in hell this very hour. God is not going to send somebody back to prove to you that hell is real. If you live without Jesus Christ, you go to hell.'

After being subjected to this rant, the congregation was rewarded with buns and hot drinks. It was a quick process, and as soon as the paper plates and mugs had been binned, the homeless were ushered into the street and the doors were locked behind them.

In this brand of Christianity, it seems that the zeal to save souls for the life to come overrides every other obligation for God's people here on earth, but as soon as we were alone with this preacher, we sensed that people like him, who are closest to these issues, were beginning to have their doubts.

Very quietly, he told us: 'These people are important to God and every time I leave here, I leave thinking about them. Some will just sleep on sidewalks, some in parks, some on freight trains, some underneath bridges, some in the warehouses. I keep asking myself, was there more I could do?'

Unfortunately, there was little he could do without breaking the rules of the 'Mother Church'. As we would discover, less than one third of one per cent of the vast resources of First Baptist was set aside for work amongst the destitute of Dallas.

****

Criswell's church, with its emphasis on power, material success and racial difference, stood at the hard edge of Christian fundamentalism, but a softer brand of the faith was being offered by TV ministries and independent 'mega-churches', headed by charismatic pastors capable of attracting congregations of thousands.

Like Criswell, they emphasise the literal truth of the *Bible*, but unlike him, they speak of a God who cares for each and every one of us, regardless of status. Some of these churches provide food, clothing and accommodation for the homeless, but most of the effort is directed inwards, towards their own people. There are play schools for children, ministries for teenagers, married couples, the elderly and the disabled, and most important of all, serious efforts are made to help those in crisis.

We interviewed church members who had been struggling with alcohol and drug addiction for decades and others whose marriages had failed or who had lost their jobs and, in one case, had even lost the will to live. One young woman told us how she used to spend 'days and nights, jumping in and out of cars with complete strangers, doing unthinkable sexual acts for money so that I was able to pay for crack.'

In these churches, people like her are not dismissed as 'the flotsam and jetsam of society'. In their moments of despair, they are encouraged to open their hearts to Jesus, and in response, they told us: 'He took me into His arms and lifted me out of the abyss'. 'Through His abiding love', families had been brought back together, addictions had been cured, and 'the sound mind, which my psychiatrist said I would never have', was finally restored.

I don't know whether these were permanent changes or brief emotional experiences with no lasting effect, but I have kept in touch with some of them, and although I can't say whether their stories are representative, they are certainly compelling.

Angel Dague, the reformed prostitute, has stayed off drugs, saved enough money to buy her own home, and now works in a rehab centre treating victims of sex trafficking.

Her emails to me are always punctuated with quotations in 'caps'. 'I am doing AMAZING. GLORY TO GOD He SAVED me through his Son JESUS … WITH GOD ALL THINGS ARE POSSIBLE.'

While these churches are willing to give their full support to people suffering from job insecurity, mental problems and addictions, they are much closer to Criswell's First Baptist on issues of race and politics. During all the services we filmed, it was hard to spot a black face in the congregation, and when scores of church members came forward to share their transformative experiences with us, there wasn't a single African American among them.

I raised this issue with several pastors, who assured us that all races were welcome in their churches. The problem, as they saw it, was cultural. African Americans preferred a different form of worship: 'more emotional', 'lots of community singing' and 'preaching all day long'.

There's a partial truth here. After decades of segregation, it is understandable that blacks and whites should have developed their own distinct forms of worship, but there was one crucial issue that these preachers overlooked: the increasing politicisation of their brand of the faith. Most prominent black preachers follow in the footsteps of Martin Luther King, with racial equality and social justice high on their agendas, but something very different was happening in the churches where we filmed. In the wake of Reagan's famous campaign speech in 1980, a huge effort was now being made to bring all evangelical Christians – the privileged and the disadvantaged – into the Republican fold.

At the time we were filming, the big TV ministries and many churches were sharing contact details of their members with right-wing pressure groups like The American Coalition for Traditional Values, Christian Voice and The Heritage Foundation, who were sending out millions of messages, urging church members to get out and vote for specific candidates at local, state and federal level.

And there was another unifying force bringing these Evangelic Churches together: compete rejection of abortion and homosexuality, and at the top of the list, belief in the literal truth of the *Bible*. To quote a typical sermon: 'We did not evolve out of something that is less important. God created man on the sixth day, created us separately, created us distinctly.'

It was a response we would hear again and again.

'To put man down as an animal, that we are no different from a dog or a horse or a cat, is totally preposterous.'

But not all the answers were so self-centred. There are other, more challenging issues facing those who are trying to reconcile their Christian belief with the theory of evolution.

In the words of one of the more thoughtful fundamentalist pastors: 'If all we are is a product of this random mutation process, then where does morality come from? Where does hope come from? Where does love come from? Where does anything that makes us human beings really come from?'

There are two ways of wrestling with these questions. We can hold firmly to our belief in God, and set the complex question of creation aside as 'a subject too profound for the human intellect',[1] placing our trust instead in 'those inner feelings that we are in a presence of something greater than we can conceive'; … 'A Father who brings love, meaning and a moral sense into our lives.'[2]

The other option is to deceive.

****

All these issues would come to the fore when we revisited fundamentalist territory with our 2013 documentary *Questioning Darwin*.

---

1 From Darwin's letter to Asa Gray, 22 May 1860.
2 Extracts from interview with Rowan Williams, former Archbishop of Canterbury, and Cardinal Vincent Nichols, head of the Catholic Church in England and Wales, from our 2009 film *How Do We Know that God Exists?*

In part, this was the story of a man who had devoted nearly thirty years of his life to painstaking research before he felt ready to submit his magnum opus, *On the Origin of Species*, for publication.

It was also a film that would give a voice to those who believe that his theory of evolution is a falsehood and an assault on their faith.

As a young man, Darwin was a committed Christian who thought seriously about being ordained in the Church, but he was also a passionate naturalist and geologist. As he gathered more and more evidence, it slowly became clear to him that creation was a 'clumsy, wasteful, blundering ... and horribly cruel'[3] process,

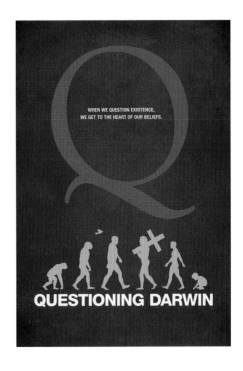

which had taken many millions of years to bring plant, animal and human life 'from some lowly organised form'[4] to their current levels. He couldn't believe that 'a beneficent and omnipotent'[5] God had taken any part in this. He may have set the whole process in motion, but the rest was left to the laws of nature.

When *On the Origin of Species* was finally published, Darwin expected a furious response. To this day, his theory of evolution is rejected by Muslims and Orthodox Jews, but the Christian world is divided, with the strongest opposition coming from the evangelical Church.

In early 1900s, legislators in twenty American states introduced motions banning the teaching of evolution in any of their schools, and in six southern states, these were passed into law.

But everything changed with the launch of Sputnik on 4 October,1957. At a time of increasing Cold War tensions, the Soviet Union had beaten the United States in the race into space, sending a clear message to the American people that their country was falling behind in science.

There was an immediate call for massive investments in science education and radical changes to high school curricula. This not only meant strong support for

3 From Darwin's letter to J.D. Hooker, 13 July 1856.
4 Darwin, *The Descent of Man*, 2nd ed, p. 618.
5 From Darwin's letter to Asa Gray, 22 May 1860.

subjects like advanced physics, but the teaching of evolution as the framework for a better understanding of anatomy, biology, genetics, zoology and the other life sciences.

Faced with a challenge on this scale, Christian fundamentalists refused to give up without a fight, and it would take another twelve years and a whole series of Supreme Court rulings before all state laws banning the teaching of evolution were annulled.

Having lost the first battle, fundamentalists changed tactics. They would fight orthodox science with creation 'science'.

****

The Creation Museum in Petersburg, Kentucky, was built at a cost of 27 million dollars, money raised largely through private donations. It was opened in 2007 and receives more than eight hundred thousand visitors a year.

In the main viewing theatre, audiences can watch stunning images of animal and plant life while the commentator takes them through the 'six days of creation', culminating in a dramatisation of Adam rising out of the dust on the sixth day.

Close by, there is another visual display with an accompanying commentary that makes a crucial addition to the Genesis account of creation.

'The Bible reveals that God created all the animal and plant kinds in the beginning, and we are now learning that God placed a huge amount of information within each created kind, allowing them to diversify into the myriad of plants and animals we see today.'

This would be my first lesson in 'creation science'. Yes, there was an evolution of sorts, but it was pre-planned by God, and all the variations in lifeforms we see today have developed over a period of just six thousand years.

The main feature of the museum is a recreation of the Garden of Eden, where we are given a taste of the world that a loving God had originally created.

Adam and Eve stand waist-deep and facing each other in a small pond with their genitalia discreetly hidden underwater. Nearby, today's carnivores and their traditional prey coexist peacefully side by side and a small dinosaur is chewing a pineapple, all on its own.

When I raised this with Ken Ham, the museum's founder, he explained that 'dinosaurs were land animals, therefore Adam and Eve and the dinosaurs lived side by side. God created a perfect world, no death, no disease; animals, man and the dinosaurs were all vegetarian', but of course, all this came to end when Adam and Eve incurred the wrath of God by eating the forbidden fruit.

The fossil record has been a consistent problem for fundamentalists, who have offered several different explanations. Initially, it was God who planted fossils to test our faith. Subsequently, it was the work of Satan, but today the devil has largely disappeared from the narrative. The current story is that fossils are the relics of animals drowned in the great deluge of 2348 BC, more commonly known as 'Noah's Flood'. The fact that fossils have been discovered at so many different levels within the rock strata is somehow overlooked.

The story of the flood raises difficult questions, particularly about the nature of God. According to the Book of Genesis, he was so incensed by the 'wickedness of man' that he called for the mass destruction of 'man and beasts and creeping things and birds of the air',[6] including, of course, an entire generation of innocent children and virtually all animal life.

And there are other anomalies. Based on the dimensions given in Genesis,[7] the ark was about a tenth of the size of a typical cruise ship today. We are also told that the flood prevailed for 'a hundred and fifty days'.[8]

It is hard to understand how pairs of all known creatures (living and extinct) as well as the huge amount of food necessary to sustain carnivores and herbivores for nearly five months could have survived in such a small space.

And if there were dinosaurs living at the time of the flood what happened to them? Why did they disappear?

I posed that question to our guide while we were filming the museum's recreation of a segment of the ark. He gave me a quizzical look. 'Antony, don't you know your history – Saint George and the dragon? That was a dinosaur.'

But the most astonishing claims came over the speakers in the museum's planetarium. Here visitors can lie back and watch stunning Hubble images of the universe on an overhead screen while the commentator guides them on their way:

> Further up we see a massive grouping of galaxies called the Virgo Cluster. It contains over 2,000 galaxies and is 50 million light years away from Earth.
>
> Critics of the *Bible* have suggested that it is impossible for the light from these galaxies to reach earth in only six thousand years, but there are several different ways to get light to travel these distances in a short period of time. These include gravitational time dilation, alternative synchrony conventions and others.

Einstein was the first to discover variations in the speed of light, but the possibility of increasing that speed 8,000 times is frankly delusional.

****

---

6 Genesis 6:7
7 Genesis 6:15
8 Genesis 7:24

Creating and subsequently politicising a brand of the faith that ignores some of the basic tenets of Christianity is serious enough, but disseminating lies and falsehoods on this scale is even more dangerous.

According to a recent Gallup poll, 40 per cent of Americans believe in the Genesis account of a six-day creation. If such a huge proportion of the population can be made to believe that the country's leading scientists and medical experts are liars, there is no knowing how far distrust can spread.

It would be absurd to blame Christian fundamentalists for all the fabrications and distortions that are becoming such a serious threat to contemporary democracy, but they made the ground fertile for those who believe in conspiracy theories. From the early 2000s, social media and online platforms added fuel to the flames, but back in 1980 when Ronald Reagan consecrated the marriage between politics and fundamentalism, he was setting his country on a course that would eventually lead to the election of Donald Trump. Although a man with no obvious Christian credentials, Trump was brought to power on a wave of fundamentalist support, and the message he took from them was that any fabrication is permissible provided it supports your narrative.

Trust is crucial in a functioning democracy, but, stage by stage, Trump undermined people's faith in all branches of government.

He ignored early warnings from medical experts about Covid dangers and weakened America's bonds with some of its closest allies. Under his leadership, the United States withdrew from the World Health Organization and the Paris Climate Agreement. In one tweet, Trump dismissed global warming as a 'money-making hoax'.

Most serious of all were his unsubstantiated claims of voting fraud, which began six months before election day.

There wasn't a shred of evidence to support this, but by flooding American society with disinformation, he was undermining people's confidence in the whole system and attracting all kinds of extremists to his cause.

Fired by an intensive campaign on their websites, a huge crowd converged on the nation's capital on 6 January 2021, the day the Senate and the House were due to certify Joe Biden's electoral victory.

After a series of incendiary speeches, culminating in Trump's instructions to his supporters to 'fight like hell', if they do not want to see our election victory stolen by emboldened radical-left Democrats', they set off to the Capitol, where they rampaged through corridors, broke into offices and sought out legislators they loathed. Five people died as a result of this assault.

In Russia, Iran and China, state media gloated over democracy's descent into chaos.

At this stage, it is hard to know how much permanent damage has been done, but one thing stands out.

If you make a complete break with the truth in the service of religion or politics, there is no knowing where this can finally take you.

Chapter Nineteen

REMEMBER: GOD DOESN'T TAKE COINS

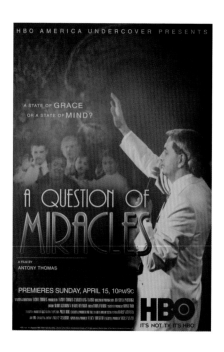

The nine films we made on religious subjects involved in-depth discussions with leading figures within many religious faiths – from the Dalai Lama to the Archbishop of Canterbury. It also required close study of the sacred texts, including, of course, the *Bible* and the *Qur'an*, but the experience that had the greatest impact on me was a very personal one.

It began with an invitation from Sheila Nevins to join her at HBO's New York headquarters to discuss a proposal that had just been submitted to her.

Like David Fanning, her equivalent at PBS Frontline, Sheila was an inspiring Head of Documentaries, and thanks to them both, I had co-production support from two of America's most prestigious channels for most of the films I made for British television.

Sheila had been approached by people with close links to two highly successful charismatic preachers, Bennie Hinn and Reinhard Bonnke.

Hinn commanded the heights of the fiercely competitive business of international television evangelism and claimed to perform miracles of healing at services held in stadia and public squares across the world. A single service he had recently held in in Manila had attracted over a million people.

Reinhard Bonnke was another Christian 'miracle worker'. German by birth, he claimed to have experienced a recurring dream in his early twenties. He would see a map of Africa coloured a vivid red, and hear the voice of God telling him, again and again: 'Africa shall be saved.'

At the age of twenty-seven, Bonnke began his African ministry in the small mountain kingdom of Lesotho. Seven years later, he founded 'Christ for All Nations', and by the late 1990s was holding massive rallies across the continent. By that time, he claimed to have brought seventy-five million people to Christ.

Clearly, both men were now hoping to spread their message beyond the conventional Christian TV channels.

I had to admit to Sheila that I hadn't heard of either of these 'miracle workers'. But I had visited Lourdes, the famous Catholic shrine in the French Pyrenees, where people come in search of miraculous cures, but the clergy who officiate there see their role – and indeed, the whole purpose of the shrine – very differently.

Their duty is to provide peace, compassion and comfort to the terminally ill, not to perform miracles, and they were very frank about this. I was told that there had only been sixty-six authenticated cures during the entire 150-year history of Lourdes. Apparently, this was proportionally lower than the number of unexplained cures recorded in the French population as a whole.

Before making any commitment, I had to take a close look at some of Bonnke's and Hinn's TV programmes. Although there were compelling images of people throwing away their crutches or claiming that sight and hearing had been restored, there was no way of knowing whether these were genuine cures without thorough research, but one thing was strikingly clear. These two preachers were drawing massive numbers of people to their brand of Christianity, and I felt it was a subject that deserved careful investigation.

The first priority was to meet them both. I had to ensure that we would be given full and free access when the time came to film, and I promised Sheila, as I would promise them, that I would approach the subject with an open mind.

Hinn was happy to receive me in his home in Grapevine, Texas. He was a small man in his late forties with one striking feature: his hair. It was clipped close to the scalp on either side of his face, then rose in a carefully coiffured wave which flowed over the back of his head and across his collar.

In a one-to-one meeting, Hinn was very different from the strident preacher I had watched on his TV programmes. He was quiet, almost humble, and encouraged me to speak frankly about my beliefs. At that time, I could honestly say that I was a Christian, but I was also frank about the issues that concerned me.

'Why', I asked him, 'would an all-powerful, all-seeing God, who knows the anguish of the sick and has the power to cure them, need Benny Hinn to nudge him into action?'

'That's a powerful question', he answered, after a long pause. 'I can only go back to the *Bible*, because the scriptures are clear that God called human vessels, whether it's Peter, the Apostle, John or Paul, to deliver his message to the crowds.'

It was hardly a satisfying response, but Hinn assured me that all my doubts would be resolved when I witnessed the astonishing cures that took place during his 'miracle crusades.' As well as promising me free access to his services, he also agreed to my second request. To confirm that these were genuine cures with long-term consequences, I would be given the contact details of those who had been miraculously healed. I could even consult their doctors, if necessary.

Reinhard Bonnke had agreed to meet me in Nakuru, a town in Kenya's Great Rift Valley, where he was holding one of his 'miracle crusades.' It was a hundred-mile drive from Nairobi, the capital, and by the time I arrived the service had already begun.

Reinhard Bonnke in action.

Again, I was astonished at the huge numbers of people who had gathered there and the emotional pitch that had been reached at this early stage of the service.

For the next half hour, I worked my way slowly through the crowds towards the high platform where Bonnke was striding back and forth, exhorting his followers to lift their hands and 'Shout, shout, shout Hallelujah!' On either side of him, black and white acolytes were skilfully moving out of his way whenever he made a move. One was holding a microphone and translating Bonnke's words into Kikuyu, the common language in that part of the country.

Reinhard Bonnke was a large man in every sense. Then in his early sixties, his face was flushed and wet with sweat, which glued his dark hair close to his scalp.

Quite suddenly, the mood changed. A choir, standing below stage, sang a sweet, gentle melody, while groups of young men moved through the crowds, collecting donations in plastic buckets.

As the choir sang, Bonnke shouted out: 'Remember! God doesn't take coins!'

He was addressing some of the world's poorest people. All around me, I could see men, women and children on crutches or clinging to others for support. In a country that could only afford the most basic medical care, the prospect of a sudden cure must have been overwhelming, and I am sure there were people in that congregation who emptied their pockets in the desperate hope that God would reward them with a miracle.

Once the donations had been gathered, Bonnke made a passionate call for all cancers to be cured, for the lame to be given the strength to throw away their crutches or to rise out of their wheelchairs and walk. On cue, people started moving towards the stage, but again, it was impossible to gauge whether there were any genuine cures. My responsibility that day was to ensure that we would be given the closest possible access when the time came to film.

Bonnke had agreed to meet me in a nearby hotel late that evening. Like Benny Hinn, he was a man with two distinct personalities – on and off stage. In private, he was warm and gentle, and as he talked about the remarkable recoveries he had witnessed that day, I felt he genuinely believed everything he was telling me. I repeated the promises I had made to Hinn, but at this early stage did not raise my concerns about the service I had seen. That opportunity would come later.

Regardless of my feelings at that time, I was determined to approach the subject with an open mind. If we found genuine recoveries, our duty was to report them, but if that evidence was lacking, we would have to find out what was really happening during these highly emotional events.

And there was another important issue. Were the millions attending these services only there in search of miraculous cures, or were Hinn and Bonnke offering a brand of Christianity that touched something deep within them, something that a privileged Westerner like me might have lost sight of?

****

Filming began in Portland, Oregon, where Benny Hinn's 'miracle crusade' was set to run for three consecutive evenings.

The chosen venue was the vast auditorium of the Veteran Memorial Coliseum, which had filled to capacity by the time Hinn appeared on stage to acknowledge the ecstatic response of the crowd.

For the next hour, the service followed a carefully orchestrated progression, with extreme swings of emotion, building and building towards the climax. There were moments when everyone stood in silence, eyes closed and hands raised, while Hinn delivered his message into the microphone in the softest whisper. Then he would lead them into bouts of boisterous cheering or singing. During one of those transitions, Hinn ordered a group of men waiting below stage to step up and join him, while the congregation sang a joyous version of Leonard Cohen's *Hallelujah*.

Benny Hinn.

Once the men were in place, Hinn flung out an arm in their direction, and shouted a single command: 'Substance!' The whole group fell backwards.

Another group was called, and the procedure was repeated. Hinn then pointed towards the congregation and repeated the command several times. 'Substance! Substance! Substance!' In response, whole rows of people collapsed in their seats. Apparently, we were witnessing the power of the Holy Spirit, moving through Hinn and touching God's people.

'Substance! Substance! Substance!'

Sometime later, we showed unedited film to a neuroscientist who had completed a major study of hypnotic techniques. He explained that the whole procedure followed a well-established pattern. First, there is the classic hypnotic induction, a time of peace and calm, when the audience is lulled into a highly suggestible state. Then the hypnotist selects those in the crowd who are most susceptible to his commands. Once on stage, these people confirm and re-confirm everyone's expectations until the whole audience has fallen under the hypnotist's spell.

As soon as the spell was cast, Hinn sent his ushers into the crowd to collect donations. He didn't just tell his followers that the more they gave, the more likely they were to be rewarded with a miracle. In fact, he went much further, prophesying that great tragedies were about to hit the world and only those who 'increased their seed' would be spared.

On stage, a violinist broke into a vivacious solo piece, which set the congregation swaying from side to side as the ushers moved through their ranks, handing out envelopes. When a lady nearby opened hers, I asked if I could see the contents. It was a request for credit card details with an invitation to tick one of six small squares, indicating the amount of money the donor would like to contribute. I am sure readers will be familiar with similar charitable requests, which usually start at about a hundred pounds or dollars and go down to five or less. This appeal started at ten thousand dollars and stopped at five hundred.

Once the envelopes had been circulated, Hinn offered some practical advice.

'If you're using your credit cards, make sure to put your name, your account number, your expiration date and sign where it says signature. Whether you're giving that seed through a cheque or through cash or credit card, just put your hand on that seed after you sow it, and pray that nothing will touch your children, nothing will touch your home, nothing will touch your finances. Whatever happens economically will not affect your people; in the name of Jesus.' Then, after a brief pause: 'If you're ready to give to the Lord's works, say "I am."'

The whole congregation responded with a resonant 'I am.'

Once the donations had been gathered, it was time for Hinn to commission God's Holy Spirit and his legions of angels to sweep through this crowd, casting out demons – yes, demons – of sickness. There was no suggestion here that human suffering was the price we have to pay for Adam's sin. Hinn was connecting to pre-Christian beliefs in the powers of evil spirits to spread disease and destruction.

'You, unclean spirit of sickness, go out of this place. Go!' he shouted. Then, after a brief pause, 'I see an animal, half man, half animal, literally walking out of this building in fear and trembling.'

Once the evil spirit had been cast out, Hinn sensed miraculous cures all around him.

'A brain tumour is being healed to my right.' (*Huge round of applause*). 'A man with cancer has been healed. I rebuke that cancer in Jesus' name. Now somebody's legs are being healed, especially the left leg. (*More applause*). Someone in a wheelchair has just been healed. Another heart disease has been healed. Another back problem is being healed. Many of you feel a warmth in your body. It's the power of God. Whether I'm calling your healing out or not, quickly begin making your way down to the front.'

And up they came at his bidding. A former lumberjack was now able to squat down and rise for the first time since the logging accident which had damaged both hips ten years ago. A little child had been 'cured' of a brain tumour. A woman could hear for the first time in fifty years. On and on they came, a ceaseless flow of men, women and children, convinced of a miraculous healing. But what were we really witnessing here? It would take several months to find out.

The most harrowing scenes we witnessed that evening are never included in Benny Hinn's TV programmes. Close to where we were filming, a woman struggled for nearly thirty minutes to rise out of her wheelchair, only to sink back in exhaustion. All around us, people were desperately trying to walk without crutches and leg braces, scene after scene of failure and distress.

How must it feel, we wondered, to be told again and again that God has the power to heal you, but chooses not to?

We showed these scenes to Harold Kushner, an eminent rabbi and author, who expressed everything we felt that evening.

'I hope there's a special place in hell for people who try and enrich themselves on the suffering of others. To tantalise the blind, the lame, the dying, the afflicted, the terminally ill; to dangle hope before parents of a severely afflicted child is an indescribably cruel thing to do, and to do it in the name of God, to do it in the name of religion, is unforgivable.'

Among those we met at that first service were Amendra and Urmila Prakash, an Asian couple in their mid-thirties, who had come here with their two boys. Alvin, their younger son, was just ten years old, and throughout the service, remained in a wheelchair in a semi-conscious state.

Amendra and Urmila were a dear couple, who invited us to join them in their modest home the following day. They had recently emigrated from Fiji to the United States, but within a month of their arrival, Alvin had started to develop problems with speech and mobility. By that time, they had seen Benny Hinn's TV programmes, and when Alvin was diagnosed with brain cancer, they converted to Christianity and joined a local church.

Over the months that followed, Alvin's condition deteriorated until he could no longer move, talk or feed himself. Finally, the doctors told his parents there was nothing further they could do. The kindest thing would be to let him go, but Urmila and Amendra had just received news that Benny Hinn was about to come to Portland on one of his 'miracle crusades'. The timing seemed like an act of God.

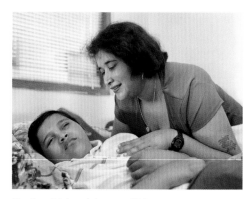

Urmila with her dying son Alvin.

'We told the doctor, no. Alvin is not going to leave us, and we are not going to let him go. We believe in God. We have faith, and there's nothing impossible for God.'

Although there were no signs that Alvin's condition had improved on the first evening, there were two more services to come, and Urmila was convinced that her son would finally walk out of the stadium with them, provided she had sufficient faith.

This was not a rich family. Amendra was working in a canning factory, and Urmila had given up her job to provide round-the-clock care for Alvin. Yet they had been persuaded by Benny Hinn's TV appeals to pledge a hundred dollars a month to his ministry.

In Hinn's presence, the urge to make an even greater gift was overwhelming, and when the envelopes were handed out, Amendra put his cross in the third square, committing himself to a further payment of $2,000.

When I interviewed Hinn after the 'crusade', it was the first question I raised:

IN THE LINE OF FIRE

Imagine this scene. I'm a recent immigrant. I have no job security. By my side is my adored son, and he is dying of a brain tumour. The medical profession cannot do anything further to help. I am at the end of the road. I cannot put a cross at the low end of this scale because that makes me feel I'm not doing the best for my son, so I put it in the middle, at $2,000. I don't have the money to pay for this, but I'm in a credit card culture where I can go into debt.

I don't think that's fair.

Hinn was unapologetic. 'I don't see any problem with the way we raise our funds. Most people give only because they believe God is leading them to give, not because somebody has asked them to.'

Not because somebody has asked them to.

It was an outrageous claim. Under American law, churches and ministries like Hinn's are exempt from paying federal, state and local taxes, and by his own admission, Hinn received 'a handsome salary' and 'lived comfortably'. He also flew everywhere in a private plane, but 'if I did not fly privately, I would wear out very quickly, and so I see that as a plus, that I would last longer in that way. I would be more productive for God's kingdom.'

There wasn't a hint of sarcasm in that reply.

By the time the 'crusade' was over, and Hinn had flown out of Portland in his private plane, Alvin was showing no signs of recovery, but Urmila hadn't lost hope.

'We believe that the regrowth of tumour has been dissolved completely and we know that God is working on Alvin so that today, tomorrow, or the day after tomorrow, He is going to do it. God has his plans. He has his dates. We just have to have our faith.'

Seven weeks later, ten-year old Alvin died. We flew back to Portland to be with the family when they scattered his ashes on the waters of the Columbia River, near the place where he had first learnt to swim.

Urmila was devastated.

'I just asked God: "Why did you take my kid away from me?" We were only a very little family, four people in the house, and I loved Alvin so much. After he died, I just couldn't take it. My dearly beloved boy had gone.'

I have stayed in close touch with her ever since. Rather sweetly, she always calls me 'Dad'. After Alvin's death, the family moved to Florida, but life has not been easy for them. Amendra was out of work for long periods of time, and he and Urmila finally separated.

Before writing this chapter, I asked Urmila what she felt about Benny Hinn, and indeed, about Christianity all these years after Alvin's death. She replied:

'Hi Dad. To be honest, I don't believe Benny Hinn anymore. As for Christianity, I know there is Jesus whom I pray to, but I don't trust any pastors or people from the Church.'

****

Three weeks before Amendra and Urmila scattered Alvin's ashes, Reinhard Bonnke was ready to meet us in Benin City, Nigeria, where he was about to hold another 'miracle crusade'. This time, I would be there with the full team.

It was Bonnke's first visit to the country in eight years. On his 1991 'crusade' to the Nigerian city of Kano, remarks he allegedly made about Islam sparked riots in the city. Muslim protestors burned down churches and attacked Bonnke's followers. No deaths were reported, but many people were seriously injured.

Benin City is over five hundred miles from Kano, and Bonnke felt safe to come here after an eight-year gap. Outside the airport, his chauffeur-driven Mercedes was ready and waiting for him with a long line of vehicles in its wake. After addressing the crowds, Bonnke stepped into the lead car, and the cavalcade pulled away with hundreds of cheering people running alongside as it made its slow progress through the city.

Hours ahead of time, we arrived in the vast open space that had been chosen for that evening's 'miracle crusade'. Seriously disabled people were already trying to make their way towards the stage before the crowd started to build. Among them was an elderly man, painfully crawling across the rough ground on all fours.

The service began at dusk, by which time hundreds of thousands had gathered to hear Bonnke, who strode back and forth across the stage in his usual style, under a huge overhead banner that carried the message: 'Jesus Christ sets you free.'

Nigerians were a conquered people. Within living memory, they had been ruled by white men contemptuous of their beliefs and superstitions, but Reinhard Bonnke was a different kind of white man. Like Benny Hinn, he connected with the old religions, and this was the source of his great strength in Africa. He was here to call upon Jesus to protect the crowd from witchcraft, devils and demons. At one point in the service, he told the story of four witchdoctors who had tried to disempower him with their curses, but as soon as he shouted 'Hallelujah', their leader suffered an asthma attack. On hearing this, the crowd roared with approval.

There was a collection, of course, but I'm happy to report that on this occasion, no mention was made of God's preference for notes.

Once the money had been gathered, Bonnke began to cast out the demons of cancer, blindness and a whole host of other afflictions, and, within minutes, there was a steady movement of people towards the stage. One small child was supposedly hearing and speaking for the first time in her life. An elderly man claimed that his sight had been restored.

Our main concern, though, were the heartbreaking scenes unfolding below stage, where Bonnke's acolytes were auditioning the sick and maimed for their performance value. An elderly woman was told that if God had really healed her, she would be walking properly, and she was advised to try again the following evening. A teenage girl, who claimed to be seeing for the first time in her life, failed a simple eye test, and received the same advice. But the most distressing incident occurred at the end of the service.

In an emotional finale, Bonnke summoned the Holy Spirt to enter the hearts of his people, and in response, whole groups started 'speaking in tongues.' They were following the traditions of Africa, where for centuries, men and women in a state of ecstasy have called upon the spirits to possess them and to speak and prophesy through them in the languages of the spirit world.

The noise continued to build until the crowd was whipped into a frenzy. By the time the service was over, calm hadn't been restored, and during the mass exodus that followed, fifteen people were crushed to death.

Early the following morning, we contacted the police and learnt that some of the families were so poor that they could not afford to pay the necessary bribes to retrieve the bodies of their loved ones from the morgue. When we visited the families affected, we were able to remedy this, but were shocked to discover that nobody from Bonnke's ministry had contacted any of them.

I questioned Bonnke about this when we interviewed him in Germany a month later. 'That shakes me', he said. 'I think if anything could stop me from doing my work, it is something like that. It really shakes me.'

I believe this was a genuine response. The problem, though, is that men like Bonnke are so bound up in a peculiar system of rituals and beliefs that the realities of life escape them.

But the nightmare in Benin City wasn't over on that first evening. While we were filming below stage at the next service, a distraught father appeared, carrying the body of his daughter, one of the victims of the previous night's disaster. He clearly believed that Bonnke had the power to bring her back to life, but, for obvious reasons, he failed the audition.

We were in a difficult position. If we tried to fight for his right to join Bonnke on stage, we knew that this grieving father would only suffer further disappointment and distress. Instead, we tried to comfort him, but he quickly spun away and disappeared into the crowd.

Later, we learnt that he had laid the child's body on the bonnet of Bonnke's Mercedes, only to be ordered to remove it immediately.

It was an incredibly powerful moment for me. If Bonnke had been the leader of some minor Christian sect, this would not have affected me in the same way, but Bonnke and Hinn represented one of the fastest growing brands of Christianity, and on that night, I made a complete break. I have never said a prayer since.

Despite those feelings, I was determined to make an honest and unbiased assessment of these 'miracle cures'. Without reliable records and medical testimony, it was not possible to reach any conclusions in Africa, but we did have opportunities in the United States.

At Benny Hinn's Portland 'crusade', seventy-six miracles were claimed, and we asked for as many names and addresses as possible. Thirteen weeks later, five were provided, but after a thorough investigation, we found no evidence of any cures. Of greater concern were the damaging consequences in three of those cases.

A young mother was so confident that her daughter, Sabrina, had been cured of severe breathing difficulties that she assured the excited congregation that there was no need for any further medication or treatment. But the symptoms were still evident on stage, and her doctor confirmed that she had not come back for any further treatment.

For the first time since the logging accident that had damaged both his hips, James McCracken was able to squat down, rise again, and repeat the movements several times. When we consulted his doctor, we were told that those antics had caused further bone damage, and movement was now so painful that James could no longer dress himself. Yet he remained so convinced of a miraculous cure that he had refused prescribed medication and the operation his doctor considered essential.

Susan Norquay had come all the way from Canada in the hope of a miracle. When she joined the others on stage, the congregation was told that she was a 'walking dead woman' when she entered the stadium that night, but her lung cancer was now cured.

When we contacted her oncologist, we were given a different version. Susan had been suffering from 'an unpredictable form of lung cancer that was stable at the time of the "crusade"'. After her return to Canada, she was so convinced of a miraculous cure that she had refused to see him again. Her condition deteriorated, and she died six months later.

And yet something significant was happening in the heat of the moment. What was the real power at work here?

For answers, we turned to some of the world's leading scientists and theologians. Apart from the insights they gave about hypnotic techniques, they made another important comparison. While not suggesting any moral equivalence, they compared Hinn's and Bonnke's healing crusades to Hitler's rallies and Stalin's parades in Red Square.

According to Professor Kinsbourne, an eminent neurologist: 'The parade, the acclaim of the leader in the enormous square, the chant of the song, the gesture, the salute; all these elements have the effect of submerging the individual into the group. This is the pitch to which leaders bring their people. They persuade them to do something which they might not do individually – to charge into battle, to risk death, to bayonet the enemy … or to rise up out of their wheelchair and walk.'

Kinsbourne and his colleagues went on to explain that in the charged atmosphere of a faith healing service, the brain releases opiates, which increase suggestibility and resistance to pain. People not only experience temporary relief, but in some cases, are able to cling to their belief in a miraculous cure, even when the original symptoms return.

Clearly, we are not talking here about the power of God or the Holy Spirit, but the power of the human mind, and after all our experiences, I was beginning to wonder whether all religions were simply constructs of the human mind or, rather, many different minds over the centuries.

There is compelling evidence that religion follows where culture leads, and it's not always a step forward. Whether we take the examples of Hinn and Bonnke spicing up their Christian messages with stories of confrontations with evil spirits and witch doctors, or Muslims incorporating gruesome ancient customs like female genital mutilation into their faith, the issues are the same.

Religious values and beliefs can also change very quickly in response to changing political and social conditions.

All these issues would come to the fore when we made our two-hour documentary *The Qur'an*.

Chapter Twenty

THE QUR'AN

There are at least 14 brilliant programmes tucked inside this scrupulously fair-minded, definitive, magisterial programme … You could read about 80 books on the history of the Qur'an and learn less than in this documentary by Antony Thomas. Placidly, logically, he tells the story of love gone sour: love for humanity, as originally enshrined, and love for other religions … Thomas tells this story with consummate grace and understanding … Please set this Monday night aside, and learn it all, and think, and rejoice, and weep, and think again.

The Times, 14.07.08

Over the years, press reviews of my programmes have been very supportive and encouraging, and although the *Times* reviewer may have been overgenerous, he does express everything I was hoping to achieve with my 2008 film *The Qur'an*.

My interest in the Muslim faith goes back to my Cambridge days when I acquired my first copy of the *Qur'an* and made several visits to the oldest mosque in the UK, the Shah Jahan in Woking, some thirty miles from London. In those days, Islam was not considered threatening in any way. Even in the late Seventies, a pop star like Cat Stevens was happy to convert to the Muslim faith while others like him were reaching out to Buddhism and Hinduism in their search for peace and fulfilment.

Violent Islamic extremism, in the form we are familiar with today, was not a serious issue until the 1990s when groups like the Taliban and Al-Qaeda came to the fore. Many of their fighters had been armed and trained in camps in Pakistan, set up by the United States to help drive the Soviet army out of Afghanistan, but it didn't take long for the US administration to realise that this had been a grave mistake. Yet it needed an outrage on the scale of 9/11 for all of us to grasp the extent of the threat we were facing. On that single day, 2,996 people (including the 19 hijackers) were killed and over 25,000 injured.

Four years later, Islamist suicide bombers detonated three explosive devices on the London Underground and a fourth on a double-decker bus, killing 52 people and injuring dozens of others. It was one of the most serious terrorist atrocities committed on British soil but worse was to follow, not only in the UK, but in Spain, France, Belgium and eleven African countries.[9] Meanwhile, the numbers killed in Afghanistan, Pakistan, Iraq, Yemen and Syria were running into the hundreds of thousands and most of the victims were Muslims.[10]

What seemed particularly outrageous were claims made by the perpetrators and their supporters that the indiscriminate murder of people of all faiths was an act of obedience to God's command.

Muslims believe there is one true source they can turn to for moral guidance: the *Qur'an*. According to tradition, this is the authentic word of God as passed down to the Prophet Muhammed by the Angel Gabriel.

Yet across the Muslim world today, there are profound differences in the status and treatment of women, in attitudes to peace and violence, punishment and forgiveness.

Islam is also a faith undergoing constant change.

When we filmed *The Arab Experience* in the mid-Seventies, couples were walking hand in hand on the streets of Cairo, and several young women were in miniskirts. We could have been in any city in any Mediterranean country.

When we returned to those same streets thirty-three years later while making *The Qur'an* documentary, the contrasts were striking. Nearly every woman was veiled. Some were wearing *hijabs* that covered hair, arms and chest, while others were completely enveloped in black *niqabs* that revealed only their eyes. There wasn't a miniskirt or a courting couple in sight.

By far the most troubling development during those intervening years has been has been the rise of violent extremism.

But if God's word is clearly set down in the *Qur'an*, how are these conflicting interpretations and sudden changes possible?

That simple question was at the heart of our inquiry.

As well as scrutinising the text, we engaged leading Muslim scholars across the world. For a better understanding of the schisms within Islam, we interviewed a cross-section of believers from humble peasants to Grand Ayatollahs and filmed major ceremonies and rituals performed by different branches of the faith.

We also delved deeply into Islamic history, reaching back to an era when the *Qur'an*'s message of openness, tolerance and free inquiry inspired astounding developments in mathematics, philosophy, medicine and astronomy, and

---

9 Somalia, Mali, Niger, Nigeria, Burkina Faso, Ivory Coast, Togo, Benin, Cameroon, Chad and Mozambique.
10 Figures given by the Watson Institute of International & Public Affairs (Brown University) updated August 2021

encouraged persecuted Jews and dissident Christians to seek the protection of Islam.

As early as the ninth century, Muslim scientists had calculated the circumference of the earth, while most Europeans still clung to the notion of a flat earth. Muslim merchants established a sea route to China via the southern tip of Africa centuries before Vasco da Gama was acclaimed in Europe as the first mariner to reach India by the sea route.

Arabic numerals were developed from their Indian origins into the basis of a new arithmetic. Trigonometry, algebra and geometry were wholly or largely Muslim inventions. Islamic medicine remained standard practice for a thousand years.

And that stimulus came from the *Qur'an*, which, in verse after verse, calls upon mankind to 'examine the heavens and the earth', 'to reflect on creation', to 'look and look again'.[11]

But when the Muslim world feels threatened – either by external enemies or internal disruption – that dignity and courtesy can give way to an explosive mixture of rage and hatred, impelling spokesmen for a great spiritual and ethical religion to seek approval in the *Qur'an* for violent confrontation.

In the minds of many Muslims, we are now living in such a time.

Economic stagnation, unemployment and the failure of many Muslim countries to achieve any semblance of democracy have been major factors. The Palestinian issue remains high on the agenda, as do the catastrophic mistakes in Western foreign policy, from the imposition of artificial colonial borders in the 1920s to the military interventions in recent years.

But one of the most powerful forces driving the Muslim world towards extremism is the huge investment King Faisal and his successors made to promote an extreme form of Islam that denigrates women and has inspired Al Qaida, the Taliban, Islamic State, Al Shabaab, Boko Haram and other terrorist groups.

In this film, we explored all those issues in depth, before returning to the central question.

If God's word is clearly set down in the Qur'an, *how are these conflicting interpretations and sudden changes possible?*

A leading Muslim scholar gave a very frank answer. 'The *Qur'an*,' he told us, 'Is like a big supermarket', with many different choices on the shelves. 'You are able to make peace, according to the *Qur'an*. You are able to declare war, according to the *Qur'an*. Moderate people have their support in the verses of the *Qur'an*, as do radical people with different verses.'

---

11 Q: 67:1-5. Q3:191. Q16:65-69, etc

These contradictions are apparent throughout the text. In one verse we are told that 'whoever kills a human being … it shall be as if he hath killed all mankind, and whoever saves the life of one, it shall be as if he saved all mankind'.[12]

Suicide is explicitly forbidden in the *Qur'an*, but the suicide bomber is also quoting the text when he says that those who die fighting in God's cause achieve martyrdom, and their reward is in Paradise.[13]

But even with all the choices on offer, it is difficult to find verses that support causes which are vitally important to educated and enlightened Muslims in today's world.

High on the list is the question of a woman's obligation to wear the veil. The verse that is always quoted calls upon them to 'guard their modesty … to draw veils over their cleavage' and not to 'display their beauty and ornaments' except to their husbands and close family members.[14] There is sufficient ambiguity here to allow many different interpretations, but other verses are more explicit and pose a huge challenge to those who try to reconcile 'the Word of God' with modern notions of gender equality.

But there are devout Muslim women who have taken this on. Among those we interviewed was Dr Souad Salah, dean of Islamic Jurisprudence at Al Azhar, one the world's leading Muslim universities.

Every contentious verse I quoted received the same confident response.

Q Men are a degree above women.[15]

A But the woman is equal to the man in everything that touches human feelings – love, trust, confidence, pride, respect and honour.

Q Those wives you fear may be rebellious, admonish them, banish them to their couches and beat them.[16]

A This teaching applies to the woman who disobeys her husband, and refuses to live in her house, and refuses to raise her children, and wants to go out wherever she pleases and wants no one to control her and is unwilling to fulfil her duties.

Q Your wives are land to be tilled, so till your land when and how you will.[17]

A This is an honouring of women. Women are not the property of man. They are like the fertile land that a husband takes care of and does not exhaust.

---

12 Q: 5:32
13 Q: 22:58,59
14 Q: 24:31
15 Q: 2:228
16 Q: 4:34
17 Q: 2:223

People of faith may attribute their moral sense to the message they take from their sacred texts, but after many similar experiences, it was becoming increasingly clear that what matters most are the values they *bring* to the text, which are largely shaped by their upbringing, their experiences in life and the prevailing culture.

Some of the world's greatest leaders and reformers were – and still are – people of faith, but the key question is this. What brought them there in the first place? Was it the power of 'Holy Spirit' or the 'Word of God', or something we might call 'the human spirit at its finest'?

Christians who believe that compassion, humility and service to others are our primary duties will find strong support and endorsement in the Gospels, but there are verses in the *Bible* condoning slavery,[18] misogyny,[19] human sacrifice[20] and violent retribution.[21]

And there is another difficult question within the Christian context. How many of the reforms which we regard as key stages in human progress were instituted by the established Church?

At the top of my list would be the abolition of slavery, torture and the death penalty, as well as the struggle for gender and racial equality.

Christians were, and still are, at the forefront of these campaigns, as are those who bitterly oppose them. In the days of William Wilberforce, there were slave owners and traders who were committed Christians and made generous donations to charities. One of them used his profits to establish and fund a religious community.

It has been a similar story in the fight for racial equality. On one side, Martin Luther King, with a vision of a country free from racism and segregation, and on the other, Dr Criswell, dismissing 'integrationists' as 'infidels, dead from the neck up'.

In his case, definitely not the Word of God or the guidance of the Holy Spirit, but 'the human spirit' at its worst.

---

18 Leviticus 25:44, Exodus 21:7
19 Ephesians 5:22–23, 1 Corinthians 14: 34,35
20 Genesis 22:2
21 Deuteronomy 20:16–18

Chapter Twenty-one

FOR NEDA

Every chapter in recent history has had its own defining image.

1943 Jewish families are marched through the Warsaw ghetto towards the main railway station, where cattle trucks are waiting to transport them to Treblinka.

1972 A naked child, severely burned by napalm, runs out of her Vietnamese village, screaming and in tears.

1976 A terrified high school boy carries the body of thirteen-year-old Hector Pieterson, one of the first victims of police violence against student protestors in Soweto.

1989 A man stands alone in front of a line of tanks, blocking their way into Tiananmen Square, Beijing.

2009 A young Iranian woman lies in the street, eyes wide open, bleeding through her nose and mouth, while someone desperately tries to save her with CPR.

That final scene was unlike the others in one important respect: it had been captured on three cell phones. As well as seeing these tragic moments, we can hear the voices of unseen people calling out: 'Neda please … stay with us … Neda don't go!'

After a few seconds, all attempts to revive her suddenly stop. A second person moves in and gently touches Neda's face, but her expression tells us everything. Neda has died with her eyes wide open.

Within hours, that scene was flashing up on computer screens across the world. President Obama called a press conference the following day and described what he had seen as 'heart-breaking' and a clear sign that the situation in her country was 'fundamentally unjust'.

Several days passed before this young woman was identified as twenty-six-year-old Neda Agha-Soltan, and by then, her death had already focused world attention on the cause she had died for. Like millions of other Iranians, she had taken to the streets to protest a rigged election in her country. Soon, others were marching 'with her' in more than a hundred cities across the world.

Neda's blood-spattered face appeared on T-shirts and placards. In Paris, the celebrated photographer Reza Deghati set his entire staff to work creating Neda masks, and soon that beautiful young face would be seen again and again among crowds rallying to the cry: 'We are Neda.'

But how much did we really know about this young woman? Who was she? What did she stand for? Why did she risk her life in this way?

Those were the questions posed by Sheila Nevins, HBO's outstanding head of documentaries, when she invited me to New York to discuss the possibility of making a film that would turn Neda 'from an icon into a living and breathing human being; someone we would come to know and understand'.

It was a huge challenge. To achieve this, we needed to gain the full cooperation of Neda's family. There was also the problem of access. All foreign media had been banned from Iran since the start of this crisis, and even if we had managed to cross the border illegally, there was no way that a group of foreigners could slip in and out of the family homes without attracting attention and putting all of them at risk.

My first thought was to approach two Iranian filmmakers we had met while making *The Qur'an* documentary a year earlier. They were people I trusted, and we had already established a secure way to communicate, but both responses were negative. To quote one of them: 'Any kind of journalism in this country means spying, and I would prefer to spend my summer by my swimming pool rather than in a foul cell in Evin Prison.'

The next option was to contact Iranian journalists based outside Iran but still free to return to their country. For obvious reasons, backgrounds would have to be thoroughly checked, and I would also need a serious face-to-face meeting before disclosing our plans.

After a long search, a strong candidate finally emerged: 24-year-old Saeed Kamali Dehghan, a stocky and rather inscrutable young man with one obvious passion: his work. In spite of government bans, he had managed to stay in Iran throughout the protests, reporting for the *Guardian* and CNN. He was also the first person to discover Neda's family name and her parents' address.

Saeed had no filmmaking experience, but he was quick to learn the basics: how to operate the camera, frame images and handle interviews. The next priority was to work out a code that would allow us to communicate securely throughout his time in Iran. We also needed to find a safe way to get his material out of the country on a regular basis. I was helped here by one of my filmmaker friends, who had a tried and tested method, but as a further precaution he agreed to make copies of everything Saeed shot in case any shipment went astray.

Finally, we needed an emergency strategy, but I'm afraid the one we devised was not up to much; just a list of the names and numbers of people Saeed had asked me to call if he was silent for more than two days.

On 17 November 2009, Saeed left for Tehran, armed with a list of questions for Neda's family and a camera that looked sufficiently amateur to pass through customs and security in Iran. The following day, he emailed back to say that he had arrived safely and was ready to start.

The first person he contacted was Neda's brother, Mohammed. Four days later, he received the message that the family had agreed to meet him.

At this point, I'll let Saeed take over the story:

> I remember that first night so well. I was very nervous. My stomach was churning. I would be walking into the home of the girl who had become the symbol of freedom for our nation. I was carrying flowers, and as I went in, I saw Neda's photo on the wall. I was so tense that I burst into tears and the family had to calm me down.
>
> Neda's mother was immediately warm towards me. At first, I addressed her by her full name, but in no time, I was calling her 'mother'.

The family agreed to let Saeed film, and on the following day he returned with his camera. It was clear from the first material we received that he had won the trust of a family holding tight to Neda's memory and determined to hold nothing back.

Neda's mother, Hajar, was the main contributor. A warm and passionate woman in her early fifties, she was constantly on the move, tidying beds, washing dishes and preparing meals. In a country where any woman who makes a public appearance is compelled to cover her hair, Hajar was prepared to compromise. Her favourite headdress was a black scarf, dotted with silver disks, which was always pulled back far enough from her forehead to reveal a sliver of hair, but Neda's older sister, Hoda, refused to compromise. She was stunningly beautiful and proud to display a head of hair carefully coiffured with blonde highlights.

Hoda lived in another apartment with her husband and children, who did not participate. Neda's story would only be told by her closest family.

****

The one quality they all stressed was Neda's courage. According to her mother, 'Neda was a rebel almost from the moment she was born. From the age of three, she never accepted control.'

In a deeply respectful tribute, Neda's father, Ali, described his daughter as 'a fearless child with no fear in her body. I loved her and respected her so much for that.'

Neda's younger brother, Mohammed, was particularly close to her. As a sign of mourning, he had neither cut his hair nor shaved since her death. He told Saeed that the one issue that was most important to his sister was the treatment of women in Iran.

'She used to say to me that women in this country cannot live like human beings. "As a woman, I can't even go outside without being covered up."'

As we had seen on the streets of Cairo, the veil takes many different forms in the Muslim world. At one extreme, there is the all-enveloping black shroud, known as the *niqab*, which only reveals the eyes and is mandatory in Saudi Arabia. The Iranian version, the *chador*, is not quite as repressive. Women are allowed to show their faces, but everything else is covered, and the *chador* has to be worn whenever they are worshipping in mosques or venturing into the sea for a 'swim'!

On the streets of the main cities, many women, particularly the young, wear something much closer to the Egyptian *hijab* – a scarf, usually in vivid colours, which covers the hair, neck and chest. Like Neda's mother, some push the boundaries further, easing the scarf back a few inches to expose a wave of hair, but if they do this in a public place, they risk arrest by the police or the notorious *Basij* militia; men and women charged with maintaining 'public order and decency'.

According to Hoda, Neda hated the veil in any form, and on entering high school at the age of twelve, 'she fought with the school authorities not to wear it, and she won that battle … Neda was the first girl in her school not to wear a *chador*.'

Neda longed to dress as she wanted, to swim in the sea and roam freely with family and friends. Turkey was the closest country that would give her those opportunities, and after taking a language course, she started working there regularly as a tour guide.

The family took every opportunity to share photographs, stories and memories. One could sense their relief in having this chance to tell the world who Neda really was, and to be as strong and optimistic as she had been, even in their grief.

The huge range of books in Neda's library was proudly displayed. They included *Siddhartha*, *The Last Temptation of Christ*, *A Hundred Years of Solitude* and *Wuthering Heights*. Some were considered subversive and were banned by the regime, but Neda didn't care. She was a young woman with an urge to know.

That thirst for knowledge and what her mother described as strong religious faith brought Neda to Tehran's Azad University to study Islamic philosophy, but after two terms she dropped out.

According to her sister Hoda, 'She used to say, "The God they are teaching us at these universities is different from the God I worship." Her professor taught them about a vengeful God, but Neda said, "This is not my God. The God I worship is a compassionate and loving God."'

Saeed was free to read Neda's poems and her personal diaries. In one of them, a single entry – 'Meet Amir' – was repeated day after day. According to her mother, Amir was the man Neda had loved since she was a teenager and had married in 2004, but they were from 'opposite cultures', and after three and a half years, they had divorced.

According to Hoda, Neda fought hard to save the marriage, and never stopped loving Amir. 'She had such high expectations when it came to affections and emotions. Amir, even I, couldn't love her in the way she expected from us.'

Neda, outspoken and brave, a girl who worshipped a loving and compassionate God, who had a thirst for knowledge and dreamed of a relationship where all the love she gave would be given back to her in return; a free spirit confined by a regime that doesn't value any of those qualities in a woman.

****

Between them, Neda's family and Saeed had created a strong personal core for the film. The next challenge was to set Neda's story in a wider context and give viewers a real sense of the world outside the family home and insights into the way people were forced to live their lives under this regime.

At one level, we had first-hand witnesses, most of them Iranians now in exile. Many had taken part in the 2009 demonstrations and been forced to flee during the fierce crackdown that followed. Among them was Dr Arash Hejazi, the young man who is seen gently touching Neda's face during her dying moments.

Others were still living in Iran, but willing to talk to us when they came through London, provided we concealed their identity. They included a young woman who had been a student at Azad University. She gave us a hilarious account of the way Neda dealt with the black-clad women, lined up at the entrance of every girls' school and college, to ensure there wasn't a hair showing or a trace of make-up on any of the young faces they were scrutinising.

As well as interviews, we also needed a whole range of visuals to help us tell the wider story. The 2009 demonstrations and the brutal response of the police and the *Basij* militia had been captured again and again on phones. We also had important footage from *The Qur'an* film and other sources. These included shots of twelve-year-old girls sitting in class wrapped in *chadors*; inspections outside a girls' college; and the extraordinary spectacle of a woman cautiously entering the sea, dressed in a full black *chador*.

Two sequences we acquired, shot secretly on phones, affected me deeply. The first was a court scene. Under Sharia law, the weight of a woman's testimony is worth only half that of a man's, which is particularly unjust in cases of violent assault or rape. Divorce is also the exclusive right of the husband, who automatic-ally takes possession of the children at the age of seven, and at an even younger age if the woman marries again.

In one scene, a young woman is in tears as she stands before a judge and begs him to 'let me keep at least one of my children, for God's sake, your honour.'

The judge shakes his head. 'You remarried, and when you remarry you lose your child.'

Clutching her child even closer, she pleads: 'I'll go mad, sir. Please, just look at this child. She's only four and a half years old.'

The judge shakes his head again.

Even more distressing was the public stoning of a woman, wrapped in white cloth and partially buried in sand. Andreas Moser, a human rights lawyer who had witnessed such an execution, explained the rules. 'If you are a man, found guilty of adultery, you are buried in sand until your waist is covered. If you manage to get out while people are throwing stones at you, you are free. That's the rule. However, women are buried up to their breasts with their arms also buried.'

****

I was about to say that a gap of centuries seemed to separate Neda's family from those who governed their nation, but when I think of some of the achievements during the early centuries of Islam, I feel it would be more accurate to describe this as a gap of millennia.

Through his interviews and close observations of their daily lives, Saeed gave us a real sense of a family, living in a contemporary world, with values we respect and hopefully share – people we would be proud to have as our friends. The problem, though, is that this world of theirs can only exist behind closed doors.

There was one spontaneous moment that said so much. While Saeed's camera was rolling, Hajar suddenly entered the sitting room, holding up a striped blue and red dress. In tears, she told Saeed: 'This is the last dress Neda bought, but she never had a chance to wear it.' She shook her head and stared at it in silence.

The dress was not even knee-length and could never have been worn in the streets outside, but Neda had planned to wear it in her other life, the life behind closed doors. She loved partying with her brother, her sister and their friends in the secrecy of the family homes. Dancing, especially Arab dancing, was an obsession, and Mohammed had taken some great shots of his sister in action.

Neda had her own singing teacher and loved music across the whole range, from classical opera to Western and Turkish pop, but her greatest idol was the Iranian singer, Googoosh, a superstar who had been imprisoned, banned from performing in Iran, and finally expelled. She paid a special tribute to Neda in the film.

Googoosh was honouring a young woman who wanted to listen to music and read the books she loved, who danced and partied at every opportunity and indulged in the coolest fashions. In so many ways, she was like any young woman anywhere. But what distinguished Neda from millions of others in her country was her exceptional courage and strength, and in the summer of 2009 those qualities were put to the test.

****

In early May, Mahmoud Ahmadinejad, the hard-line incumbent, began his campaign for re-election to the presidency, but the whole process was suspect from the start. Four hundred and seventy people had put their names forward as potential challengers, but after the all-powerful Guardian Council had worked through the list, only three opposition names remained. All of them, or so it seemed, were safe establishment figures.

Then something remarkable happened. For the first time ever, rival candidates were allowed to challenge Ahmadinejad in a series of televised debates.

Those moments defined what everyone disliked about Ahmadinejad, who came across as deeply unpleasant, conceited and abusive. At one point, he threatened to reveal secret dossiers about the wife of one of his opponents, Mir-Hossein Mousavi, a former prime minister, whose immediate response was: 'This is exactly what we don't want government officials to do, building up dossiers about our citizens and then threatening to reveal them.'

Neda had been watching the first debate with Hoda, and the moment it was over, they went out onto the streets together, where huge crowds were starting to gather. The small hope that things could change had created enormous energy, especially among the young.

Mousavi soon emerged as the opposition front-runner, attracting massive crowds to his rallies, but it was his wife, Zahra Rahnavard, who gave real lustre to his campaign, even holding rallies of her own.

A woman, playing a major role in a political campaign! This was an incredible breakthrough in the Islamic Republic of Iran.

June 12, Election Day. There was real optimism in the air and people went off to the polls early in the morning, but suspicions soon began to build. Opposition candidates complained that their phone and email communication had been obstructed and that their observers had been denied access to polling stations.

Neda went to vote with her mother and her brother, but when she saw that there were no representatives of opposition candidates in any of the polling stations they visited, she told Hajar: 'This is nonsense', and she didn't vote.

That evening, while people were still voting, the *Basij* militia raided Mousavi's headquarters and closed it down, confiscating files and documents. All this was captured on phones.

Just two hours after the polls closed, State Television announced that Ahmadinejad had secured over 60 per cent of votes already counted and was heading for a resounding victory. In the early hours of the following morning, that victory was confirmed.

It was a blatant fabrication. There was no digital or online voting system in Iran, only paper ballots. It would have been impossible to gather these from towns and villages across the country and have all votes counted just eight hours after the polling stations closed.

If the rigged election was not provocation enough, on the following evening police and the *Basij* militia mounted an attack on Tehran University. One policeman was so appalled at what they were doing that he recorded this on his phone and posted the evidence online.

Five students were killed. Over 130 were arrested and imprisoned.

The next day, some of the largest crowds ever seen in the capital took to the streets in protest. According to witnesses: 'All ages, all classes; religious, non-religious, all of them were there. They didn't shout slogans. They didn't say, "Death to this", "Death to that". They just held up their hands, showing the victory sign. In those four days, I think we really witnessed the political maturity of the Iranian people.'

Neda was in the protests every day, sometimes with her mother, brother or sister. On one occasion, three *Basij* women approached her in their black *chadors*. Her mother described what followed.

Very politely, one of these women asked Neda: 'Dear, please don't come out looking so beautiful, because the *Basij* men target beautiful girls, and they will shoot you. Then she said: "I'm also a psychologist, and I know the danger of beauty to these men."'

'And I know the danger of beauty to these men'! – a dreadful omen and such an insight into the fundamentalist mind. Reza Deghati, the celebrated photographer, made the point very clearly in his interview. 'Feminine beauty,' he told us, 'is the greatest threat to those who believe that the path to paradise and all its promised pleasures will be blocked forever if they fail to control their desires. The surest way to deal with that threat is to kill it.'

****

June 19, one week after Election Day. During Friday prayers the Supreme Leader, Sayyid Ali Hosseini Khamenei, addressed the nation. Unelected by the people, he was, and still is, considered to be above politics – God's representative on earth. On that day, he warned the nation that he had instructed his security forces to crush those peaceful demonstrations 'by all means possible'. It was a declaration of war against his own people.

On the following day, Neda's mother begged her not to go out onto the streets, but she said, "I have to go. I have to go. If I don't go out, who will?"

According to her father, 'Neda had thought about all the consequences. She knew there was a risk that she would be tortured or imprisoned or even killed, but she was not afraid.'

The violence on the streets was appalling. One of our witnesses was 'beaten six times with a baton' and saw 'people being pushed against a wall and beaten. What made me so angry was that this was absolutely unprovoked.'

Then the shooting started. Neda's university friend was moving with the crowds, when 'a very young boy, just a few meters away, was shot and killed. I've had nightmares ever since.'

To suppress the evidence, journalists had been cleared from the streets. Some were imprisoned, others expelled from the country, but the authorities failed to understand that the Iranian people had the courage and the know-how to get the evidence out to the world. The random beatings and shooting were captured on hundreds of phones, clearly showing that the violence on the streets did not come from the demonstrators, but from government-sponsored thugs.

When Neda left the family apartment in the early afternoon, her mother decided to call her every half hour. The second time they spoke, 'Neda told me, "There are so many government forces out here. I've never seen so many in my life before." I asked what they were doing, and she said, "What do you think they're doing? They're chasing us and beating us." I pleaded with her to come back home. She said, "Mum, I will – Don't worry."'

But Neda returned to the fray. She had gone to the demonstrations with her singing teacher, and their last moments together were captured on phones. For her safety, Neda was wearing a full *chador*, topped with a baseball cap. Her elderly teacher was wearing a distinctive blue and white striped shirt.

I'll leave to Dr Arash Hejazi to describe those final moments:

What grabbed my attention was that she was so active, shouting 'Death to the Dictator', supporting others, moving around while her music teacher was trying to pull her back, but she didn't want to give up. I was really looking at her with admiration, because she was a young woman, so courageous, while I was dying out of fear.

The anti-riot police then took up their batons and rushed towards the crowds. People scattered, but as all the streets were blocked, they didn't know which way to go. It was chaos. We all ran, and Neda was running beside me, but her music teacher couldn't keep up, so Neda kept turning back to see if he was OK. And then we heard the blast.

Neda was standing about a metre away from me, and I saw her looking up in astonishment and surprise at the blood gushing out of her chest.

I'm sure she was shot in her aorta. It is the major blood vessel coming out of the heart. No one could save her. In a minute, she bled out. Her eyes lost their light. Her heart stopped beating, and I knew she was dead.

No one has ever been charged with Neda's murder.

****

When we made the film, all those we interviewed were sure that the government would never risk reigniting public anger by harming Neda's family, and mercifully, they have so far been proved right.

There was also a strong feeling that Neda's death, and the worldwide response, would change the situation in Iran forever, but conditions in that country have only gone from bad to worse.

Just as they had done in 2009, members of the all-powerful Guardian Council disqualified scores of potential candidates in the lead-up to the 2021 presidential election, and the Iranian people were finally given a choice between six virtually unknown contenders and Ebrahim Raisi. Back in the late Eighties, he had been a key member of one of the notorious 'death committees' that ordered the mass execution and torture of thousands of political prisoners, but in spite of his murderous past, Raisi now enjoyed the full backing of the Supreme Leader.

Once again, Iranians took to the streets in protest and called for an election boycott, while distraught parents posted online videos describing how their children had been 'shot in the head', 'pierced in the heart' or 'left to die under a huge pile of dirt' for daring to take part in protests.

On polling day less than half the population bothered to vote, and of those who did, a significant number posted blank ballots in protest.

But this time, there were no supportive marches outside Iran's borders, nor was any foreign leader prepared to stand up and describe the situation in that country as 'heart-breaking' and 'fundamentally unjust'.

And there was another upsetting sequel to this story.

In late 2018, nine years after the broadcast, Saeed wrote two articles for the *Guardian* newspaper which would have been well received by the Iranian regime. In these, he revealed that Iran International, an anti-regime broadcaster based in London, was secretly funded by the Saudi Crown Prince Mohammed bin Salman (MBS).

The first article was published on the day Jamal Khashoggi was brutally murdered in the Saudi consulate in Istanbul. A month later, Saeed claimed in a tweet that Khashoggi was killed 'because of speaking to me about the Iran International issue'. By this time, the *Guardian* had already decided that they could no longer commission him to write articles on Iran.

On 3 March 2020, a major article appeared in *The Tehran Times*, an official regime publication, with an online version in English. In the article, Saeed accuses the *Guardian* of 'silencing my voice' and imposing 'a de facto ban on me writing on Iran, which has led to my current severe mental health state.'

He also denounces the Neda film, claiming that he was 'deeply upset' when the programme was broadcast, 'even though I didn't show that at that time'.

This doesn't sit well with the congratulatory emails he sent me immediately after the broadcast. 'It really is a great film and I'm very proud to have had the experience of working with you and learning a lot from you. Thank you for making *For Neda*, thank you, thank you.'

The young man who tells us in the film that he was 'walking into the home of the girl who had become the symbol of freedom for our nation' was now claiming that 'the reality is that I have no idea who killed Neda whereas Antony Thomas's film points the finger at the Iranian leaders'.

Saeed was free to join us at any time he chose while we were editing the film and approved every step we took. It would have been clear to him from the start that no member of Neda's family or any of the witnesses to the violence on the streets had doubts about who bore responsibility for Neda's death.

Saeed also knew that he would be banned from Iran as soon as the film was broadcast, but thanks to the support he was given by lawyers for the *Guardian* and Central Television, his application for British citizenship was secured.

Saeed and I kept in touch for several years and in 2016 he joined me and other friends for my retirement party, but by then his personal life was not going well and he desperately missed his family in Iran. In one of his emails, he writes about his 'huge depression as the result of me not to being able to return to Iran which led to a suicide attempt and months of being ill.' Apparently, he was 'off work for several months, and even hospitalised'.

Eventually, he broke off all contact with me and my emails were ignored. When the *Tehran Times* article appeared, I wrote to the *Guardian* hoping to get their reaction to Saeed's claims but received no reply. All I know is that they have treated him generously. He has kept his job but has been transferred to another section, 'Global Development', where he no longer has an opportunity to write articles on Iran.

The rest, I'm afraid, is conjecture, but I know enough about the mishaps in his personal life and his despair at being separated from his family in Iran to believe that he is trying hard to ingratiate himself with the regime. Whether he will succeed and be allowed to return to the country is another question.

I have never been in a position where my personal life was in a mess and I was cut off from family and all those close to me, and I can only hope that I would not have responded in the same way, but I can't be sure. All I can say is that there would have been no film without Saeed, and I am still very grateful to him.

EPILOGUE

When planning this book, one of my earliest decisions was to end with a chapter that would not only honour Neda and her family, but also make the important point that documentary filmmakers are totally reliant on the contributions of others.

Saeed's role in the Neda film was the most obvious example and this was fully acknowledged. As well as receiving the Peabody Award, the Clarion Award and Foreign Press Association's Documentary of the Year Award, the film also won the FPA's Journalist of the Year Award, which Saeed and I were proud to share.

As I write this, the top feature on Saeed's website is still a series of photographs showing him (in a dinner jacket and black bow tie) standing with me on the night of the award!

That recognition was as important to me as it still is to him. It was the first time that the contribution of another member of my team was formally acknowledged in this way, but there were many others who deserve similar recognition.

From the mid-80s onwards, Jonathan Partridge, an outstanding director of photography, worked with me on every film except *The Qur'an*, because of his commitment to another project at that time. Paul Lang, another fine DOP, stepped into the gap and made a very important contribution. I also had two excellent sound recordists, Simon Palmer and Paul Paragon, who worked with me at different times across a span of thirty years.

When you are working closely with a team like this, you soon reach the point where you start thinking with one mind. Whether we were filming some dramatic scene that none of us had anticipated or sharing a very personal moment with someone who trusted us, I never had to intrude or waste time with instructions and explanations. All that was required were a few nods and gestures to ensure that we were all in step.

That close sense of partnership continued right through to editing, where I had outstanding contributions from Barry Reynolds at Yorkshire Television and Roger James at ATV/Central Television. When Roger was promoted to head of documentaries, McDonald 'Mc' Brown took his place, and I owe a huge debt to the editor who worked with me on every project from the mid-Eighties onwards. There were moments when the two of us would sit staring at the screen, trying to work out the right linking thought between one sequence and the next. Suddenly, 'Mc' would scribble a sentence on a scrap of paper and slide it across the table towards me. And there it was, clear as daylight!

Another key contributor in those final stages is the composer. At its best, film music can add another layer, conveying feelings that cannot be easily expressed in words and images, and here I would like to thank the late Dimitri Tchamouroff, who worked with me on most of my later documentaries.

While major technical advances continued to make the documentary process far less cumbersome and intrusive from the late Sixties onwards, these changes had other consequences. With higher film speeds and the eventual switch to digital cameras, it was no longer necessary to have a team of electricians handling all the interior lighting. Wireless technology also eliminated the need for an assistant sound recordist, and although the unions fought hard to maintain numbers, their power was finally broken in the Thatcher era, but the pressure to thin down documentary crews did not end there.

With the massive increase in the numbers of TV channels and competition from streaming platforms like Netflix and Amazon Prime Video, BBC and ITV no longer had the monopoly they enjoyed during my early days in television, and as viewing figures fell, there was increasing pressure to cut budgets and reduce team numbers. Although production of a small number of outstanding documentaries has been maintained, self-shooting directors are fast becoming the norm.

While some have done excellent work, this is not a safe route to quality programming. If you are preoccupied with focus and the correct exposure, you cannot concentrate on content and the most creative ways to communicate this. Nor are you able to observe what is happening outside the frame of your camera.

A successful documentary depends on collaboration, meticulous research and, above all, empathy. People who entrusted me with their personal thoughts and feelings often told me that they began to feel that the two of us were the only people in the room. Interviewing them from behind a camera would have been out of the question.

And there are other problems. Budget constraints have deprived many self-shooting directors of the necessary time to think and prepare. In this digital age when filmmakers are no longer constrained by the cost of film, there's a tendency to shoot and shoot in the hope of covering every option. Documentary editors often have a huge amount of material to sift through and precious little time to give shape and meaning to the content. As 'Mc' always used to say: 'The best cameras have an "off" button.'

For me personally, research was the most exciting stage in the process. In this context, I am especially grateful to those like Salah Jaheen and Yukiko Shamamura who helped me reach people at all levels in their own societies, as well as the local 'fixers' who took great risks on our behalf when we were working in countries like China and Iran. But at the top of my list are three colleagues who worked with me at different times in the United States, the UK and Canada: Barbara Multer, Elizabeth Klinck and Carleen Hsu.

Researchers like these are not just fact-checkers; they are co-creators. Long before filming began, we used to go our separate ways to meet people whose lives and experiences were relevant to the subject we were investigating. Along the way, there were frequent surprises, and preconceptions often changed, but through this process we became increasingly confident that we were getting closer and closer to the truth, until we finally reached the point where we could agree on the people and places that would give the viewer the deepest insights.

Of course, this whole approach would have been impossible without the creative and financial support I received from the heads of the various documentary departments I worked for, and I hope I have given proper credit to all of them throughout the book.

Finally, and most importantly, I would like to thank Elsa, my grandmother, who gave me the confidence to set off on these extraordinary journeys with her message that anything is possible if you set your heart on it.

INDEX